THE SUBURBAN ENVIRONMENT AND WOMEN

THE SUBURBAN ENVIRONMENT AND WOMEN

○ Donald N. Rothblatt
○ Daniel J. Garr
○ Jo Sprague

PRAEGER

PRAEGER SPECIAL STUDIES • PRAEGER SCIENTIFIC

Library of Congress Cataloging in Publication Data

Rothblatt, Donald N
   The suburban environment and women.

   Bibliography: p.
   Includes index.
   1.   Women--United States--Social conditions.
2.   Suburban life. 3.   San Jose metropolitan
area, Calif.--Case studies. 4.   Women--
California--San Jose metropolitan area--Case
studies. 5.   Urban policy--United States.
I. Garr, Daniel J., joint author. II. Sprague,
Jo, 1943-   joint author. III. Title.
HQ1426.R77   301.41'2   78-19797
ISBN 0-03-041031-2

Published in 1979 by Praeger Publishers
A Division of Holt, Rinehart and Winston/CBS, Inc.
383 Madison Avenue, New York, New York 10017 U.S.A.

9 038 987654321

Printed in the United States of America

For Ann, Mylvia, Syreeta, and Doug

ACKNOWLEDGMENTS

The completion of this book would not have been possible without the help of numerous individuals, public institutions, and representatives of private business. In gratitude, we would like to thank Melanie Freitas, Nancy Geilhufe, Deana Dorman Logan, Mara Southern Plant, and Serena Wade for their advice and criticism of the conceptualization and design of our San Jose study of women in suburbia. We are also grateful to Timothy Chalmers, Mark Curran, Susan Fallis, Vivian Hobbs, Zelko Pavic, Karen Schirle, and Patricia Stadel for their assistance with the data analysis of our study. In addition we would like to thank the many graduate students at San Jose State University who helped us conduct our field work and the many women who were willing to be interviewed and share a part of their suburban world with us.

Our special thanks are due to our colleagues in the Departments of Urban and Regional Planning and Speech Communication at San Jose State University, especially Earl G. Bossard and Marie Carr; to the former coordinators of the Women's Studies Program, Ellen Boneparth and Sybil Weir; and to the past and present Deans of the School of Social Sciences James Sawrey and Gerald Wheeler, for their support and encouragement while we were completing this study.

For financial support we are grateful to the California State University and Colleges, which provided funds for research assistants and computer services, and the National Science Foundation, which provided assistance with a Faculty Research Grant.

We would like to express our appreciation to Sheila Brutoco, Christine Haw, Ann Rothblatt, and Douglas Stuart for their invaluable editorial assistance. Special thanks also go to Carolyn Danielsen, Kathryn Hill, Linda Garbesi, Merrilee DeWitt, and Ellen Leiner for their diligent typing and retyping of the original manuscript. All errors are, of course, our own responsibility.

CONTENTS

LIST OF TABLES

LIST OF FIGURES

INTRODUCTION

Sprawling housing tracts, shopping centers, and office complexes relentlessly continue to consume open land at the edges of the United States' urban areas. Indeed, few research topics have proven more intriguing or controversial than the ongoing postwar suburban boom, still vigorous as it passes a quarter century's longevity. Early popular sociological studies emphasized what appeared to be the shortcomings intrinsic to suburban life.[1] What is most interesting about these excoriating reactions to the expansion of the suburbs was the consistent penchant to fabricate myths which this then novel "aberration" of urban living seemed to foster. Rather than attempting to understand the significance of suburbia within the context of the continuing transformation of U.S. society (and its physical habitat), many observers dismissed it with their sometimes grotesque sketches of the individual and collective dysfunctions mysteriously triggered by the move from the central city. As Greer has observed, "Those who criticized suburbia were simply depressed with conditions in a mass democracy whose affluence was expressed, not by policy, but through the marketplace."[2]

Even today, there are but a few serious studies of the impact of suburbia on its residents and consequently on society as a whole despite the fact that suburban living is no longer a unique living condition. The suburban United States has evolved with such force and vigor that it is now the dominant form of urbanized living and promises to reinforce this supremacy with no indication of abatement. Presently the suburban population represents a majority of metropolitan residents and projections indicate that it will have doubled its 1960 total by the end of the century.[3]

A workable definition of "suburbia" is an elusive quarry defying categorization by political, economic, or social criteria alone. Perhaps this elusiveness is the point of departure that distinguishes the suburbs of the 1970s from that of the 1950s. According to Masotti, the difference is one of a dependent urban fringe of 20 years past evolving into the independent "neo-city" of today.[4] Neither respecting nor ignoring the existence of political jurisdictions, suburbia is now viewed as a metropolitan aggregation of many urbanized suburbs. This collective entity embodies those processes which have marked the evolution of the postwar metro United States: the decentralization of manufacturing, services, and commerce resulting from the obsolescence and rejection of the central city as well as efforts to garner and aggrandize a tax base by entities seeking to strengthen their respective fiscal positions; the resulting independence of the suburbs from the central city; and the growth of a larger and more spatially dispersed population in terms of employment and residential location.

On an individual functional level, suburbia is an area of relatively low land costs which permit a less dense environment than that of the traditional city. This fosters more individual and dispersed land consumption and thus inhibits mass transit in favor of an auto-based pattern of commutation. These spatial factors create a family lifestyle in which one or two adults must often spend considerable time in intra or inter-metropolitan commutation and which in turn has a bearing on the very structure of the family and its participation in the community.

Aesthetically, the suburbs have been vilified over the years. The salient suburban feature of sameness, or cheerful mediocrity, is the direct result of the activities of a newly-emerged group of large merchant builders, who sought to satisfy the housing market's pent-up demands, which had gone unmet from the Great Depression to the postwar era. Visually reflecting the economic organization of its progenitors, the suburbs represent everything not embodied in a Jane Jacobs or Lewis Mumford definition of urbanity: diversity, charm, visual surprise, and pedestrian scale. But, in fact, we are not a nation of cities, as aesthetes and intellectuals would have it be. Omit the Bostons, New Orleans, San Franciscos, Chicagos, New Yorks, and Philadelphias, and one is at a loss to recommend urban communities that are urbane. The urbanized suburbs are the new urban United States, which has delivered and continues to promise economic success for its developers and seeming contentment for more of its consumers than any prior form of social and physical organization.

Although older empirical work has demonstrated that many if not all of the characterizations of 1950s suburbia are myths based on distorted perceptions, it is not surprising that in retrospect the literature on suburban United States generally fails to provide adequate perspectives on the essential features implicit in the suburbs-as-haven for increasing pluralities of affluent Americans.[5] Investigators have usually avoided the basic issue of whether the suburbs are viewed as a satisfactory environment by the suburbanites themselves. Rather than pursuing the question from a general vantage point, they appeared to accept the notion that the suburbs are an adequate if not ideal place to live and that this largely unquestioned dictum should provide a basis for future social policy formulations.[6] Consequently, while the design of the physical environment has been studied with some adequacy,[7] often with female respondents, the social and psychological satisfaction of middle and upper middle-class suburbia has been largely neglected.

Suburban studies have usually focused either upon lower-income dwellers or the more privileged upper class. Berger examined the changes occasioned by a move to the suburbs by automobile workers in the San Francisco Bay area.[8] Gans studies the early years of a lower middle-class, large-scale tract near Philadelphia.[9] Seeley et al., on the other hand, investigated the culture and lifestyle of an older upper-class suburb proximate to downtown Toronto, [10] while Sternlieb et al. described the traditionally crusty and elite orb of Princeton.[11] Only in a few recent studies[12] and in a vivid and sensitive photo essay have the social, psychological, and environmental concerns of middle America been confronted.[13] How these people feel about their way of life and environment is critical, and Owen's photographs in particular leave us with the uneasy feeling that at least a minority is dissatisfied. The recent impact of inflation and the accompanying petroleum shortage may have magnified this number as millions have been compelled to reevaluate the benefits and costs of their living situation.

This book provides a framework for making such a reevaluation by examining the opportunities for creating satisfying living environments for women in suburbia. First, the study presents the historical framework of the suburbanization process in the United States, from the beginnings of a mass movement in the nineteenth century to the predominant mode of today's middle-class life, and discusses where suburbia is likely to take us in the future. Chapter Two explores the relationship between the status of women and the suburban environment. Major questions addressed are: How do male designers of suburbia view the role of women? How does this view compare to the archetypal women of the feminist mystique or the new feminism? How well is suburbia adapting to the changing occupational, social, and interpersonal needs of contemporary women?

Chapter Three presents a study of the satisfaction that women have with various dimensions of suburban life in a range of social and physical environments in the San Jose metropolitan area characteristic of much of American suburbia. The dimensions of suburban life examined are concerned with the level of satisfaction with four of the major aspects of the quality of urban life: housing environment, community services, social patterns, and psychological well-being. We also attempt to measure demographic and environmental characteristics, such as education, income, and housing density and design features, which seem to be related to such levels of satisfaction. That is, we examine relationships of variables which are expected to help explain changes in these levels of satisfaction.

In Chapter Four we discuss the findings of our San Jose study and address our conclusions to the major question underlying our research: What is the comparative importance of environmental and various social influences on women's satisfaction with suburban life?

The book closes with a discussion of the implications of our case study and literature review for women and urban America. In this last chapter, we focus on the public policy implications of our research for improving the quality of metropolitan living environments for women and society at large.

NOTES

1. William H. Whyte, *The Organization Man* (Garden City, N.Y.: Anchor Books, 1957); John Keats, *The Crack in the Picture Window* (Boston: Houghton Mifflin, 1956); A.C. Spectorsky, *The Exurbanites* (Philadelphia: Lippincott, 1955); R.E. Gordon et al., *The Split Level Trap* (New York: Dell, 1962); and David Riesman et al., *The Lonely Crowd* (New Haven, Conn.: Yale University Press, 1950).

2. Scott Greer, "The Family in Suburbia," in *The Urbanization of the Suburbs*, ed. Louis H. Masotti and Jeffrey K. Hadden (Beverly Hills, Calif.: Sage, 1973), p. 156.

3. Leo F. Schnore and Vivian Zelig Klaff, "Suburbanization in the Sixties: A Preliminary Analysis," *Land Economics* 40 (February-November 1972): 23–33.

4. Louis H. Masotti, "Suburbia Reconsidered—Myth and Counter Myth," in Masotti and Hadden, eds., *Urbanization of the Suburbs*, pp. 15–22.

5. T. Ktsanes and L. Reissman, "Suburbia: New Homes for Old Values," *Social Problems* 7 (Winter 1959–60): 187–94; Leo F. Schnore, "The Growth of Metropolitan Suburbs," *American Sociological Review* 22 (April 1957): 165–73; T. Caplow and R. Foreman, "Neighborhood Interaction in a Homogeneous Community," *American Sociological Review* 15 (June 1950): 357–65; Jerome Manis and Leo Stine, "Suburban Residence and Political Behavior," *Public Opinion Quarterly* 22 (Winter 1958): 483–98; Wendell Bell, "Familialism and Suburbanization," *Rural Sociology* 21 (September-December 1956): 276–83.

6. Anthony Downs, *Opening Up the Suburbs: An Urban Strategy for America* (New Haven, Conn.: Yale University Press, 1973).

7. Edward P. Eichler and Marshall Kaplan, *The Community Builders* (Berkeley: University of California Press, 1967); John B. Lansing et al., *Planned Residential Environments* (Ann Arbor: University of Michigan Press, 1970); William Michelson, *Environmental Choice, Human Behavior, and Residential Satisfaction* (New York: Oxford University Press, 1977); Robert B. Zehner, *Indicators of the Quality of Life in the New Communities* (Cambridge, Mass.: Ballinger, 1977).

8. Bennett M. Berger, *Working Class Suburb* (Berkeley: University of California Press, 1971).

9. Herbert J. Gans, *The Levittowners* (New York: Vintage Books, 1967).

10. John Seeley et al., *Crestwood Heights* (New York: Basic Books, 1956).

11. George Sternlieb et al., *The Affluent Suburb: Princeton* (New Brunswick, N.J.: Transaction Books, 1971).

12. See Michelson, *Environmental Choice*; Zehner, *Quality of Life*; and Mark Baldassare and Claude S. Fischer, "Suburban Life: Powerlessness and a Need for Affiliation," *Urban Affairs Quarterly* 10 (March 1975): 314–26.

13. Bill Owens, *Suburbia* (San Francisco: Straight Arrow Books, 1973).

THE SUBURBAN ENVIRONMENT AND WOMEN

1

BACKGROUND OF
U.S. SUBURBANIZATION

Suburbia and metropolitan decentralization together comprise a topic at least as venerable as a Brahms symphony. Before the Spanish-American War, the consolidation of New York City, and the flight of the Wright brothers, the nineteenth century had spawned a generation or more of rapidly growing peripheral metropolitan communities. Yet, when conversations turn to this still timely and provocative topic, it is the post-World War II era that invariably comes to mind, with its visions of crabgrass, split-levels, PTAs and Little League.

However, what is of recent memory may not serve us well when we are confronted by the future. The survey which we have conducted is designed to assess where we stand as the postwar generation comes to a close. Its implications will be useful in helping us prepare for the difficult period that lies ahead. If we can bring into clear focus the most successful and adaptable elements of what now exists in the suburban environment and align these with a firm hand on the pulse of trends that will maintain their societal prominence, an agenda for future actions may begin to coalesce.

The events of the last decade provide a perspective on the "once and future suburbia," a topic treated in depth below. What is now viewed as the over-valued postwar dollar is gradually and at times painfully reaching an equilibrium with the stronger currencies of the other industrialized nations. The price of fossil fuels has soared, and the traditional "gas wars" of yesterday's memory have merged with that of queues of early-morning commuters at beleaguered service stations. The prospect of continued instability in the Middle East is a sobering question for energy planners. A mood of fiscal restraint has gripped the nation. There is growing pressure to reject Keynsian deficit spending in favor of California Proposition 13-type tax reforms and grassroots demands for balanced budgets. The government-generated subsidies for land development and highway construction on which we coasted in the 1950s and 1960s are dwindling. The talk now is of an era of limits, development by in-filling, paying-as-you-go expansion on the urban fringe, and the wise use of scarce and finite resources.

This period of constraint evokes parallels with a century ago. Changing lifestyles, high costs for housing and transportation, and other curbs on today's lifestyle to which we were once so blithely immune all made their impression then. They are still central to present discussions as we stand on the threshold of the 1980s.[1] What occurred a century ago may help us focus more clearly on the next decade or two.

Similarly, just as the past can serve as a selective guidepost for our future actions, so is it important to document how we arrived at the circumstances that have given rise to the present study. The decentralization of population which created an urban metropolitan nation by 1920 has continued, giving rise to what Zimmer terms the "urban centrifugal drift" and today's suburban society.[2] As shown in Table 1.1, total metro population has increased consistently since the turn of the century, but most of this increment has been captured by communities outside the central city. This phenomenon has evolved from an almost equal rate of urban-suburban growth from 1900–20, to spectacular suburban population booms in the two postwar decades. From 1950 to 1960, for example, the rate of growth outside the central city exceeded that within by a factor of nearly five. During 1960–70, suburban areas came close to repeating this performance.

TABLE 1.1

Population Change in Metropolitan Areas in the United States, 1900–70

	Percent Change in Metropolitan Population		
Time Periods	Central Cities	Outside Central Cities	Total
1900–10	33.6	38.2	34.6
1910–20	25.2	32.0	26.9
1920–30	22.3	44.0	28.3
1930–40	5.1	15.1	8.1
1940–50	13.9	35.9	22.0
1950–60	10.7	48.6	26.3
1960–70	6.5	26.7	16.6

Source: Basil Zimmer, "The Urban Centrifugal Drift," in *Metropolitan America*, ed. Amos H. Hawley and Vincent P. Rock (New York: Halsted Press, 1975), p. 25.

However, these figures are understated due to the annexation practices of some central cities. Indeed, 86.3 percent of their population increases has been due to territorial aggrandizement. Without annexation, central cities would have grown by only 0.1 percent from 1960–70, and by 1.5 percent in the preceding ten-year period.[3] Such a practice has somewhat obscured the eclipse of the central city, although most of our older and more distressed urban centers are hamstrung by the gauntlet of other incorporated units of government. But for those of more recent vintage, such as San Jose, the technique has prevented political fragmentation to a degree. Yet, as Bollens and Schmandt have observed, this practice has not succeeded in achieving congruence with the entire metropolitan complex. Although annexation has limited the number of political units within a metro area, it has stimulated geopolitical warfare among communities and thus the "defensive formation" of new units of government.[4]

This is precisely what occurred within the San Jose Metropolitan Area. Simultaneous to their embarcation on an aggressive program of annexing adjacent unincorporated territory, the first new municipalities in over forty years were formed within Santa Clara County. Table 1.2 illustrates the postwar annexation phenomenon, which has fueled the growth of many of our newer urban centers. Note that San Jose ranks twelfth nationally in land area absorbed since 1950 (excluding city-county consolidations).

Later in this chapter we shall discuss in more detail how a bountiful agricultural valley grew into a vigorous urbanizing metropolitan community of well over one million inhabitants. Although aspects of this growth have their local idiosyncracies, its explosion in population and urban land uses is not unique. Thus, the chronicling of the growth of the San Jose metropolitan area constitutes the bridge between the Suburbia that once was and that which will be.

THE ONCE AND FUTURE SUBURBIA

The French have an apt way of expressing the essence of the "once and future suburbia": "Plus ça change, plus la même chose." We would like to suggest the notion that U.S. suburban life in the last quarter of the twentieth century will share rather striking parallels with the so-called streetcar suburbs of 100 years ago. Further, these will begin to eclipse the continuity that the present era shares with those communities which traversed the crabgrass frontier of our metropolitan fringes during the 1950s and 1960s. In particular, the tenacious economic struggle to secure home ownership and the resultant array of stresses this quest will place on the nuclear family—and particularly on the working woman with children—will be central to this discussion. In addition, three other points warrant emphasis.

TABLE 1.2

Increase in Land Area of at Least 40 Square Miles among U.S. Cities with Populations of 100,000 or More, 1950–72

City	1970 Population (thousands)	Land Area (square miles)		
		1950	1972	1950–72 Increase
Jacksonville, Fla.	529	30.2	766.0	735.8[a]
Oklahoma City, Okla.	366	50.8	635.7	584.9
Nashville-Davidson, Tenn.	448	22.0	507.8	485.8[a]
Indianapolis, Ind.	745	55.2	379.4	324.2[a]
Houston, Tex.	1,233	160.0	439.5	279.5
Phoenix, Ariz.	582	17.1	257.0	239.9
Kansas City, Mo.	507	80.6	316.3	235.7
Virginia Beach, Va.	172	1.8	220.0	218.2[a]
Dallas, Tex.	844	112.0	266.1	154.1
San Diego, Calif.	697	99.4	246.8	147.4
Corpus Christi, Tex.	205	21.5	166.8	145.3[b]
Tulsa, Okla.	332	26.7	171.9	145.2
Memphis, Tenn.	624	104.2	235.7	131.5[b]
Fort Worth, Tex.	393	93.7	223.2	125.5
Columbus, Ga.	154	12.0	141.0	129.0[a]
San Antonio, Tex.	654	69.5	198.1	128.6
San Jose, Calif.	446	17.0	142.0	125.0
Columbus, Ohio	540	39.4	147.1	107.7
Huntsville, Ala.	138	4.2	109.2	105.0
El Paso, Tex.	322	25.6	122.3	96.7
Atlanta, Ga.	497	36.9	131.5	97.6
Columbia, S.C.	114	12.8	106.6	93.8
Mobile, Ala.	190	25.4	116.6	91.2
Kansas City, Kans.	168	18.7	107.7	89.0
Sacramento, Calif.	254	16.9	93.9	77.0
Tucson, Ariz.	263	9.5	82.9	73.4
Colorado Springs, Colo.	135	9.3	80.2	70.9
Tampa, Fla.	278	19.0	84.5	65.5
Lubbock, Tex.	149	17.0	82.0	65.0
Newport News, Va.	138	4.2	69.1	64.9[c]
Wichita, Kans.	277	25.7	90.5	64.8

TABLE 1.2 (continued)

City	1970 Population (thousands)	Land Area (square miles)		
		1950	1972	1950–72 Increase
Hampton, Va.	121	1.0	54.7	53.7[a]
Knoxville, Tenn.	175	25.4	77.3	51.9
Springfield, Mo.	120	13.6	61.5	47.9
Charlotte, N.C.	241	80.0	76.1	46.1
Milwaukee, Wis.	717	50.0	95.0	45.0
Austin, Tex.	252	32.1	75.6	43.5
Toledo, Ohio	384	38.3	81.2	42.9
Amarillo, Tex.	127	20.9	63.4	42.5
Greensboro, N.C.	144	18.2	59.7	41.5

[a]Most or all of the increase resulted from the consolidation of the city with a county.

[b]Includes an undetermined amount of water area.

[c]Resulted from intercity consolidation.

Source: John C. Bollens and Henry J. Schmandt, *The Metropolis: Its People, Politics, and Economic Life,* 3rd ed. (New York: Harper and Row, 1975), pp. 242–43.

First, the literature of postwar suburban growth has tended to focus too specifically on the atypical: lower middle and working-class suburbs, areas close to the center of the city, elite communities, and so on. Ignored in the unbalanced inquiries of the last three decades are the forgotten people at the median or somewhat above and the broad strata of communities in which they reside. Instead, only in its largest context has the global phenomenon of postwar suburbs been discussed widely. Second is the contemporary context of the process of metropolitan expansion in the nineteenth century. Although it proceeded with its own unique conditions and constraints, it is as remarkable a development as its modern counterpart and has much to teach us about the physical, social, and economic growing pains of urban decentralization. And third, families of both eras sought similar environmental amenities and social stability, the necessary ingredients of a suitable setting for childrearing. More importantly, the conditions under which these circumstances were to be achieved involve striking similarities. In both eras, housing costs and transportation factors place the potential homeowner under severe pressure. The price of urban development is high and neither could nor can be deferred by big and bountiful government. In the past this was dictated by structure and organization, today by the pay-as-you-go fiscal constraints in an age of limits. Thus, two incomes both were and will be required in many cases. Women (married or not) were and will be expanding their roles to include employment outside the home. The impact on changing sex roles in both eras precipitated social dissonance and forced individuals to adapt in a period of changing lifestyles. The experience of the nineteenth century thus has a familiar resonance for today. This is the essence of the "once and future suburbia."

Visible Suburbs, Invisible Suburbanites

Historians and sociologists have until quite recently ignored the lives of the overwhelming majority of the population as they pursued, dissected, and interpreted the course of human events. Decision-makers and diplomats, deviants and dead-enders, these were the subjects of traditional scholarly attention. In contrast, commonplace, everyday life somehow has lacked the allure so amply possessed by existences imbued with power, pathology, or both. Such is also the case if one examines the suburban literature of the last 30 years. Suburbs of the elite and of the working class—atypical communities—have commanded a surprisingly large share of the attention.[5]

However, though intrinsically interesting, this skew in the literature to extremes overlooks the fact that by and large suburbs are and have been preponderantly a middle-class phenomenon. As such, perhaps this rampant familiarity has bred neglect, if not contempt. The latter, of course, was abundantly supplied in the 1950s by the Time-Life-Fortune axis, and by the vituperations of East Coast academic brahmins.[6] It was tempting to reduce the emergent suburban population of that day to a few trite generalizations which may still be hauntingly familiar: gray organization men recruited into a procrustean mold of corporate conformity; bored housewives drawn into a vacant spiral of consumerism and chauffeurism; a matriarchal-bred younger generation trapped in a psychological salad whose existence was trumpeted by pop soothsayers.[7] All of these portraits were encased in a standardized, mass-produced environment which both influenced and reflected its social milieu. Although a few scholars have produced reasoned analyses of this otherwise distorted view of a continuing urban process and its social setting, the residue of a portrait alien to the lives of the vast majority of suburbanites still exists. Indeed, as Richard Sennett has recently written, "Neither rebels nor leaders, the middle classes have been...the forgotten people of the American city.... Their lives have been the routine norm, rather than the arresting exception."[8]

It is therefore odd that, unlike the "forgotten people" whose lives have hewn to the "routine norm," the general phenomenon of postwar suburbs has not escaped the notice of the last generation of scholars and social commentators. What has exalted this familiar landscape to so lofty a pedestal? Had there been no Great Depression or World War II, S. D. Clark has stated, a continuous process of migration from the city would have occurred unimpeded.[9] Thus, he continues, "the suburbs gained their social significance because they were areas into which great masses of people suddenly moved."[10]

A prime current example of suburbanism that well fits this description is the city of San Jose. The population of San Jose, formerly an agricultural processing center for a valley of unsurpassed productivity, grew from 90,000 in 1950 to 600,000 in 1978. Although annexation was a key tool in this growth, it should be noted that it was orchards, not existing communities, that were absorbed in order to bring urban services to land ready for development. Aided and abetted by a willing city government, a vigorous era of freeway construction, and the unshakeable faith that growth was desirable and financially self-sustaining, San Jose exploded and sprawled.[11] Today, thoughtful citizens are debating the implications of this legacy, and "quality of life" concerns resound through the corridors of civic centers, universities, and corporations, obscuring the unvarnished optimism and boosterism of the 1950s and 1960s. The waves and ripples of this generation-old explosion have not yet been subdued and will continue to provoke, frustrate, and stimulate students of society and its physical setting. Its legacy is the challenge of the urbanized suburbia of the future— a vista of increasing densities and escalating housing costs. How this situation evolved in recent decades is discussed in greater detail later in this chapter.

But what of the "other" suburbia that once was? However remarkably intense and concentrated the process of urban decentralization, it is not a phenomenon limited to the postwar era, or even to the twentieth century. As Kenneth Jackson has observed, "If it is a truism to say that the United States is now a suburban nation, it is a matter of considerable confusion as to how and when this came about."[12]

The Nineteenth Century

It is not widely known that the growth of the metropolitan community in the nineteenth century was no less startling than that of the post-World War II era. Thus, Chicago doubled its population in every decade but one during the years 1850–90; and over a hundred other communities' populations multiplied by a factor of two in the 1880s alone.[13] Of course, this expansion excluded the existence of political boundaries for annexation of existing outlying communities was the most popular route for territorial and population aggrandizement. As a case in point, consider again the Second City.

In June 1889, 120 square miles were annexed to Chicago. This massive increment of expansion not only added more than 200,000 inhabitants to the city's population (thus bringing its total to over 1 million), it also appropriated a vigorous suburban ring that had far surpassed the core in dynamism.[14] While Chicago's population within the old city limits had grown from about 500,000 in 1880 to 790,000 in 1889, a jump of 57 percent, the annexed area had increased during that same period from 40,000 to over 300,000, or 650 percent.[15] The chief components of this growth were Lake Township (up 550 percent to 100,000), Lakeview (up 800 percent to 52,000), and Hyde Park (up 850 percent to 133,000).[16] Further, this rate of increase in turn is dwarfed by the expansion of population in the area three to five miles from the city center from 1860 to 1873. During that time span, a surge of 1,200 percent was recorded, with a boost from 8,000 to nearly 100,000 13 years later; nearly half of that increase occurred after 1870 alone.[17]. Suburban population growth continued to be an awesome factor in metropolitan Chicago even after the annexation of 1889. Showing no sign of flagging, its new suburbs grew from 242,000 in 1900 to over 1 million in 1930, an increase of 439 percent.[18] Reflecting the above, between 1880 and 1920, 250,000 residential lots were recorded within Chicago, while 550,000 were plotted outside the city limits.[19]

Nationally, in the decade 1910–20, population rose by one-third in the urban territory surrounding the 62 largest U.S. cities, thus eclipsing the growth of the cities themselves.[20] The gap between this suburban vigor and the more slowly expanding central city grew still wider from 1920 to 1930. During that time, the outer rings of the United States' 17 largest cities grew by two-fifths as the growth rate of the urban cores continued to slacken.[21] By the 1920s, suburbs were a striking, persistent, and venerable phenomenon.

Two key factors lie at the root of the early suburban explosion. First, the development of transportation and industry shaped the destiny of the urban community. A change in one produced an upheaval in the other, and it was not long before the interaction of these forces undermined traditional and established forms of community life. Most notably, the separation of work and residence was made possible in the last third of the nineteenth century by the evolution of mass transit.

As work and residence became physically separated, so did social classes in response to the expanding pattern of residential development. This reflects the second factor, the differential allocation of wealth. The beneficiaries of this growing and industrially based affluence were the middle class, a group which had increased substantially in size and in buying power by the turn of the century. This sector of the population was able to capitalize on the cheap labor provided by the wave of European immigrants which flooded the employment markets of the industrial centers of the East and Midwest after 1880. Able to outbid prior residents for their residential turf of dense warrens and teeming slums within walking distance of their jobs, foreign settlers were a prime factor in the expansion of the urban realm in that era.[22] As for the displaced, they were pulled more than pushed to the city's periphery, for the alternative of new homogenous neighborhoods and housing in styles à la mode were available to a large spectrum of the population. In the late nineteenth century in Boston, for example, Warner has estimated that the market for new suburban housing included the dominant half of society, only a small portion of which could be termed wealthy.[23]

The environmental dynamics of the growth of the nineteenth-century suburbs were well expressed by Charles Horton Cooley. Writing in 1891, he observed, "Humanity demands that men should have sunlight, fresh air, the sight of grass and trees.... There is, then, a permanent conflict between the needs of industry and the needs of humanity. Industry says men must aggregate. Humanity says they must not."[24] Of course, only that segment of humanity which could afford the high costs of new construction could successfully resolve that conflict. For those fortunate enough, the suburbs provided a sanitary and safe environment with stylish new houses amenable to a familial existence. Accentuating the social stratification inherent in Cooley's analysis, Sam Bass Warner writes of Boston's nineteenth-century suburbs, which were

> temporary neighborhoods of people with similar outlook. In an atmosphere of rapid change, the income-graded neighborhoods rendered...neighbors who would reinforce an individual family's effort to pass on its values to its children...a sense of community of shared experience, and thereby gave some measure of relief from the uncertainties inherent in a world of highly competitive capitalism.[25]

The suburbs of the nineteenth century, then, were not only creatures of the laissez-faire marketplace but also the locus of a social system centered on children and their conditioning by the community. Indeed, it is not entirely clear whether economics or the life cycle turned the engine of suburban growth more decisively. Charles Booth emphasized the latter in his analysis of London's expansion, published about 1900:

> One of the dangers of the growth of London...is the tendency for the better-to-do classes to fly the furthest off....Many may still move out to as great a distance as their purse permits; but others will pause, hesitating to lose central

advantages....The decision depends not so much on class or on amount of
income...as on the constitution of the family. The father of young children
finds it best to establish their home as far from the crowded parts of London as
he can afford.[26]

Earlier still, in 1874, Everett Chamberlin very perceptively recognized
that both economic factors and technology would soon align themselves
with the preference for low-density living, which commentators from Booth
and Cooley to Gans and Owens have analyzed so tellingly.[27]Chamberlin
found noteworthy, if not surprising, the strong centrifugal tendency to the
suburbs less than a decade after the end of the Civil War. He was struck by

> the rapidity with which Chicago workers are now flocking into the suburbs to
> live. The fact is thoroughly established that ninety-nine Chicago families in
> every hundred will go an hour's ride into the country, or toward the country,
> rather than live under or over another family, as the average New Yorker or
> Parisian does. This tendency will be increased in the future years, rather than
> diminished; for we may safely calculate upon the new inventions and reform
> legislation of the day to improve the means of transit, and cheapen the charges
> therefor, at least as rapidly as the distance necessary to be traveled by the new
> settler becomes greater.[28]

Thus, though the product of dramatic changes in transportation and
industrial technology, the suburb was incontrovertibly a familial phenomenon. Such a basis clearly emerges even from the murky past. "Families
who may desire to associate in forming a select neighborhood," read an
1819 advertisement for lots in Brooklyn Heights across the East River from
Father Knickerbocker's Manhattan, "cannot anywhere obtain more desirable situations."[29] Implied here, of course, is the assumption that such a
"select neighborhood" will accommodate an appropriately select stratum
of the population. Even in the absence of zoning regulations and the
massive housing tracts of postwar conglomerate merchant builders, homogenous residential neighborhoods evolved initially as the result of informal
arrangements. The chief motivation here was the security of one's
investment. In Boston's central Dorchester, during the last quarter of the
nineteenth century, for example, housing of similar costs was constructed
because builders could best market their product by fostering clusters of
people of similar lifestyle and income. A parallel uniformity of architectural
styles was a logical concomitant of minimal risk taking in a conservative and
fragmented housing industry.[30] Only a radical shift in transportation or the
expansion of an adjacent neighborhood would affect this standardization.[31]

The gradual proliferation of a dense network of mass transit opened large
tracts of land to families with two incomes who required this breadth of
services to sustain both home and livelihood. The efficacy of transit as the

spearhead for the improvement of middle-class housing opportunities is shown by an observation of Sidney Low in an 1891 periodical. "The new suburbs," he wrote, "which show the largest increase are those in which a considerable proportion of the inhabitants are artisans and mechanics."[32] This prefigures the blue-collar affluence which has so successfully fueled the housing booms of recent times.

In less central locales, transit again was an enforcer of homogeneity. The distance of the residence from downtown was an effective regulator of social distinctions. "Those who traveled the suburban route had occupations that met both the income and time requirements for suburban living," Hopkins tells us, and thus an array of neighborhoods came into existence based on these selective criteria.[33] On the other hand, suburban economic hetero-geneity did occur, but only in areas of low and medium-priced housing. This is so, Marshall asserts, because the stock in such a price range will accommodate families at different career stages and with different economic ceilings and potentials.[34] However, contrary to Marshall's con-tention that this diffusion occurred without regard to the age of the housing stock, it must be noted that new construction excluded at least half of the economic spectrum. The expansion of housing opportunities, some call it filtering, was more a reflection of periodic neighborhood invasion, suc-cession, decline, and obsolescence (usually after 20 to 30 years) and the continuing increased volume of construction. Prior to World War I, Woods and Kennedy observed that this vigor in the homebuilding industry allowed Boston's black community to better significantly its housing situation.[35]

But diversity in housing was the exception rather than the rule in the suburbs. Suburban life allowed, if not dictated, that one should live with equals, thereby eschewing the maintenance of a niche in the unstable and tolerantly vigilant urban neighborhood hierarchy. Once the purchase decision was made, one would be entitled to a neighborhood "with the needed services and segregation already in being."[36] One could also add to that package the social environment and the responsibilities of home ownership dictated by economics and neighborhood norms.

Points of Stress

Today's suburban resident is immersed in a complex economic and social equation, the variables of which may precipitate a long hard look at the worth of the housing product consumed. In many cases, the balance is a precarious one, currently in danger of being undermined by spiraling property taxes, petroleum costs, and alarming price inflation in markets for new housing and automobiles. Perhaps equally important, the social ledger has yet to be evaluated systematically, especially with respect to the rapidly changing status of women. Yet, even with lengthy mortgage amortization periods, low-interest home loans, real estate tax shelters, and other inducements, today's suburban homeowner is under economic seige. The suburbanite of the past was probably at least equally stressed, especially when one considers the then prevailing primitive modes of housing finance and the precarious stability of lending institutions. Like his or her present counterpart, yesterday's suburban resident could marvel at the speed of construction that created residential areas overnight and at the mass arrival of new families separated along income lines. The product of past and present is and was distinguished by high standards of light, air, sanitation, available land, and "the effect of omnipresent newness."[37]

The dwelling of a century ago was exemplary of what Warner terms "the suburban style," that is, "houses designed with their most important side toward the street."[38] In particular, rural inspiration ruled the roost of design, but this preeminence was often severely compromised by the economics of the land market. Nevertheless, the turn-of-the-century detached suburban home featured backyards, porches, front lawns, and "slavish copying of each shift in style in more expensive construction."[39] A similar progression of fashion may be observed today from the ersatz alpine chalet to angular California vistas in redwood.

But whatever the aesthetic, economics prevailed, and with it the social consequences of the housing product. The developer of the past, like today's, extracted his profit from a land-house tandem emphasizing generous internal dimensions festooned with reasonably fashionable ornamentation. Indeed, continuing this trend, the typical new house of 1977 was 15 percent larger than that of a decade earlier, measuring 1,720 square feet in living area.[40] Where did the economic crunch then come? According to Warner, land was always skimped on to keep prices down. Profit was realized in always selling small parcels of land relatively high because competition and fashion dictated a more or less standardized product. The brutality of this equation may have been somewhat softened by maturing trees and the vista of well-tended "handkerchief front lawns."[41] However, the continuing legacy of catering to the sizeable middle-income market, then, is "an array of relatively generous structures and pinched and inflexible land divisions."[42] Perhaps there has always been universal disillusionment with this "inchoate dream of spaciousness."[43] More than 20 years ago, Riesman queried, "I keep asking myself what the lots will look like when the explosion of our population doubles the numbers of the suburban hegira."[44] Janus-faced, his answer could have been equally specific to the past or to the land-efficient "no frills house" of the very near future. Indeed, in San Jose, single-family detached houses of 1,600 square feet are already offered on lots totaling only twice that in area.

But what of the social consequences of the physical product and its setting? S. D. Clark is of the opinion that "people were made into different beings by the demands of suburban living, with tastes that were inevitably simpler, standards of judgment that were narrower and more self-centered.... For what was to be gained...very real costs were involved."[45] First and foremost, suburban life exiled "the young wife to lonelyville," as Grace Goodwin observed in a 1909 issue of *Good Housekeeping*.[46] She continues, "The busy men leave on early trains and are at once plunged in the rush of their accustomed life among their usual associates," while the suburban woman remains at home, "standing behind the struggling young vines of her brand new Piazza."[47]

Secondly, trapped in her solitary opulence, the female's role was dictated by the functional territory ceded to her by her spouse, and her responsibilities were generally defined not by her own initiative but by the exigencies of conjugal life. Thus, as Sennett has suggested, the family took on substantial importance as the only immediately available mechanism to shield men from the tumult, disorder, and diversity of the rapidly growing city.[48] In his discussion of Chicago's suburban Union Park neighborhood, vintage 1879, he found that women became the authority figures as husbands withdrew from exerting power, responsibility, and energy in virtually all endeavors outside their workaday world.[49] The passivity of the male, theoretically sapped by efforts to advance in occupational and economic mobility, left the suburban woman in a role and physical environment that could have exacted a tremendous emotional cost. And, as neighborhoods expanded, a shift in social emphasis occurred which forced the woman outside the home to other and larger, less personal venues, such as churches.[50] Surely, this must be the Victorian era's version of the harried housewife condemned, like the Flying Dutchman, to the eternity of her station wagon. Robert Wood has accordingly attested to the demands of modern suburban life which comprise "an implacable array of schedules which seem to testify to the suburbanite's inability to live as an individual. ...There are no longer any options, but instead unbreakable patterns."[51]

To this, one must additionally consider the imperatives faced by the working wife. In his study of Chicago's Union Park during the 1870s, Sennett found that 7 percent of wives were employed as opposed to 25 percent of women in general.[52] Excluded from teaching and domestic work, occupations which were typically not carried into marriage, working wives usually found work as store clerks (53 percent), artists (15 percent), or office clerks (11 percent).[53] This relatively limited range of possibilities, according to Sennett, further reflects the fact that working women often had access to better jobs than their husbands but felt compelled to forego those employment opportunities; vocational self-effacement and with it financial improvement were the prices paid for marital stability.[54] If this was true in the nineteenth century, then the evidence for this situation is, according to Fischer and Jackson, overwhelming in the twentieth. Not only must women sacrifice employment opportunities, but the locational constraints on their social environment frequently work to great disadvantage.[55] Paraphrasing Gans, they conclude the malaise of Levittown and elsewhere is both female *and* suburban.[56] One could easily place the emphasis on the latter element rather than the former. Perhaps it is these factors which account for the barrenness and isolation which have been ascribed to suburban life. The struggle to achieve a modicum of housing services and economic progress has always been waged, and perhaps the two-income, stressed family of today has more in common with the tenaciously emerging middle class of a century ago than with the urban pioneers who broached the crabgrass frontier in the 1950s and 1960s. The recent suburban past came on the heels of an explosion of housing demand which had gone unquenched from the Great Depression to the early days of the Cold War. Accompanied by growing affluence, a low inflation, a generous finance package for veterans, and a seemingly endless supply of freeway-induced developable land, the suburbs offered the dream of single-family homeownership to what appears to be the broadest segment of society ever observed.

The conditions of the immediate future, then, when a new house in the western states will cost $80,000 and up, are more the norm than the aberration of the recent past. Life in the suburbs was always an economic strggle, and the female, as Sennett suggests, bore a heavy, if not the heaviest burden. With the family unit stressed by the passive male struggling to succeed and the female obliged to serve as a homemaker and supplemental wage earner, the dream of home ownership was a highly exacting quest. Riesman has written, "We have the impression that the suburbanite, tied to his house as a doctor to his practice, may actually be less likely to take off for a weekend in the country than the urban dweller."[57] It need not even be a weekend that is eschewed, but perhaps just an evening out on the town. In Union Park, Sennett discovered that the populace did not go out often; excitement and exotica were nowhere to be found, let alone bars and restaurants.[58] For some, this absence of facilities may be attributed to the newness of the environment. But it may reflect equally the preferences of the inhabitants themselves. And did the central city itself offer an alternative? If, as David Riesman avers, the city of the 1950s spelled "crime, dirt, and race tensions more than it [did] culture and opportunity," then that of 1900 far surpassed it in degradation, as readers of Jacob Riis well know.[59]

The key therefore lies not only in what that environment provided, but also in the choices made by its residents. Wood has observed, "What is striking in the lives of most suburbanites is the frequency with which they choose *not* to avail themselves of the variety of experiences the metropolis affords, the way they decline contacts with the larger society, and the manner in which they voluntarily restrict their interests and associations to the immediate vicinity."[60] Paramount in the nineteenth century was the struggle to acquire and maintain the small suburban house. The Dreiserian scenarios of the male wage earner and the accompanying but lesser-known stresses on working mothers with children on their own without supervision clearly made their impression on contemporary writers, such as Robert A. Woods and Albert J. Kennedy. (The latter concern is still a factor. It has been estimated that the number of small children of working mothers in California alone is expected to increase by 30 percent between 1979 and 1984.)[61] Their portrait of life in the declining streetcar suburbs of Boston was termed by Warner one of "a kind of desert in the middle of American society."[62] These early suburbanites were solid citizens. Employment for them was regular and well paid, and, although a few were in poverty, overall they enjoyed a high incidence of homeownership, including those in "blue-collar" occupations. Most spoke English and had finished at least the sixth grade. Yet, their residential turf was characterized as "drab," "monotonous," and "deadly commonplace."[63]

Indeed, as Warner has observed, suburban Boston was a failure in many respects that modern commentators might find equally appropriate. Streets and houses were built, not neighborhoods or communities. Housing tracts were the economically efficient way of dividing large parcels of land as they were placed on the market. The centerless commercial strip slithered across the landscape, following the extension of lines of transportation. Schools were partial loci, Warner tells us, but because they were located on inexpensive land on side streets they were often isolated from potential nuclei of community and social interaction. Conditions may have varied from place to place, but the common denominator of the suburban environment of 1900 was fragmentation.[64]

Conclusion

The terms fragmentation, decentralization, and isolation still resound with significance today. They are severe points of stress in the tenuously understood triangle of the individual, society, and the physical environment. We have now reached a point where this intricate set of relationships is coming under careful scrutiny. With the dust of the suburban boom of the 1950s and 1960s beginning to settle, and with residential growth opportunities shrinking through skyrocketing costs and scarcities in land and materials, a period of slow growth affords an opportunity for evaluation and introspection. We can now pause and look back into the recent past in order to ascertain what has or hasn't worked—for whom and under what conditions.

While outlying suburban growth continues,[65] it seems likely that such growth will occur with increasing restraint in the future. As we have shown, restraint and suburban growth usually are not familiar traveling companions. However, the key point to remember is that, unlike that of the late nineteenth century, the growth of the past two to three decades has proceeded with a relative lack of constraint. Abundant land, easy money, and a supply of housing which successfully contained a vast demand are now as extinct as the gas guzzlers which propelled commuters on their diurnal journeys. In the future, housing will probably be a hard-won symbol of economic progress, and the struggle waged to gain it is likely to be fought on many fronts. It appears that two wage earners will be necessary; the family unit, already under siege, will have to become more adaptable and resilient. It is therefore desirable that we establish an awareness of the forces that have set the historical precedent for the pressing contemporary concern with the quality of our existence as a suburbanized society. It is hoped that the familiarity of the past context may better prepare us for an uncertain future.

THE SUBURBANIZATION OF THE SAN JOSE METROPOLITAN AREA, 1940–75

Aficionados of dried fruits, particularly prunes and apricots, might well imagine the changes that have transformed the Santa Clara Valley since 1950. Once a reasonably priced healthful snack, these products are now luxury items for an affluent sector of natural foods connoisseurs. Such treats ranked high among nature's cornucopia of produce that once flowed from the valley in legendary abundance. However, in the last 30 years, thousands of acres of orchards have disappeared, and the former "Fruit Bowl of America" is now an urbanized phantasmagoria of housing tracts, industry, and shopping centers. These uses have engorged themselves on a rich diet of freeways and mighty but sometimes dismal boulevards encrusted with extroverted, strip-commercial development. The prunes and apricots are but a memory possessed by few of the valley's current residents, many of whom would be surprised to learn that they, indirectly, are the reason for the high price of the crops that once grew on the very ground they now inhabit. One is reminded of the anonymous English ditty of the 1870s, recently resurrected by Kenneth L. Jackson:

> The richest crop for any field
> Is a crop of bricks for it to yield

> The richest crop that it can grow
> Is a crop of houses in a row.[66]

This fertile valley lies within the 1,300-square-mile Santa Clara County at the southern end of San Francisco Bay and comprises 300 square miles of area (see Figures 1.1 and 1.2). Its unsurpassed topsoil is a fine loam of 30 to 40 feet in depth which sits upon a vast underground water aquifer. Aided by a mild marine climate, the valley enjoys a year-round growing season which, historically, has favored the agrarian economy first instituted by Spanish colonizers during the 1770s. It was recognized long ago, even before the Gold Rush, that the Santa Clara Valley, as one American traveler observed, "if properly cultivated, would alone produce breadstuffs enough to supply millions in population."[67] In its bucolic heyday, the county ranked as one of the 15 most productive agricultural counties in the United States. Within it flourished more than 200 food-processing plants and an extensive container and packaging industry. Indeed, it was truly the "Valley of Hearts's Delight," a beautiful and wholesome place to live.[68]

In 1940 there were nine incorporated jurisdictions in the county of which San Jose, with 68,500 residents, was the largest (see Table 1.3). It served as the county seat and the hub of agriculture, with many canneries, food machinery industries, and supportive businesses and services. The other towns, with one key exception, were the scattered service centers for 100,000 acres in orchards and 8,000 in vegetables. "The urban half of the population," former County Planning Director Karl Belser recalled, "was the exact counterpart of the farm community," for their relationship was deeply intertwined. The towns, Belser continued,

> provided the financial, retail, professional and personal services. They were also the market for some of the farm produce. However, the key to the economic life was the joint activity where the produce of the farm was processed and prepared for delivery to the world market. Each dollar of value produced on the farm was recycled through the economy several times.[69]

The one atypical community, Palo Alto, would be the point of genesis for the great changes that were to engulf the agrarian world that had existed in Santa Clara County until the 1940s. Palo Alto, 20 miles northwest of San Jose, grew up around Leland Stanford's great university, which had been established in 1885. In 1940 it had less than 17,000 residents, most of whom were affiliated with the university or who sought the genteel tranquillity of gracious living within a railroad commute of the office towers of San Francisco. A more opposite ambience from that of San Jose and surroundings could not be imagined, yet their fates were already intertwined

By the 1930s, Frederick Terman, a visionary electrical engineering

FIGURE 1.1
The San Francisco Bay Region

Note: "Localities" include cities and unincorporated places of 2,500 or more population in 1970 Census. Unincorporated localities are indicated (u).

Source: 1970 USGS—San Francisco Bay Region Map; Association of Bay Area Governments, 1976.

FIGURE 1.2

The San Jose Metropolitan Area (Santa Clara County)

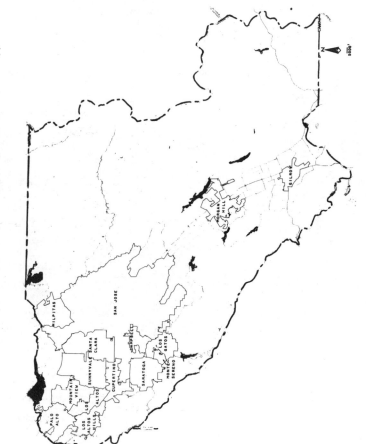

Source: Planning Department, Santa Clara County, 1979.

19

TABLE 1.3

Population of Cities and Unincorporated Area in Santa Clara County, 1920–75

City	1920	1930	1940	1950	1960	1970	1975
County Total	100,700	145,100	174,900	290,500	642,315	1,065,313	1,169,006
Alviso	500	400	700	700	1,174	[a]	[a]
Campbell	—	—	—	—	11,863	23,797	25,108
Cupertino	—	—	—	—	3,664	17,895	22,023
Gilroy	2,900	3,500	3,600	4,900	7,348	12,684	15,589
Los Altos	—	—	—	—	19,696	25,062	26,260
Los Altos Hills	—	—	—	—	3,412	6,871	6,993
Los Gatos	2,300	3,200	3,600	4,900	9,036	22,613	23,882
Milpitas	—	—	—	—	6,572	26,561	31,666
Monte Sereno	—	—	—	—	1,506	2,847	3,111
Morgan Hill	600	900	1,000	1,600	3,131	5,579	8,882
Mountain View	1,000	3,300	3,900	6,600	30,889	54,132	55,095
Palo Alto	5,900	13,700	16,800	25,500	52,287	56,040	52,623
San Jose	39,700	57,700	68,500	95,300	294,196	459,913	551,224
Santa Clara	5,200	6,300	6,700	11,700	58,880	86,118	82,978
Saratoga	—	—	—	—	14,861	26,810	29,150
Sunnyvale	1,700	3,100	4,400	9,800	52,898	95,976	102,154
Total unincorporated	40,000	53,000	65,700	129,500	160,882	142,415	132,268

[a] Annexed into the city of San Jose.

Note: Dash indicates city not yet incorporated.

Source: Santa Clara County Planning Department, *Housing Characteristics, Cities, Santa Clara County, 1970* (1971), and Santa Clara County Planning Department, *1975 Countywide Census, Santa Clara County* (1976).

20

professor at Stanford, had perceived the lucrative partnership that could be shared by industry and the academy, and he encouraged his talented students to establish their fledgling enterprises nearby rather than pursue employment in the East. Thus, he convinced David Packard to return to Palo Alto from Schenectady, New York, and General Electric. There he joined William Hewlett, another Terman protege, and, in a small garage shop, the Hewlett-Packard Company began operations in 1939; it now employs about 30,000 worldwide, 40 percent of whom are in Santa Clara County. About the same time, Sigurd and Russell Varian, with $100 for supplies from Stanford and free use of its laboratories, developed the radar-essential klystron tube. The university's royalties on this one item have amounted to more than $2 million over the last 30 years. Today, the multitudinous spinoffs of the Stanford atelier are staggering in their proliferation. For example, an offshoot of William Shockley's pioneering transistor firm became Fairchild Semiconductor, which has in turn spawned at least 38 other enterprises. Similarly, Varian alumni formed Spectra-Physics, now the world's largest laser company.[70] The list goes on ad infinitum.

With the outbreak of World War II, the die was cast for the Santa Clara Valley. Proximate to Stanford's technology watershed and the nearby Moffet Field military base and only a short distance from the industrial centers of San Francisco, Richmond, and Oakland and the military installations ringing the northern sector of San Francisco Bay, urbanization in Santa Clara County awaited only the benign influences of a peacetime economy.

Even before the end of World War II, it was clear that a new order of conditions would be directing the course of events in the county. War-related manufacturing and the burgeoning technology that provided the successful underpinning of the Allied victory would reach as pervasively into the postwar era as it had during prior years. The regrouping of international belligerence after 1945 and the eruption of the Korean conflict generated even more momentum in what was already a prodigious cradle of sophisticated scientific advance. Brimming over with ingenuity, industrial leaders also found it was not a difficult matter to make defense-related technology applications amenable to domestic consumption.

Population growth followed apace. The personnel imported by war materiel industries during the early 1940s and returning military contingents from the Pacific Theater found that the San Francisco Bay area could absorb them into its expanding labor force. Indeed, many of the new jobs were located in the northern portion of Santa Clara County, particularly in the swath from Palo Alto southeast to Sunnyvale and Santa Clara. San Jose interests had recognized the enormous potentials for growth heralded by the postwar era and had mobilized to aggressively attract its share. In 1944, local politicians and businessmen formed the Progress Committee in order to achieve that mandate. Landowners, the construction trades, retailers, bankers, realtors, and other mercantile groups managed to elect the first in a long succession of city councils with an enthusiastic commitment to growth. In the 1950s, when questions were raised concerning the impact of this policy and the concentration of wealth and influence perceived to be its prime mover, a similar axis emerged with the thinly veiled title of the "Book of the Month Club." Although it was averred that the main purpose of this clique was to discuss certain literary works, its membership of businessmen, builders, realtors, land speculators, the publisher of the San Jose *Mercury* and *News* (the city's only morning and afternoon papers), San Jose's city manager, councilmen, and planning commissioners, among others, signalled an interest in matters far less altruistic.[71] Indeed, they had much to occupy them, for the county's population had grown to 290,000 in 1950, an increase of two-thirds since 1940. The lush farmlands on the valley floor were being sold for development, and attendant residential services followed in rapid order. Unable to garner the industrial base, which tended to cluster around Palo Alto area agglomerations, San Jose cast its lot as the bedroom community for individuals working in the north county technology belt. Perceiving this aggressive posture on the part of San Jose, officials of other communities moved to secure their share of the prosperity.

Perhaps the key reason for the ensuing scramble in Santa Clara County's helter-skelter land market in the early 1950s was the aggressive program of annexation pursued by San Jose. Between 1950 and 1972, it engulfed 125 square miles, thus increasing its total area to 142. Not an insignificant portion of this turf was brought into the city by means of extending fingers of city land to outlying tracts deemed ripe for development. One of these corridors was no less than three miles in length and a mere roadway in width.[72] This situation was viewed with alarm not only by proponents of rational growth but by other local interests as well. As a result, existing municipalities, such as Santa Clara and Sunnyvale, moved to consolidate their geopolitical holdings, while seven other localities experiencing sufficient nascent awareness, tempered by a reluctance to become swallowed up by San Jose, moved to implement a policy of incorporation. Thus, Campbell, Milpitas, and Cupertino, adjacent localities directly threatened by the expansion of San Jose, carved out their spheres of influence. It had been 40 years since the last incorporation had occurred in the county. Table 1.4 details the progression of this activity.

Simultaneously, the eruption of hostilities in Korea had acted to provide additional momentum to the vigorous industrialization that was proceeding in the county. Sylvania, Fairchild, FMC, Admiral, Kaiser, General Precision, and Lockheed made their move into the area, and San Jose

TABLE 1.4

Dates of Incorporation for Santa Clara County Municipalities

Community	Year of Incorporation
San Jose	1850
Santa Clara	1852
Gilroy	1870
Los Gatos	1887
Palo Alto	1894
Mountain View	1902
Morgan Hill	1906
Sunnyvale	1912
Campbell	1952
Los Altos	1952
Milpitas	1954
Cupertino	1955
Los Altos Hills	1956
Saratoga	1956
Monte Sereno	1957

Source: Santa Clara County Planning Department (1978).

managed to attract facilities that included Ford, General Electric, and IBM, among others. This industrial pattern, consolidated in the post-World War II years, continued to develop in the 1950s and beyond and provided the structural underpinnings for future developments. The entrepreneurial and scientific vigor of local researchers spawned the aerospace industry and then a burgeoning of electronics and other related high technology enterprises. Mergers and acquisitions further increased the number of significant operations.

Perhaps the ultimate in Terman's industry-academy tandem is represented by the Stanford Industrial Park. Because its founder prohibited the sale of the land in his bequest, Stanford developed its industrial park on 660 acres adjoining the campus. With 55 tenants, including Hewlett-Packard and Varian, the park employs over 17,000 persons and has been an important factor in the continuing creation of a swarm of smaller firms, many of which have grown into major corporations which in turn have spawned other enterprises. By 1977, Santa Clara County was the established national center of electronics and high technology, with nearly 200,000 employed in that sector alone.[73]

Population growth was a simultaneous response to the rapid industrialization that was occurring. While each new manufacturing job

TABLE 1.5

Distribution of Owner-Occupied Houses by Value Class, for Cities and Unincorporated Area, Santa Clara County, 1970

City	Total Housing Units	Distribution of Owner-Occupied Houses (percentage)								Median Dollar Value
		Under $4,999	$5,000–$9,999	$10,000–14,999	$15,000–19,999	$20,000–24,999	$25,000–34,999	$35,000–49,999	$50,000–and Over	
Total county	181,177	0.1	0.6	2.9	12.6	25.8	35.2	16.0	7.0	27,300
Total incorporated	155,112	0.1	0.5	2.6	11.4	25.8	36.7	16.3	6.6	27,600
Campbell	4,291	0.2	0.8	2.4	11.5	34.4	44.7	4.9	1.1	25,100
Cupertino	3,342	0.1	0.2	0.7	2.9	9.7	39.9	40.8	5.7	34,100
Gilroy	1,910	0.3	2.3	10.5	24.3	28.4	24.7	7.7	1.8	22,200
Los Altos	6,182	0.0	0.0	0.3	1.3	5.4	24.6	41.4	26.9	41,600
Los Altos Hills	1,585	0.1	0.1	0.1	0.2	0.5	3.2	12.4	83.3	50,000+
Los Gatos	4,318	0.1	0.4	2.2	6.9	15.4	31.5	28.7	14.9	33,000
Milpitas	4,698	0.0	0.2	1.5	17.3	45.6	32.6	2.3	0.4	23,400
Monte Sereno	789	0.0	0.3	1.3	4.2	7.9	19.9	25.6	40.9	44,700

Morgan Hill	887	0.2	1.9	7.3	23.0	27.7	21.6	14.2	3.9	23,200
Mountain View	5,381	0.1	0.6	1.6	9.8	20.3	44.6	18.1	4.9	23,900
Palo Alto	10,407	0.1	0.2	0.6	3.4	12.8	36.9	30.3	15.7	33,900
San Jose	76,119	0.1	0.6	3.5	14.2	29.8	39.0	10.9	1.7	25,400
Santa Clara	13,726	0.1	0.5	2.9	15.3	37.7	37.8	5.4	0.3	24,100
Saratoga	6,281	0.0	0.1	0.3	2.8	7.5	13.9	33.3	42.1	46,400
Sunnyvale	15,196	0.2	0.2	1.2	8.3	22.9	41.2	24.9	1.2	29,200
Total Unincorporated	26,065	0.2	1.0	4.7	19.3	25.4	26.2	14.2	9.2	24,800

Source: Santa Clara County Planning Department, *Housing Characteristics, Cities, Santa Clara County, 1970* (1971).

TABLE 1.6

Minority Population, By City, Santa Clara County, 1970 (percentage)

City	White Race		Negro	Other Races						
	Spanish American	Non-Spanish American		Total	Amer. Indian	Japanese	Chinese	Filipino	All Other[a]
Total county	17.5	76.8	1.7	4.0	0.4	1.6	0.7	0.6	0.7
Campbell	10.5	86.2	0.2	3.2	0.3	1.7	0.4	0.4	0.4
Cupertino	6.4	89.9	0.3	3.4	0.2	1.7	1.0	0.1	0.3
Gilroy	46.1	47.5	0.2	6.2	0.6	1.8	0.5	1.0	2.2
Los Altos[b]	5.1	92.3	0.4	2.2	0.1	1.2	0.7	0.2	0.2
Los Altos Hills	n.a.	n.a.	0.4	1.6	0.2	0.7	0.5	—[c]	0.2
Los Gatos	4.9	93.5	0.2	1.5	0.2	0.5	0.4	0.1	0.3
Milpitas	18.6	70.4	5.2	5.6	0.9	0.6	1.0	1.6	1.6
Monte Sereno	n.a.	n.a.	0.1	1.9	—	1.0	0.2	0.3	0.4
Morgan Hill	28.5	65.6	0.2	5.7	0.7	2.6	0.3	0.5	1.5
Mountain View	14.0	78.1	1.3	6.5	0.3	2.8	1.1	1.6	0.7

Palo Alto[b]	5.7	87.1	2.6	4.6	0.2	1.7	1.8	0.4	0.5
San Jose[b]	21.8	71.7	2.5	3.9	0.4	1.6	0.6	0.6	0.8
Santa Clara	18.1	77.3	0.8	3.8	0.5	1.1	0.5	0.9	0.8
Saratoga	5.3	92.5	0.2	1.9	0.1	1.1	0.5	0.1	0.2
Sunnyvale	13.3	81.4	0.8	4.6	0.3	1.6	1.3	0.8	0.7
Total Unin-corporated	n.a.	n.a.	1.2	3.9	0.4	1.8	0.6	0.5	0.6

[a]Includes 748 Hawaiians and 685 Koreans. Available countywide only.

[b]Does not include later total population corrections by the Bureau of the Census. Revised figures on minority population have not been received.

[c]Dash indicates less than 0.5 percent.

Source: U.S. Census of Population 1970, Single Area Tabulation 11-2, Census Service Facility, U.C. Berkeley. General Population Characteristics, California, 1970 U.S. Census of Population, PC (1)-B6 California; Santa Clara County Planning Department, Housing Characteristics, Cities, Santa Clara County, 1970 (1971).

generated about 1.2 additional positions in the matured economy of the San Francisco Bay area in 1975, this multiplier was two to three times higher in the early 1950s, when Santa Clara County was beginning to urbanize.[74] Because of these jobs, people came to the valley in large numbers. Table 1.3 illustrates the dimensions of an immigration that swelled the county's population from 290,500 in 1950 to nearly 650,000 in 1960, an increase of 121.1 percent. Numerically, San Jose was the single largest recipient of that growth.

The county's other cities, as noted above, each reacted to the aggressive expansion of San Jose. For example, Santa Clara and Sunnyvale, two of the most proximate, consolidated their territorial spheres of influence and effectively capitalized on their convenient access to the Palo Alto technology orbit by attracting a large industrial base as well as encouraging substantial residential construction of reasonable cost. It is hardly surprising that these two communities experienced the highest rates of growth in the frenetic pace of urbanization that inundated the county during the 1950s.

On the other hand, Cupertino incorporated so that its destiny could be better controlled than if San Jose were allowed to assume jurisdiction. The legacy of this action is obvious. By preempting San Jose, Cupertino could achieve a more balanced tax base by eschewing dependence on a broad-based residential growth and create a more exclusive housing stock by allowing the market to establish more costly land prices. Consequently, Cupertino has joined Los Gatos as an upper middle-class enclave, while San Jose has grown to accommodate a broad range of housing markets. Table 1.5 illustrates the impact of this policy as one views the distribution of housing prices for owner-occupied units in 1970. Well before the end of the decade, inflation in California's housing market has been so rampant that by 1978 one could treble those values for a more contemporary assessment of the real estate market and distribution of housing prices. A byproduct of this situation is the distribution of racial minorities in Santa Clara County. Table 1.6 provides data concerning the distribution of minorities—the most numerous of whom are the Chicanos—who find that San Jose's housing market is far less restrictive than the other communities contained within the ensuing study.

The development of housing in the 1950s, 1960s, and early 1970s, proceeded apace as all conditions were favorable to the development of large tracts of single-family housing. The valley floor was easily urbanized and highly accessible once the circulation system developed and matured. Financing was readily available, and the large supply of land kept housing prices low, even though the demand generated by immigration was vigorous. The single-family house was the preferred mode of living under these bountiful circumstances, and it was a goal attainable by nearly three-

TABLE 1.7

Distribution of Housing Units, by Year Structure Built, for Cities, Santa Clara County, 1970

City	Total Units	Percentage Distribution						
		1969 to March 1970	1965–68	1960–64	1950–59	1940–49	1939 or Earlier
Total county	336,192	6.4	15.1	25.4	32.5	8.6	12.1
Total incorporated	289,628	6.6	15.7	27.1	31.3	7.5	11.7
Campbell	7,436	1.5	11.4	35.8	32.8	11.0	7.5
Cupertino	5,687	18.3	21.6	38.1	16.9	2.4	2.6
Gilroy	3,726	5.6	14.9	18.1	25.0	12.3	24.2
Los Altos	7,817	2.1	9.0	19.6	47.8	12.2	9.4
Los Altos Hills	1,903	3.1	16.2	24.5	35.5	7.6	13.1
Los Gatos	8,147	3.4	16.0	29.7	22.7	7.9	20.2
Milpitas	6,794	5.9	29.4	39.2	22.9	1.1	1.6
Monte Sereno	912	2.9	12.5	9.8	33.7	16.3	24.9
Morgan Hill	1,896	6.2	16.0	19.0	28.1	7.2	23.5
Mountain View	21,129	7.3	18.5	28.5	32.0	7.0	6.7
Palo Alto	21,353	3.4	4.9	13.7	38.7	15.2	24.1
San Jose	136,268	7.6	17.8	27.7	26.2	6.9	13.9
Santa Clara	27,851	5.5	9.2	26.4	46.6	6.0	6.3
Saratoga	7,237	4.3	17.6	25.5	38.5	5.9	8.2
Sunnyvale	31,472	7.1	16.6	30.3	36.0	6.5	3.6
Total unincorporated	46,564	5.0	10.8	14.7	40.0	15.4	14.2

Source: Santa Clara County Planning Department, Housing Characteristics, Santa Clara County, 1970 (1971).

29

quarters of the population by 1970.[75] Table 1.7 illustrates the rapid pace at which building proceeded after 1950. Based on 1970 figures, nearly half of Los Altos and Santa Clara were built between 1950 and 1959. Two-thirds of Sunnyvale, Saratoga, Campbell, and Los Altos and three-fourths of Santa Clara were in place by 1964. Over 90 percent of Milipitas and 80 percent of San Jose emerged from 1950 to 1968, and more than three-fourths of Cupertino was built after 1960.

However, in the early 1970s, there were signs that the supply of developable land was taking on finite proportions. As land costs began to escalate, lots became smaller, and townhouse and condominium projects emerged. Further, environmental and fiscally inspired moratoria put a brake on housing supply, thus fueling the flames of inflation in the market. The supply of large parcels began to dry up, and "in-filling" developments of less than 50 units started to appear. The northern half of Santa Clara County is now a mature, fully urbanized community with most of its growth already accomplished. Redevelopment to higher densities in some areas is now the only alternative posed by the near future.

On the horizontal plane, then, one can perceive the increments of growth of each period in the two centuries that the county has been inhabited by other than its indigenous population of the California Indian group, collectively known as Costanoan. There are old nineteenth-century kernals in Campbell, Los Gatos, downtown San Jose, and so forth. There is the development that accompanied the agrarian and food-processing centers before World War II. The suburban sprawl that consumed most of the valley after World War II is the dominant feature of the landscape today. Finally, here and there are the in-fillings of the mid and late 1970s, small projects, mostly of higher density. This last group will probably evolve into the type of unit that will be defined by economic constraints and by the lifestyle preferences of the population to be served. It will be a formidable challenge to translate these circumstances effectively into an attractive, functional, and socially supportive environment.

NOTES

1. See, for example, William Alonso, "Metropolis Without Growth," *The Public Interest* 53 (1978): 68–86.

2. Basil Zimmer, "The Urban Centrifugal Drift," in *Metropolitan America in Contemporary Perspective*, ed. Amos H. Hawley and Vincent P. Rock (New York: Halsted Press, 1975), pp. 23–92.

3. Ibid., p. 26.

4. John C. Bollens and Henry J. Schmandt, *The Metropolis: Its People, Politics, and Economic Life*, 3rd ed. (New York: Harper and Row, 1975), p. 245.

5. See, for example, Bennett M. Berger, *Working Class Suburb* (Berkeley: University of California Press, 1971); Herbert J. Gans, *The Levittowners* (New York: Vintage Books, 1967);

George Sternlieb, et al., *The Affluent Suburb: Princeton* (New Brunswick, N.J.: Transaction Books, 1971); and John Seeley et al., *Crestwood Heights* (New York: Basic Books, 1956).

6. William H. Whyte, Jr., *The Organization Man* (Garden City, N.Y.: Anchor Books, 1957); David Riesman et al., *The Lonely Crowd* (New Haven, Conn.: Yale University Press, 1950); David Riesman, "The Suburban Sadness," in *The Suburban Community*, ed. William M. Dobriner (New York: G.P. Putnam's Sons, 1958), pp. 375–408; A.C. Spectorsky, *The Exurbanites* (Philadelphia: Lippincott, 1955).

7. Whyte, *Organization Man*; Vance Packard, *The Status Seekers* (New York: Dell, 1962); R.E. Gordon et al., *The Split-Level Trap* (New York: Dell, 1962); John Keats, *The Crack in the Picture Window* (Boston: Houghton-Mifflin, 1956).

8. Richard Sennett, *Families Against the City: Middle Class Homes of Industrial Chicago, 1872–1890* (New York: Vintage Books, 1974), p. 44.

9. S.D. Clark, *The Suburban Society* (Toronto: University of Toronto Press, 1966), p. 8.

10. Ibid.

11. Stanford Environmental Law Society, *San Jose: Sprawling City* (Stanford, Calif.: Environmental Law Society, 1971).

12. Kenneth L. Jackson, "Urban Deconcentration in the Nineteenth Century: A Statistical Inquiry," in *The New Urban History*, ed. Leo F. Schnore (Princeton, N.J.: Princeton University Press, 1975), pp. 110–11.

13. Stephan Thernstrom, "Urbanization, Migration and Social Mobility in Late Nineteenth Century America," in *American Urban History*, ed. Alexander B. Callow, 2nd ed., (New York: Oxford University Press, 1973), p. 399.

14. Homer Hoyt, *One Hundred Years of Land Values in Chicago* (New York: Arno Press, 1970), pp. 153–54.

15. Ibid., p. 195.

16. Ibid.

17. Ibid., p. 109.

18. Ibid., p. 282.

19. Howard P. Chudacoff, *The Evolution of American Urban Society* (Englewood Cliffs, N.J.: Prentice-Hall, 1975), p. 76.

20. Robert C. Wood, *Suburbia: Its People and Their Politics* (Boston: Houghton-Mifflin, 1958), p. 60.

21. Ibid.

22. David Ward, *Cities and Immigrants: A Geography of Change in Nineteenth Century America* (New York: Oxford University Press, 1971), ch. 4.

23. Sam Bass Warner, *Streetcar Suburbs: The Process of Growth in Boston, 1870–1900* (New York: Atheneum, 1969), p. 157.

24. Quoted in Joel Arthur Tarr, "From City to Suburb: The 'Moral' Influence of Transportation Technology," in Callow, *American Urban History*, p. 202.

25. Warner, *Streetcar Suburbs*, p. 157.

26. Quoted in Peter J. Goheen, *Victorian Toronto, 1850 to 1900* (Chicago: University of Chicago Press, 1970), p. 19.

27. Gans, *Levittowners*; Bill Owens, *Suburbia* (San Francisco: Straight Arrow Press, 1973).

28. Everett Chamberlin, *Chicago and its Suburbs* (New York: Arno Press, 1974), p. 188.

29. Christopher Tunnard and Henry Hope Reed, *American Skyline: The Growth and Form of Our Cities and Towns* (New York: Mentor Books, 1956), p. 62.

30. Warner, *Streetcar Suburbs*, p. 76.

31. Ibid.

32. Sidney J. Low, quoted in Goheen, *Victorian Toronto*, p. 18.

33. Richard J. Hopkins, "Status, Mobility, and the Dimensions of Change in a Southern City: Atlanta: 1870–1910," in *Cities in American History*, ed. Kenneth L. Jackson and Stanley K. Schultz (New York: Alfred A. Knopf, 1972) p. 217.

34. Harvey Marshall, "Suburban Life Styles: A Contribution to the Debate," in *The Urbanization of the Suburbs*, ed. Louis H. Masotti and Jeffrey K. Hadden (Beverly Hills, Calif.: Sage, 1973), p. 145.

35. Warner, *Streetcar Suburbs*, p. 80; Robert A. Woods and Albert J. Kennedy, *The Zone of Emergence*, ed. and abridged by Sam Bass Warner, 2nd ed. (Cambridge, Mass.: M.I.T. Press, 1969), p. 38. The original manuscript is dated 1905-14.

36. Sam Bass Warner, *The Private City: Philadelphia in Three Periods of Growth* (Philadelphia: University of Pennsylvania Press, 1968), p. 174.

37. Warner, *Streetcar Suburbs*, p. 156.

38. Ibid., p. 148. This may now be difficult to evaluate aesthetically with the auto(s) now dominating much of the house environment.

39. Ibid., p. 90.

40. San Francisco *Chronicle*, November 28, 1977, p. 1.

41. Sam Bass Warner, *The Urban Wilderness* (New York: Harper and Row, 1972), p. 206.

42. Ibid.

43. Riesman, "Suburban Sadness," p. 399.

44. Ibid., p. 398.

45. Clark, *Suburban Society*, p. 144.

46. Quoted in Peter J. Schmitt, *Back to Nature: The Arcadian Myth in Urban America* (New York: Oxford University Press, 1969), p. 21.

47. Ibid., p. 22

48. Sennett, *Families Against the City*, pp. 141-42.

49. Ibid., p. 49.

50. Ibid., p. 51.

51. Wood, *Suburbia*, p. 6.

52. Sennett, *Families Against the City*, pp. 122-23.

53. Ibid.

54. Ibid., pp. 146-67.

55. Claude S. Fischer and Robert Max Jackson, "Suburbs, Networks and Attitudes," in *The Changing Face of the Suburbs*, ed. Barry Schwartz (Chicago: University of Chicago Press, 1976), p. 286.

56. Ibid.; see also Gans, *Levittowners*, p. 226.

57. Riesman, "Suburban Sadness," p. 389.

58. Sennett, *Families Against the City*, pp. 52-53.

59. Riesman, "Suburban Sadness," p. 381., Jacob Riis, *How the Other Half Lives* (New York: Hill and Wang, 1957).

60. Wood, *Suburbia*, p. 107.

61. See the Child Care Act of 1979, S.4 (introduced by Alan Cranston) and/or H.R. 1121 (introduced by Edward R. Roybal).

62. Woods and Kennedy, *Zone of Emergence*, p. 23.

63. Ibid., pp. 21-22.

64. Warner, *Streetcar Suburbs*, pp. 158-59.

65. Alonso, "Metropolis Without Growth."

66. Quoted in Jackson, "Urban Deconcentration," p. 142.

67. Quoted in Daniel J. Garr, "A Frontier Agrarian Settlement: San José de Guadalupe 1777-1850," *San Jose Studies* 2 (November 1976): 102.

68. Karl Belser, "The Making of Slurban America," *Cry California* 5 (Fall 1970): 1-4.

69. Belser, "Slurban America."

70. For more details on the role of technology in the growth of the Santa Clara Valley, see Gene Bylinsky, "California's Great Breeding Ground for Industry," *Fortune* 89, no. 6 (June 1974): 129-35, 216-24.

71. See Stanford Environmental Law Society, *San Jose*; ch. 2.

72. Ibid., p. 26.

73. James M. Carney, "How to Evaluate the Impacts of the Combined General Plans of the Cities of Santa Clara County, California" (M.U.P. thesis, San Jose State University, 1978), p. 28. Note that many jobs are held by residents of adjoining San Mateo County and thus are not reflected in Santa Clara data.

74. Santa Clara County Housing Task Force, *Housing: A Call for Action* (San Jose, Calif.: Santa Clara County Planning Department, 1977), p. 4.

75. In 1970, detached single-family homes comprised 72.6 percent of all housing in the San Jose Standard Metropolitan Statistical Area (Santa Clara County). See Santa Clara County Planning Department, *Housing Characteristics, Cities, Santa Clara County, 1970* (San Jose Calif.: Santa Clara County Planning Department, 1971).

2

WOMEN'S STATUS AND SUBURBIA

Women have lived intimately with men through all of history, we may assume, or there would be no history to report. Yet men and women may well live in two different cultures. They have shared in the tasks of creating an advanced civilization, but in their internal psychological worlds they have frequently focused on their differences rather than their similarities. And because men have held positions of power and control, women's lives have always been seen as tangential to and supportive to theirs. The story of women, until very recently, has been a story told by men. How, then, have men perceived women, and how does this perception relate to how women see themselves? A thorough answer to these questions would involve plumbing the mysteries of the mythical consciousness of generations, through Eve and Lillith, Athena and the Eumenides, the Virgin Mary, Mona Lisa, and Miss America. Such studies have been undertaken elsewhere and have come to the conclusion that the greatest commonality among all the images of woman is that the woman is the Other.[1] She is different from men, unknowable,perverse,a bit dangerous. Her sphere of life is apt to be kept separate from the male sphere. Beyond this essential differentness there is little consistency in the images of women that have passed through the generations. Women are spiritual and holy. They are the guardians of religion and ethical values. Women force men to clean up their language around the children. They remember to send flowers when someone is sick. They stand for temperance, graciousness, and restraint. But women are temptresses, men also tell each other. They represent raw sexuality. They'll lure you away from your work, play on your weaker nature, and squander your money. Women waste your time with endless vanities and sap your precious body fluids. Women are servants. They will plow the fields, type your term paper, clean the toilet, bring you a beer when you're thirsty.

Women are weak and fragile. They need to be protected from the harshness of life. They cry easily. They cannot open car doors or light their own cigarettes. They are to be cherished and pampered. The list goes on and the contradictions compound as they pass from generation to generation, confusing men and women equally. The concept of woman as Other pervades every culture and every social class. Many have described the status of women as a caste status.[2] The blend of the various myths may change from group to group, but in every case the woman is seen as different, and in every case the woman's own self-concept is manipulated, leading to her self-denigration so that she appears to contribute to her own subordination. This tacit cooperation between oppressor and oppressed is part of the definition of a caste.

The women's liberation movement, the second major feminist movement in the United States, has challenged the underlying ideology that has perpetuated the oppression of women as a caste. Like the earlier feminist movement, it had its beginning among well-educated, middle-class women. Unlike the earlier movement, which came to center on the political issue of suffrage, the new feminism appeared to spring out of a discussion of the most personal and trivial issue imaginable—housework. In 1963, Betty Friedan spoke about the unspeakable, the problem that has no name. Women who had achieved the American dream, an affluent lifestyle in a lovely suburban home with a devoted husband and two darling children, these women, were not happy. The problem that could no longer be ignored, Friedan said, was the voice within each woman which said, "I want something more than my husband and my children and my house."[3]

The movement started with middle-class women who had many advantages over their working-class sisters, but perhaps those very privileges of education and financial comfort served to point out to them the essential waste of their lives. In comparing the women in two Santa Clara County suburbs, Susan Grumich found that the working-class women in Milpitas were fairly content with their lives. Although most of them worked, many on the assembly lines at the auto plants, they described themselves in terms of their family roles of wife and mother. In elegant, upper middle-class Saratoga the women who were predominantly housewives described themselves in terms of professional roles, "I'm a teacher who hasn't taught in ten years," for example. The women were asked what animal they would like to be if they were not human beings. The Milpitas women often expressed the desire to be pampered domestic pets, especially kittens. The Saratoga women wanted to be birds, to soar away to freedom.[4] Maybe one needs the luxury of living as a coddled kitten for a while before one can confront the ideological implications of that life.

The present study examines mothers of school-age children in commodious suburban homes, women who appear to lack few comforts in their surroundings. Many of these women are married housewives; others work full time, and some are single or divorced. Our interest in these women is in their lives at home, as consumers of housing in a suburban setting. The remainder of this chapter explores the concepts of home, house, and family as they relate to the concrete experiences of women and help us to understand the women interviewed in our study, women whose lives for 20 years have paralleled and perhaps intersected with the awareness of a new feminist movement, yet who function in institutions that reflect centuries of a traditional doctrine.

WOMEN AT HOME

Historians are not in agreement about the earliest family structures. An indirect source of evidence on early family life lies in anthropological data regarding modern pre-industrial societies. Nearly every society recognizes a family unit of some sort as the prime instrument of childrearing and socialization. Every society appears to make role distinctions and to divide labor along sexual lines. Moreover, the biological necessity of women's bearing and nursing children tends to prescribe that the female's sphere will be close to the home. Beyond this one limitation, however, no cross-cultural generalizations can be drawn. Tasks that are considered woman's work in one culture are firmly held to be men's work in another.[5]

Engels argues that both Greek and Roman civilizations progressed from promiscuous to monogamous relationships and from matriarchal to patriarchal forms. He observed that the word "family" derives from the Roman *famulia* meaning the total number of domestic slaves belonging to a man. "The term was invented by the Romans to denote a new social organism, whose head ruled over wife and children and a number of slaves, and was invested with rights of life and death over them all.... "[6] Through this mechanism men were guaranteed a clearly defined line of parentage and inheritance. Sexual fidelity was demanded of women though not of men. Engels viewed the establishment of the family as the first step toward the subjugation of women and the elimination of the matriarchal line of inheritance. Other historians, notably Westermarck, claimed that patriarchal monogamy was the original form of the household unit.[7]

The medieval family structure is believed to have been "large, loose and undemanding."[8] Children were treated as small adults. They wore adult clothes, played adult games, and were expected to share in the work of society.[9] Family members had few obligations to one another. Women were allowed considerable freedom of movement and participated in government, crafts, and trades.[10] In the sixteenth century changes began to occur in the concept of family life. According to William O'Neill,

The family concentrated itself and turned inward, privacy became important, the education of children assumed major proportions, and women acquired a great many new duties and responsibilities.... In the seventeenth and eighteenth centuries as domestic life became, from the woman's point of view, more demanding and confining, the alternatives to it diminished. They were squeezed out of certain traditional occupations, and by the early nineteenth century women, and especially married women, possessed few legal or political rights of their own.[11]

With the industrial revolution came changes which accelerated the constraint of women's social and familial positions. In colonial America, women worked at crafts and "ran self sufficient domestic factories producing, among other things, clothes, candles, soap, quilts and mattresses."[12] As industrialization advanced, "the separation of the workplace from the home caused a major shift in the functions of the family and the household."[13] Whereas the home had previously served a number of social functions—workshop, school, church, hospital, asylum—it came to be increasingly private. The family gradually changed from the production unit to a consumption unit.[14] The focus of the home because primarily domestic. Christopher Lasch has described the function of the new family unit as the haven in a heartless world. This view

found ideological support and justification in the concept of the family as an emotional refuge in a cold and competitive society.... This ideal took for granted a radical separation between work and leisure and between public life and private life. The emergence of the nuclear family as the principal form of family life reflected the high value modern society attached to privacy, and the glorification of privacy in turn reflected the devaluation of work.[15]

The male head of household went out into the world and faced a harsh marketplace. He then returned to his private haven to replenish his strength. It follows that the woman would play a complementary role, making only an indirect contribution to the production of society by providing a comfortable home for her husband and children. A contemporary analysis of this relationship has been described by Beverly Jones:

The husband...wants in the home to be able to hide from his own inner doubts, his own sense of shame, failure, and meaninglessness. He wants to shed the endless humiliation of endless days parading as a man in the male world, pretending a power, control, and understanding he does not have.... All he asks of his wife, aside from hours of menial work is that she not see him as he sees himself. That she not challenge him, but admire him and desire him, soothe and distract him.[16]

Most significant to the present analysis is not the motivation of the husband or of the larger marketplace but the psychological reality for each woman. The ideology of the family as haven and the woman as nurturer and spiritual guardian has been accepted since biblical times. The relative status of American men and women in the nineteenth century is typified by this dialogue between feminist Margaret Fuller and a trader. After she challenged his right to speak on behalf of his wife, he countered:

> Am I not the head of my house?
> You are not the head of your wife. God has given her a mind of her own.
> I am the head, and she the heart.[17]

For centuries women have been socialized for the role of the heart of the household, the angel of consolation to husband and children. Rousseau wrote:

> The whole education of woman ought to be relative to men. To please them, to be useful to them, to make themselves loved and honored by them, to educate them when young, to care for them when grown, to counsel them, to console them, and to make life agreeable to them—these are the duties of woman at all times and what should be taught to them from their infancy.[18]

In more recent years women have come to be seen as important adjuncts to their husbands' professional advancement. Whyte, for example, discussed the importance of the appropriate wife for an ambitious young executive and described how wives as well as husbands were screened to be sure they projected the desired image.[19] Does this mean that the contemporary housewife is truly an equal partner in her husband's career, participating in the decision making and providing valuable counsel? Apparently not, according to Helen Z. Lopata's interviews with Illinois housewives. When asked how they felt that they influenced their husbands' careers the women most commonly answered by entertaining, being seen socially, and providing a happy home where the husband could relax. Other contributions such as discussing issues related to work and giving advice were rated much lower.[20]

The early education of females appears to be identical to that of males, yet Rousseau's doctrine is still subtly communicated throughout the educational system. By puberty a girl is beginning to receive messages that her future plans ought to be compatible with her inevitable and primary role as wife and mother. Simone De Beauvoir, Virginia Woolf, and Mary Wollstonecraft are among the feminist writers who have commented on the conflicts created in females by educating them for intellectual independence while indoctrinating them with a stronger mandate toward domesticity.[21] In a contemporary feminist novel the heroine Norma Jean muses on this training.

> She thinks how, as children, boys and girls move in and out of a house with a passable degree of equality, move outward from the home toward what they perceive as eventual goals, eventual freedom. Their late childhood and early adolescence is a continuous rehearsal for autonomy. Then, by some invisible arrangement, on reaching adulthood—usually at the time of marriage—the woman moves abruptly backwards, assumes the management of a home herself, occupies its center as her mother before her, becomes that mother, reverts to and displaces her, revokes whatever goals for achievement and involvement she may have entertained, and whatever freedom she may previously have enjoyed. The man's life, by contrast, continues to move in a direct and logical line—a continuum of the outwardly moving pursuit of freedom and explorations begun in childhood. He embraces the world, to the extent of his ability, and no one questions that this should be. Only the woman renounces it, trading whatever dreams she had for the isolation and certainty of her enclosure.[22]

Descriptive research appears to be in accord with this description of the male and female life cycle. The changes that men experience are frequently gradual ones, while women experience a series of sharp discontinuities at the points of marriage, childbirth, and departure of children, for example.[23] These changes also affect men, but not as dramatically. Men's career cycles usually shift at different points than do their personal life cycles, each thus offering some continuity to the other. More often shifts in a woman's personal life lead to dramatic changes in all areas of her existence. Marriage is one such dramatic change in a woman's life. Most women agree that the greatest and the most unanticipated changes accompany the birth of the first child. Studies show that a loss of freedom and a feeling of being tied down are mentioned by almost all new mothers.[24]

Although women have been socialized from birth to assume the roles of homemaker and mother, most report feeling totally unprepared for the sudden demands placed on them.[25] Playing with Barbie dolls is no training for the realities of raising a child. High school home economics classes offer scant help in managing a complex household. Even a young girl who anticipates the demands of her future role finds little within the formal educational system to prepare her for it. If she foregoes the courses in literature and trigonometry to take advanced classes in home economics, she will find that they have become professionalized, training the dietician, the professional interior decorator, the clothing designer, reflecting further our societal assumption that no particular education is needed to become a housewife or mother. Housewives report that the main source of their information comes from women's magazines (surprisingly little from their own mothers or their friends).[26] Factory workers, grocery clerks, and fast food chain managers all undergo some period of formal training. The skills of managing a home and raising a child are either assumed to be innate or so trivial that they can just be picked up on the job.

Apparently housework is assumed to be easy because it is often dull and repetitious. It does not produce anything tangible but merely maintains life. One cleans the kitchen in order to fix dinner. Two hours later one stands among the same dirty dishes and pans. Beds are made, rugs are vacuumed, laundry is done, rooms are straightened. Tomorrow, like Sisyphus, the housewife starts over in her endless cycle. Women's magazines in recent years have featured articles by "househusbands" who have taken over the tasks of housekeeping and childrearing temporarily or permanently. These men somewhat incredulously report what many women know: A great deal of housework is tedious, unpleasant, and thankless. Above all, it is relentless and draining. The tired housewife syndrome is a combination of physical exhaustion, lack of social and mental stimulation, and, often, simple lack of sleep attendant to caring for young children.[27] Men or others unaccustomed to caring for a house and children often express their surprise at the physical and emotional fatigue that accumulates after only a few days. A graduate student who spent several weeks caring for her sister's young children said,

> I took along lots of books and had planned to make major headway on my thesis. Although in one sense I had more free time than I had at school, I was never free. If the children were sleeping or playing outside, their safety, their next meal, their trail of clutter always demanded some part of my attention. After a few days I gave up trying to read anything heavier than *Redbook*. More often, if I had a few minutes to sit down, I'd turn on a game show or a soap opera. The neighbors were reasonably intelligent and educated women, yet I talked to them only of meatloaf, rashes and the Dating Game. This was very rough on my self image. I had always thought that if I became a housewife and mother I'd be different. But there I was living out the stereotype after only a few weeks. I had to admit that my concept of myself as an intellectually curious, creative, self motivated person was heavily dependent on the intense academic environment I lived in. I came to see my life as a result of choices—conscious and unconscious—rather than as a result of my unique traits. I've ceased to feel superior to women who appear to be totally absorbed in domesticity. I try harder to listen to them.[28]

These daily realities of housework seem less important somehow than the mythology that surrounds it. The mystification and glamorization of the homemaker role compounds women's problems. Not only is the female expected to take on many of life's more unpleasant and routine maintenance tasks, but she is led to believe that there is something terribly wrong with her if she fails to find happiness, stimulation, and creative challenge in her role. As Marya Mannes has written,

> The housewife image...is exalted daily by all the mass media.... In television soap operas the apron is the mark of a good woman.... Thanks largely to the brilliant manipulation of mass media, women are obsessed with an ideal of feminity as the guarantee of happiness. Be thin, be smart, be gay, be sexy, be soft-spoken. Get new slip covers, learn new recipes, have bright children, further your man's career, help the community, drive the car, smile. And if you can write a bestseller or a broadway hit too, that's great.[29]

Of course housework is necessary, and of course there is nothing inherently degrading in the tasks of cooking and cleaning. Campbell, Converse, and Rodgers's extension surveys conclude that well over half the women in the country like doing housework, that only three percent, without qualification, dislike the chores of cooking, sewing, and cleaning house.[30] There is, however, something inherently confusing about glamorizing tasks which seem to those doing them singularly unglamorous. The two real difficulties with housework, according to Meredith Tax, are that it is done in isolation and that it is not recognized as having any economic value.[31]

The loneliness and isolation of housework is in sharp contrast to earlier periods when the women of an extended family did their work together or when neighbors gathered to create small cottage industries. Myra Marx Ferree's research revealed that those housewives who were least happy in their roles were those who were socially isolated. These women were less happy than those who worked at even the most unsatisfying jobs if the latter had friends and enjoyable social contacts at work. The housewives who were happiest and who felt the most recognition for their work were the ones "who are warmly involved in social support groups. Their mothers, sisters, friends and cousins are in and out of the house all day. Their husbands value their work and think it is an important contribution to the maintenance of the family."[32]

Most women do not have access to such a support system. They spend hour after hour alone or with small children. In his book, *The Pursuit of Loneliness*, Philip Slater explored this problem:

> The emotional and intellectual poverty of the housewife's role is nicely expressed in the almost universal complaint: "I get to talking baby talk with no one around all day but the children." There are societies in which the domestic role works, but in those societies the housewife is not isolated. She is either part of a large extended family household in which domestic activities are a communal effort, or participates in a tightly knit village community, or both. The idea of imprisoning each woman alone in a small, self-contained, and

architecturally isolating dwelling is a modern invention, dependent upon an advanced technology.[33]

During a typical work day a man has extended social interaction. He returns to his "haven" seeking privacy and finds his wife starved for adult conversation. Herein lies the basis for many a comic strip and situation comedy, the husband absorbed in his newspaper or Monday night football game dutifully answering "yes, dear," to his wife's monologue. One step more serious is the tableau of the nagging wife claiming, "you never talk to me." The male, finally exaggerated, turns to his wife with a cold stare and says, "Oh, for Christ's sake, what is it you want to talk about?"[34]

After all, unless it's a matter of sexual pursuit or practical necessity ("Did you get my brown suit from the cleaners, dear?" "Bring me the Thompson file, Miss Jones."), why should a man want to talk to a woman? At the classic upper-class dinner party the men retire with brandy and cigars to discuss important matters until their host reluctantly suggests that it's time to rejoin the ladies. Informal social gatherings follow a similar pattern—men in the living room discussing business, cars, and sports, women in the kitchen talking about recipes, toilet training, and hairdos. An outrageous stereotype? At most an exaggeration. Men and women do talk about different topics. Only naturally, they talk about their own experiences and those experiences are radically different. In her novel, *The Women's Room*, Marilyn French probed this difference:

> There were two cultures—the world, which had men in it, and their own, which had only women and children. Within their own world they were there for each other physically and emotionally. They gave, through good humor and silent understanding, support and affection and legitimacy to each other and to the concerns they shared. Mira thought that they were more important to each other than their husbands were to them. She wondered if they could have survived without each other. She loved them.[35]

French's heroine Mira is an exception among both men and women in recognizing the value of women's interaction. In the culture at large it is devalued and ridiculed. We have the standing jokes of Blondie and Tootsie gossiping for hours on the telephone; women's gatherings are rendered absurd with such labels as hen parties and coffee klatches. Women themselves fail to see the significance and value of their talk with one another. They are taught to see other women as competitors. Adolescent girls talk endlessly, but they talk—directly or indirectly—about men. Girls learn that females spend time together when males are busy at other pursuits or when women need to plan their strategies related to men: "What shall I wear Saturday night?" "How can I get Ken to give me his ring?" "Do you like my hair this way?" Very early in life girls discover that their relationships with each other are secondary and learn not to be offended by "Let's go shopping Friday night unless one of us has a date."

An old African proverb states, "Women are sisters nowhere."[36] Jonathan Swift said, "I never knew a tolerable woman to be fond of her own sex."[37] These two sayings capture the folklore of generations that regard women and their conversations as trivial. Women themselves deny the importance of their relationships with one another, discrediting the empathy and emotional support they so desperately need because it comes from other women. Beverly Jones summed up the problem of the loneliness of women:

> Women see each other all the time, open their mouths, and make noises, but communicate on only the most superficial level. We don't talk to each other about what we consider our real problems because we are afraid to look insecure; because we don't trust or respect each other, and because we're afraid to look or be disloyal to husbands or benefactors.[38]

The social isolation of housewives is related to the second factor mentioned by Tax which renders housework dispiriting, the lack of any recognition of economic worth. Housewives are not paid. Their labors are not counted as part of the Gross National Product. They do not receive social security benefits, paid insurance policies, retirement plans, or unemployment benefits. As Tax observes, "the housewife's work is treated by society as though it simply did not exist as work."[39] Thus the common social faux pas persists "Do you work or are you just a housewife?" despite the irony of the fact that the average housewife works 60 to 80 hours a week and provides services worth approximately $14,000 a year.[40] There are few objective standards for success or failure in housework.[41] A woman will probably know if she's a poor homemaker but she has no sure way of knowing if her performance is fair, good, or excellent. Because there are no clear definitions and no external standards for such work her own sense of the number of hours at work blurs. Surely she's working when she's cleaning the bathroom. And surely she's not when she's playing bridge. But what about the afternoon with a friend shopping for new curtains, the time in the park with the children, the whole day spent planting a vegetable garden? Are these activities work or play? Before long, the housewife begins to doubt her own experience, declines to defend herself against the stereotypical charges that she spends her day sitting in front of the television set eating bonbons. Maybe these things she thought she was doing for her family *are* her hobbies. She certainly has few other hobbies.

Perhaps the lack of social recognition of the value of housework would be tolerable if women felt that their own husbands and children valued their contributions. Several television commercials are based on the assumption that the housewife's efforts are taken for granted. The advertised product will actualize her dream of achieving some notice. "Hey, mom, what did you do? These towels smell great!"

Selecting the laundry soap that makes towels soft and sweet-smelling in fact reflects the housewife's major value to the economy. John Kenneth Galbraith explains that "the decisive contribution of women in the developed industrial society is rather simple...to facilitate a continuing and more or less unlimited increase in consumption."[42] The steady growth of production which the United States has come to identify with economic health can occur only if there is also a steady increase of consumption. Galbraith observes that

> just as the production of goods and services requires management or administration so does their consumption.... The higher the standard of living...the more demanding the administration.... Thus suburban life sustains an especially large consumption of goods and, in consequence, is especially demanding in the administration required. The claims of roofs, furniture, plumbing, crab grass, vehicles, and recreational equipment all illustrate the point.[43]

A superb example of the pervasiveness of consumerism in the life of San Francisco Bay area Marin County is found in Cyra McFadden's, *The Serial*. The central characters, Kate and Harvey, made a great deal of money,

> but they spent it rapidly on things they hadn't known existed ten years ago: Rossignol Stratos and season lift tickets at Squaw; twin Motobecane ten-speeds; Kate's Cuisinart, which did *everything* but put the paté in the oven; Stine graphics; Gumpoldskirchner and St. Emilion (Harvey had "put down" a case in the vacuum cleaner closet); Klipsch speakers and the top-of-the-line Pioneer receiver; Brown-Jordan patio furniture; Dansk stainless and Rosenthal china; long-stemmed strawberries and walnut oil from the Mill Valley Market; Birkenstock sandals and Adidas.[44]

In this satirical exploration of the lives of Northern California's beautiful people objects are only referred to by their brand names: Kate never puts the dishes in the dishwasher, she puts the Heathware in the Kitchenaid. In the affluent household the level of consumption is so high that a full-time manager of consumption is needed. For approximately a century this management has been clearly understood to be an important part of the job description of the housewife. Torre discovered a 1912 Home Management treatise that stated, "the modern woman is chiefly a consumer, and not a producer."[45] Another such observation comes from Henry James's "International Episode" of 1878: " 'An American woman who respects herself, said Mrs. Westgate, turning to Beaumont with her bright expository air, 'must buy something every day of her life. If she cannot do it herself, she must send out some member of her family for the purpose.' "[46]

The management of consumption is a primary task of the middle-class housewife, and she takes pride in developing her skills, searching out the unknown specialty shops, taking estimates for household improvements. She decides when to shop for bargains to fill her family's needs, when only top quality goods and services will do. Consumer skills have developed to such a sophisticated level that they cannot be delegated to amateurs. The media remind us that the bungling husband or offspring, even when carefully instructed, will manage to bring home the wrong kind of paper towels or dog food.

The management of consumption has become so specialized that it can only really be appreciated by other practitioners. Galbraith suggests that "much social activity is, in primary substance, a competitive display of managerial excellence. It is like a fair ... at which embroidery or livestock is entered in competition, but for the same ultimate purpose of improving the craftsmanship or breed."[47] When a middle-class couple has a party or invites other couples in for dinner, the hostess has an opportunity to show the visiting women how well she manages consumption. The competitive nature of this sort of social event is well illustrated by a chapter in *The Serial* in which Kate worries about her first dinner party after being out of touch with the social scene for a while. She recalls the various phases of entertaining during her years in Marin. At first, "Kate and all her women friends competed with each other to serve the first really authentic couscous or the first Mongolian hotpot, complete with those little mesh dippers from Cost Plus." Later, Kate recalled, "You could just wipe everybody *out* by stuffing your own grape leaves, making your own phyllo dough or pickling your own pickled squid." Fashions changed and the "in" entertainment was to call at the last minute and invite friends to take pot luck with the family and to "dump another quart of water into the lentil soup." Now, she nervously hopes that she has made the right decisions, that Petrini's paté is not over exposed as an hors d'oeuvre, that she has not made any error that will cause her friend Martha to speak of her in the tone used to describe "the kind of people who still serve California wines."[48]

Not all social display of homemaking skills is competitive in such an anxiety-producing way. Often women are simply eager to demonstrate their craftsmanship and professionalism to someone who is capable of appreciating it. Then, as with the pie and preserve contests at the county fair, recipes are exchanged and the women go home and begin to plan for the next exhibition.

The fact that women enthusiastically search for bargains and ingeniously use their managerial role as consumers to find some sort of creative outlet within the housewife role is frequently turned against them. Ignoring the essential function of consumption in maintaining a capitalist society and the real services provided for the household, men act as if women spent money in totally selfish ways. In the classic, *A Doll's House*, Torvald taunts Nora, "It's a sweet little spendthrift, but she uses a great deal of money. One would hardly believe how expensive such little persons are."[49] In this play, of course, Nora had been using household money to pay off a note she secretly signed during her husband's illness. Nonetheless she endured being labelled as a wasteful little skylark or squirrel who abused her husband's money. In Sinclair Lewis's *Main Street*, Carol was forced to beg prettily for household money and to have her husband calling her "an extravagant little rabbit." Finally she confronted him at his office and said, "I now humbly beg you to give me the money with which to buy meals for you to eat. And hereafter to remember it. The next time, I shan't beg. I shall simply starve."[50]

The degrading process of being expected to manage a household yet having to bargain with one's husband for a fair share of "his" money to do so persists in the lives of many women. A Redstocking Sister has commented, "The pervasive image of the empty-headed female consumer constantly trying her husband's patience with her extravagant purchases contributes to the myth of male superiority."[51] As Galbraith has observed, as long as one member of a household is the primary wage earner and a different member is the primary consumer, conflict is inevitable.[52] At a primitive level both husband and wife have trouble resisting the notion that *she* is spending *his* money. One fictional woman suddenly confronts her own economic dependence on her life "partner" when he refuses to give her $300 to help a friend:

> Oh, Norm, what difference does it make? We have plenty.
>
> That's easy for you to say. That money comes out of my hide.
>
> What do you think I do all day? What have I done all these years? I work as hard as you do.
>
> Oh, come off it, Mira.
>
> What do you mean, come off it? Her voice rose wildly. Am I not an equal partner in this marriage? Don't I contribute to it?
>
> Of course you do, he said placatingly, but there was an edge of disgust in his voice. But you contribute different things. You don't contribute money.
>
> My work enables you to make that money!
>
> Oh, Mira, don't be ridiculous. Do you think I need you to do my work? I could live anywhere. I could have a housekeeper, or live in a hotel. I support your way of life by my work, not the reverse.[53]

Women may be led to believe that their contributions in the home are valued sufficiently to make them full partners in a relationship. Yet in moments of stress the underlying feelings often surface: men are paid for their work and thus it must be of greater value. Engels believed that this economic imbalance between husband and wife has served to perpetuate the historical oppression of women:

> In the great majority of cases today, at least in the possessing classes, the husband is obliged to earn a living and support his family, and that in itself gives him a position of supremacy, without any need for special titles and privileges. Within the family he is the bourgeois and the wife represents the proletariat.[54]

It is a short step fom economic dependence to servitude, and Charlotte Perkins Gilman argued in 1903 that the sharp division of labor between men and women creates a petty tyranny that is harmful to both.

> A too continuous home atmosphere checks in the woman the valuable social faculties. It checks it in the man more insidiously, through his position of easy mastery over these dependents, wife, children, servants; and through the constant catering of the whole menage to his special tastes. If a man had a private tailor shop in his back yard he would be far more whimsical and exacting in his personal taste in clothes. Every natural tendency to self-indulgence is steadily increased by the life service of an entire wife. This having one whole woman devoted to one's direct personal service is about as far from the cultivation of self-control as any process that could be devised.[55]

Contemporary feminist writings are replete with examples of males' unconscious assumption of the servitude of women. Fictional women discuss their husband's idiosyncrasies. One's husband refuses to eat any meat but beef and chicken. Another would only drink a certain brand of coffee. Still another ran his fingers along windowsills and moldings looking for dust. Marilyn French capsulized these discussions:

> Husbands were walls, absolute, in small things at least. The woman would often howl and cackle at them, at their incredible demands and impossible delusions, their inexplicable eating habits and their strange prejudices, but it was as if they were de black folk down to de shanty recounting the absurd pretensions of de white massas up to de big house.[56]

The first issue of *Ms.* magazine published a now classic article which heralded women's growing awareness of the true nature of their partnerships in marriage. "I Want a Wife," by Judy Syfers, speculated on how pleasant it would be to have a person to cook one's meals, pick up the dry cleaning, make dental appointments, keep a social calendar, raise one's children, and of course, meet one's sexual needs upon demand. "My God," concludes Syfers, "who wouldn't want a wife?"[57] Finally, a half century later, Virginia Woolf's message about £500 a year and a room of one's own was receiving wide currency among women.[58] They began to see that male genius, creativity, and accomplishment were all dependent upon a background of logistical and emotional support provided to them by women, usually wives. The problem that had no name in the early 1960s was widely discussed in the 1970s. Women realized that they needed to express themselves in ways other than childrearing and housekeeping. They rejected the historical arguments about women's lack of talent and about their economic indebtedness to their husbands. Women believed that they deserved a chance to try for a fuller life, and in order to free time and energy to go to school, take a job, or explore some creative talent at home, it was necessary to share household tasks. The era of negotiations that has ensued has revealed how deeply seated are the traditional premises about men's work and women's work. Some men simply refuse to discuss the division of labor. Pat Mainardi's essay, "The Politics of Housework," outlines several tactics of male resistance including, "housework is too trivial even to talk about. Imagine then," she counters, "how much more trivial it is to do, all day every day."[59]

Other husbands agree to try to help their wives but are unable to overcome their basic assumptions about the sexes and the appropriate behavior for each, like Darryl and Sandra Bem's illustration of the husbands who will change wet diapers but not dirty diapers.[60] In some cases the token efforts, the intellectual commitment, only served to emphasize men's basic expectations that woman's work was to care for them. This subtle double standard is explored in a well-known consciousness-raising treatise by Jane O'Reilly. "The Housewife's Moment of Truth," widely known as the "Click" essay, describes those sudden moments of awareness that many housewives were experiencing in the early 1970s.[61] A woman spends the last day of the family vacation cleaning the cottage the family has rented. Her husband spends a half hour scrubbing the bathroom. On the way home she asks herself why she is thanking him for the sixth time. If two spouses are both exhausted at the end of an evening, why should one pick the other's clothes up from the floor? O'Reilly claims that when women discuss the issue of housework with men they get agreement but not cooperation. For example, Norma Jean was a fictional housewife who longed for uninterrupted time to develop talent as a sculptor.[62] Her family tried to cooperate yet constantly intruded on her work to ask her minor questions. Through much of the novel, her husband managed to communicate nonverbally, "I'll take over *your* work for a while until you get this out of your system and return to normal." The television movie based on Erma Bombeck's, *The Grass is Always Greener Over the Septic Tank*, displays a subtler form of sabotage. The heroine's husband agreed to her plan to return to college two nights a week, yet a series of "business emergencies" arose which kept him at work. His phone calls came too late for his wife to find a babysitter.[63]

When women suggest that other members of the household share some of the drudgery of maintaining life, they confront social images that have prevailed for centuries. If by any chance men could shake off these images, women might still cling to them. A 1978 study indicates that women who attended college part time and did all their own housework were happier than those whose husbands helped substantially. Apparently, the researchers speculate, the latter group felt more guilt.[64] Helen Lopata's study of housewives revealed that what most women wished for was a maid.[65] Consider the irony of a woman oppressed and depressed with the work of maintaining her household dreaming not of a more equitable division of labor within the household but of turning the worst of that work over to another woman. "I Want a Wife" may be a tongue-in-cheek, politically aware statement. "I want a maid" is a universal lament of women who even at their most overburdened moments accept the traditional definitions of men's work and women's work.

WOMEN AT WORK OUTSIDE THE HOME

The universal conception of women's work as homemaking might lead one to believe that the history of American women has centered in the home. In fact, from the colonial era to the present, American women have demonstrated their willingness to mix their labor outside the home in various spheres of society. Whenever women's labor has been essential to survival the fragile and spiritual image of woman has been temporarily set aside. Andreas comments that "during the period preceding the agricultural and industrial revolution in the United States, women who migrated with their families from European countries worked at strenuous tasks that would both before and after this period have been considered wholly unfeminine."[66] Social upheavals in the Civil War and Reconstruction period brought record numbers of women into the labor force.[67] At the turn of the century only about six percent of American wives were employed.[68] World War I made temporary demands on women to fill the jobs vacated by men and to feed the insatiable war machine. The 1920s and 1930s saw a return to women's traditional roles. Those who were not housewives worked as teachers, nurses, and in low-paying service jobs, such as waitress, laundress, or clerk.[69] The woman's suffrage movement and the enfranchisement of women apparently had little impact on the occupational rights of women. The American labor movement, however, had made great gains for male workers during this period, gains which were to benefit the 3 million additional women who entered the labor market between 1941 and 1944 to aid in the war effort.[70] Many of the jobs in manufacturing carried high wages, seniority rights, union benefits, and advancement opportunities. "Rosie the Riveter," the symbolic World War II factory worker made her monumental contribution to the civilian and military demands of the economy. As soon as the war was over, it was assumed, Rosie would want to get out of her dirty overalls and into a frilly apron to provide a haven for the returning soldier and, incidentally, to open up a job for him. Instead, women had come to count on their higher wages and to value their new independence. A 1944 survey of female UAW workers disclosed that 85 percent would like to continue in manufacturing jobs after the war.[71] A Department of Labor survey that same year found that 80 percent of the former working women, 75 percent of the former students, and 50 percent of the former homemakers hoped to continue working.[72] Of course, this was not to be the case. In 1945 and 1946 the phase-over to a peacetime economy took its toll. In industries where women accounted for 44 percent, 39 percent, and 13 percent of the work force, they accounted for 60 percent, 89 percent, and 51 percent of the layoffs, respectively.[73] By 1946, 4 million fewer women were working than had been at the peak of wartime employment. Sheila Tobias and Lisa Anderson report that when plants began to rehire, women's seniority was often ignored; sometimes unemployment compensation was denied. Many jobs held by women during the war were reclassified as men's jobs.[74] Women had little choice but to return to the traditional woman's world: the home, the elementary classroom, the coffee shop, the typing pool.

Since the dramatic dip in women's employment at the end of World War II, female participation has increased fairly steadily. Wives, of particular interest to this section of analysis, increased their labor force participation from 23.8 percent into 1950 to 44.4 percent in 1975.[75] Nearly 30 million American mothers worked in 1978.[76] Numerous surveys have shown that the main reason women work is economic. A 1978 Nielsen survey of married working mothers indicated that 60 percent of them went to work because they needed the income or in order to make extra purchases for themselves and the family.[77] This corresponds with David Olson's finding that nearly half of all American families that have only a median income require two workers to maintain that level.[78] Interestingly, another study discloses that only 29 percent of the husbands of working women feel that their wives work because the family needs the income. Three out of five men say that their wives work because they like it.[79] Only one out of five women in the Nielsen survey mentioned personal satisfaction as their primary reason for working.

The most recent data suggest that women who work are committed to their careers. They do not consider their jobs temporary or stopgap but fully 85 percent of them intend to work until retirement.[80] Eighty-four percent of the wage-earning mothers believe their jobs make them more interesting and stimulating people.[81] Women enjoy the social contact with other adults that accompanies most jobs.[82] Hoffman reports that working women have opportunities to feel competent and important and often express higher self-esteem than do full-time housewives.[83] Working women also achieve status from their occupational roles that is unrelated to their husbands' status.[84] This research confirms an earlier finding by Weiss and Samuelson that when asked what made them feel useful and important, employed women were more likely to mention some aspect of their job than they were to mention either housework or their role in the family as wife and mother.[85] Moreover, working wives often find that their careers lead to greater power in the marriage relationship. McCall found that the higher a woman's earning power, the more helpful and cooperative her husband is. Men are more enthusiastic about their wives' jobs when their wives make more money. "One can conclude," says McCall, "that a husband's adaptation to his wife's working improves when she's a success."[86] As crass as these economic motivations may seem (recall Norm's statement to Mira, "It's not as if you contributed money"), at least two studies offer limited support for the conclusion that working women have more decision-making power in marital relationships than full-time housewives, presumably due to enhanced economic power.[87] Although researchers caution against generalizations it appears that working wives as a group are somewhat happier and better adjusted than their counterparts who are full-time housewives.[88]

The working wife and mother may have some sources of satisfaction outside the home and some additional power in the home, but she is not fundamentally different from the housewife. Rather, she is a housewife with another job. In her own consciousness and in her family's she is still the primary guardian of the home. Most women who work do not allow themselves to think of work as self-expression but rather see it as an extension of their nurturant role:[89] one further way that I care for my home and children is to take this job so that I can buy new furniture for the house, pay for the children's education. Recent research by Campbell, Converse, and Rodgers shows that among working women 41 percent say that their work is more important than their housework, 37 percent say that their housework is more important, and 22 percent say that the two kinds of work are equally important.[90] Employers, too, perceive of women's work as secondary. As Alice Rossi has explained,

Our society...expects men to aspire to jobs of the highest occupational prestige consistent with their abilities, indeed, his job should tax and stretch his ability or it will not be "challenging" enough.... By sharp contrast, we not only tolerate but encourage women to work in jobs which are below their abilities, precisely because this *does* release energies for their central roles in families.[91]

This cultural attitude towards women's work has provided the justification for the often unconscious discrimination against women in the more challenging occupations. For example, a woman may not even be considered for promotion to a job that involves travel because her superiors assume that she would not be able or willing to leave her family responsibilities.

Indeed, the family responsibilities of working women are great. Describing working women in the nineteenth century, Brown and Seitz say,

> to add to the troubles of the woman worker, the idea remained fixed that the real and happy province of the woman was a home. Despite long and arduous labors at a job, a woman was expected to assume household chores, thus fulfilling her "natural role" as wife and mother. If she was exhausted by leading both lives, her exhaustion was an expression of the natural physical inferiority of women.[92]

Actually, economist Mary Rowe has pointed out that if women, who are half the world's population, are randomly distributed in all occupations and also have total responsibility for early childcare, then women literally do three-quarters of the world's work.[93] Neither of these conditions exists, but Rowe's point is an intriguing one and suggests that perhaps it was the working wife and mother who inspired the folk saying "man must work from dawn 'til set of sun, but woman's work is never done."

In 1972, Scanzoni summarized several studies which generally confirmed that when a wife works she often "continues to perform just as many household chores as wives who do not work." It also appears that "husbands of working wives do not significantly increase their participation in these chores; instead, these wives simply add their work duties to their home chores."[94] One 1958 study indicated that husbands do about 15 percent of the housework when their wives are not employed and about 25 percent of the housework when their wives are employed,[95] a commendable increase to be sure, but far short of the 50 percent that might be considered appropriate if both partners work full-time outside the home. More recent studies show that this division of labor has not changed dramatically. The Nielsen survey cited previously revealed that 85 percent of the working mothers believe they have more household demands made on them than do their husbands.[96] McCall's research found that only one husband in four claims to help his working wife with housework, only one in five with childcare.[97] An even more recent local poll by the San Jose Mercury News discovered that the average full-time housewife spends 36.5 hours a week scrubbing and cleaning, while her husband helps out about 3.8 hours. Working women spend 17.5 hours a week on these tasks, their husbands, 5.5 hours.[98]

The woman who excells at a career, raises perfect children, and keeps a beautiful house is known as Supermom.[99] Any woman who falls short of this ideal, who is able to organize her time and marshall her energies only well enough to work a forty-hour week and maintain the bare essentials of her household is overcome with guilt. She feels torn between her desire to take care of her family at home and her desire to contribute to her family financially by working full time. Despite the evidence that working mothers have better adjustment to their children, are more relaxed in their discipline, and are generally excellent parents,[100] many feel guilty about their role as mothers. They are not concerned about the quality of their interactions with their children—indeed, working mothers often report less tension and conflict with children than mothers who are at home all day— but working mothers do feel guilty about the quantity of time they can spend with their children.[101]

There is some limited evidence that women who work experience more conflict with their husbands than do housewives. Curiously, there are many areas of the marital relationship that are unaffected by the wife's working status. Blood found that "when conflict occurs in working-wife families, it does not spread randomly over all aspects of marriage. For instance, there is no increase in difficulties over in-laws, friendships, or sexual or religious matters. Almost all the significant differences are concentrated in the 'domestic-economic' field."[102] Division of labor, childcare, household management, and financial matters cause most conflict.

It appears that working wives, especially working mothers, experience the least conflict when they keep their occupational roles clearly subordinate to their home roles. For instance, Rossi reports that women who work because they want to feel more guilt than women who work because they have to.[103] The former apparently feel a greater contradiction with the unselfish nurturant role that women are conditioned to. A recent study claims that the women who are happiest in dual-career marriages have only modest career ambitions. Those who aim higher in their professional lives experience greater conflicts amont the roles of professional, spouse, parent, and self-actualized person.[104]

WOMEN WITHOUT MEN

Another group of women, the single heads of household—widowed, divorced, or never married—obviously avoid those conflicts that housewives and working wives encounter in relating to their husband's expectations. These women, though, experience unique economic and social problems. The number of families headed by women doubled between 1940 and 1975. By that year, 7.2 million women headed one out of every eight households.[105] In previous decades widowhood was the main reason a woman assumed this role. Over the past 15 years, though, the number of divorced women heading families tripled, and the number of never-married women nearly doubled, an increase reflecting population trends and changes in the institutions of marriage and the family.[106] Consequently, the median age of female heads of household has shifted downward from 50.5 years to 43.4 years, one out of every ten such households being headed by a woman under 25.[107] The labor force participation for divorced and separated women, 64 percent, is higher than for women in any other marital category.[108]

What has been the experience of this increasing group of young divorced women? Has society responded to their needs and those of their children? Economically, it would appear that they are not faring well. Women heads of household as a whole tend, when employed, to be concentrated in the low-skilled and low-paying occupations.[109] Their unemployment rate has run three to four percentage points higher than the rate for male heads and somewhat higher than the rate for wives.[110] Women head one out of three households living below the poverty level as opposed to one out of eighteen headed by men.[111] Summarizing a number of studies dealing with the economic plight of divorced women, Brandwein, Brown and Fox write, "economic discrimination against women, and the reluctance of ex-husbands or outside agencies to aid mothers in supporting themselves and their children, often forces the families of divorced mothers to suffer severe economic hardship."[112]

Socially and emotionally, the divorced woman faces another set of problems. Campbell, Converse, and Rodgers found that divorced women were more likely than any other life cycle group of men or women to report such psychological stress indicators as feeling that life is hard (42 percent), always feeling rushed (34 percent), worrying about bills (63 percent), feeling frightened (60 percent), and worrying about a nervous breakdown (25 percent).[113] Although at any given time around one-third of the adult women in the population are not married,[114] the American culture tends to act as though single women don't really exist. Their status is assumed to be temporary, despite the fact that many of the divorced women over 40 will not remarry.[115] Substantial numbers of women of all ages are choosing a single lifestyle.[116] They are not simply between marriages or are not unlucky spinsters who have not yet found a man.

Frequently a woman alone is treated as a failure—an object of pity or contempt. One study disclosed that neighbors showed little respect for female-headed families; for example, they would borrow things without permission.[117] Other research indicates that some parents forbid their children to play with the children of divorced mothers.[118] Stephen Birmingham describes how married women in the Santa Clara County community of Los Altos seemed to freeze newly divorced women out of the social network, making them feel uncomfortable and unwelcome.[119]

Bequaert cites testimony from several divorced women who report that their neighbors are cool and unfriendly toward them. One said, "I feel sometimes as though I had a social disease, as though I don't belong here *really*."[120] Another, describing the stigma that accompanies a "broken home" said of her experience in the suburbs, "I sometimes feel as if I had two heads. If you're single and you're a parent—well, you don't fit into a studio flat in the city and you don't fit out here without a husband."[121]

Single women have financial and social problems which the suburban environment may tend to exacerbate rather than solve. Presumably, married women find the surroundings more congenial. In light of the foregoing analysis of the historical conceptions of housewives and working wives, this presumption bears further investigation.

WOMEN AND SUBURBIA

What does suburbia reflect about society's conception of the role of women? Have male planners and architects responded to the changing consciousness of the issues raised by the feminist movement? Have they adapted to the increasing numbers of single and divorced women living in suburbia, the many two-career marriages? Although undoubtedly aware of such trends, "it is unlikely that the typical planner has researched the data from the woman's perspective and analyzed what the changes mean in terms of the suburban setting," comments Marilyn Pray.[122] Janet Abu-Lughod tells about her experience as the only woman in attendance at a conference which dealt with future studies in urban design. The men became quite excited about a model wherein the shortened work week would permit men to spend three nights a week in the city and then return to the country to spend a long weekend with wife and children. Dr. Abu-Lughod objected that the model was completely designed for upper-class males, that it separated men's and women's spheres even more radically than the present and made no allowance at all for single women (unless they were supposed to stay in the cities to entertain the men on their three nights there). The male participants responded with silence and an embarrassed joke. "No woman I have told this story to has felt that it was a matter to joke about. We are frightened by this handwriting on the wall,"[123] Abu-Lughod observes. Her essay and Pray's are part of a seminal volume edited by Hapgood and Getzels which reports on a special research group of the American Society of Planning Officials and identifies several planning issues that are raised by changing trends in the lives of women.[124] A great deal of their analysis is relevant to our consideration of women in the suburbs.

Suburbia tends toward homogeneous communities of large, single-family homes. Single women, widows, childless working couples, divorced mothers all have trouble meeting their housing needs. Zoning regulations and rigid local interpretations of the term "household" (as only persons related by blood) make it difficult for unrelated adults to share housing. Too often those who fail to fit the nuclear family pattern—a pattern that in fact accounts for only about 35 percent of U.S. households[125]—are forced into multi-family, usually rental, housing on the fringe of the "residential" areas of suburbia. Pray has observed, "in such instances multi-family users frequently buffer the single-family enclave from the noise nuisance of railroads, major traffic arteries, and commercial areas. The rationale goes something like this: because multi-family occupants have no investment to be protected the nuisances are not as noxious to them."[126]

Those who do live in single-family homes may find that architects, the most predominantly male professional group of all,[127] have historically designed home environments around the traditional assumptions of women's roles. As long ago as 1896, Harriett Beecher Stowe wrote that "the real mischief with houses built to rent is that they are all mere male contrivances." If women were to design dwellings, she speculated, they "will wear a more domestic and comfortable air, and will be built more with reference to the real wants of their inmates."[128] Mrs. Stowe and her sister Catherine Beecher designed homes with movable screens as partitions and huge closets. Homes envisioned by women in the nineteenth and early twentieth centuries had such logical and functional features as basement floors that sloped downward toward a drain, kitchens with a small office area in the corner and nurseries located on the ground floor where the mother spent most of her day.[129] Modern conceptions of living space designed by women try to alter the typical suburban home's emphasis on togetherness by stressing multiple use of space allowing adults and children to be together or to have privacy as needed. Torre, Rock, and Wright point out that while "the trend has long been to centralize activity and disperse storage," a feminist analysis leads to floor plans which do the opposite. A large storage center of shelves, drawers and closets "breaks down one aspect of the role of housekeeper—knowing where things are put away."[130] Similarly, they propose a do-it-yourself kitchen which facilitates shared cooking and cleanups through a restaurant model of open storage space.[131] "The houses we live in," they write, "are designed for traditional family roles and can prevent us from experimenting with new ways of living, sharing housework, respecting others' autonomy, emphasizing personal development."[132] They report that in 1956 a 103-member Woman's Congress on Housing made a number of suggestions for more differentiation of space in homes with particular emphasis on the need for some privacy in the living areas for adults only. Builders claimed that the demands were too idealistic to be translated into action.[133]

A survey of the history of women in American architecture suggests that it is quite possible that men and women do conceptualize space differently. In addition to the modifications of floor plans for homes mentioned here, women have always shown particular interest in the design of communal living spaces. From the earliest Indian villages to the utopian Shaker and Amana colonies, to contemporary feminist communes, examples abound of proposals by women for shared cooking areas and for arrangements that allow them to work together at various household chores.[134] This message has not been heard by planners. Homes in many suburban neighborhoods are focused toward the privacy of the patio and backyards. People come and go through carports set back on the lot and sheltered by landscaping. Women complain about the sense of isolation from one another, "houses too far apart for casual neighborliness; no movie theaters or nighttime recreation; no parks or places where women can gather during the day to see other adults; no child care facilities."[135] The sidewalk culture of the urban neighborhood has no counterpart in suburbia. Nor is there any equivalent of the European pub or club.[136] Shopping centers have been mentioned by some as a possible replacement for the village square, but their huge scale, their anonymity, and their emphasis on efficiency seem to deter casual sidewalk interaction.[137] The neighborhood laundromat, Pray suggests, perhaps comes closest to providing a spot for spontaneous interaction among suburban women, a solution with obvious aesthetic limitations and one irrelevant to the affluent woman with home laundry facilities.[138] Inadequate childcare services and poor public transportation further add to the sense of isolation. The suburban woman is cut off from the centers of activity, imprisoned in her expensive, beautifully furnished dream house. Sylvia Fava concludes that "the trends toward an even more dispersed suburbia and the separation of work and residence are founded on deep seated sexist assumptions about the role of women."[139]

In the fictional community of Stepford, the husbands belong to a private men's club on the hill. After a family has lived for a short time in Stepford, the woman undergoes a change. She becomes neater, and her figure is a little more rounded. Her house is cleaner, and she is cheerful all the time, even though she is so busy cleaning, cooking, and nurturing her children that she no longer has any time to waste visiting with other women. In fact, the women have been killed and replaced by passive humanoid robots devised by the technological experts of the Men's Club to serve as the perfect wives, free from the troublesome selfhood and individuality of real women.[140]

Is the contemporary suburban scene a conspiracy like the one described in this melodrama? It seems unlikely that male planners and architects and politicians actively scheme to arrange living patterns to keep women in their traditional place. It is far more probable that men just think like men and that people in power tend to think in ways that preserve their comfortable supremacy. Men have not solved the problem that has no name, but neither have they created it alone. As Friedan foresaw in 1963, "it is easy to see the concrete details that trap the suburban housewife, the continual demands on her time. But the chains that bind her in the trap are chains in her own mind and spirit. They are chains made up of mistaken ideas and misinterpreted facts, of incomplete truths and unreal choices. They are not easily seen and not easily shaken off."[141] Since 1963, the feminist movement has made great progress in identifying and severing many of the chains that bind women and men in their stultifying roles. Changes in employment, education, and government may come easier than changes in daily personal living. The consciousness of recent decades has caused some women to say, don't call me a housewife. I'm not married to a house. A deeper and more chilling awareness is that for all practical purposes many women are married to houses. Lopata reported that at certain points in the life cycle women stress their role of housewife in the first rank, above their roles as wife and mother. Caring for the home, keeping it straight, are the primary goals that they mention for their existence.[142]

In an ideological sense, women and houses are married in the collective consciousness and unconsciousness of Western culture. The nature of this alliance is discussed by Torre.

> In our society "the ideal happiness has taken material form in the house," says Simone de Beauvoir, "the house stands for permanence and separation from the world." Woman, the domestic keeper of that ideal happiness, has herself taken on the house's traditional attributes of enclosure and isolation. No other building type embodies such symbiotic association between occupant and object.[143]

The historical outline in this chapter has illustrated the depth of the connection between women and domesticity, the tenacity with which both men and women have held to the image of woman as "guardian of the hearth, carrier of tradition, influencer of morality...salve for men's consciences, symbol of stability."[144] The contemporary studies reviewed have indicated that women, employed or not, married or single, are still perceived as the center of domestic life. A successful professional woman will still do more housework than her husband, and, if help is hired, will no doubt be the one to make the arrangements, buy the cleaning materials, give directions to the cleaner, and nag the family to pick up their belongings so that cleaning is possible. The attorney makes shopping lists as she drives to court, the professor puts in a load of laundry as she sits down to prepare a lecture, the business executive runs back from the driveway to defrost something for dinner, the doctor skips lunch to buy a gift for her son to take to a birthday party. In short, all women are housewives because they are the ones who worry about housework. Men value neatness, order and graciousness, too, and of course they are able, even willing, to do particular tasks to insure a pleasant domestic life. What men aren't willing, or perhaps able, to do is to *worry* about domesticity. Women worry about dust and dirty dishes and about making appropriate gestures at ritualistic moments. They worry because they always have and because their mothers and grandmothers before them worried about these things. They worry because no matter how successful a woman is in other areas of life, she feels that she is a failure unless she is a good housewife too. Unless her home is sparkling and warm, unless her children have handmade Halloween costumes, unless she cooks her company meals from scratch, it seems that her basic sexuality and her humanity are somehow deficient.

The mantle of masculinity is heavy, too, and oppressive in its own way, a burden which has been discussed at length as part of the increasing feminist awareness. Most relevant to the concept of suburbia as domicile is the fact that men not only connect "house" with "wife" but "woman" with "domestic service," carrying into all social institutions the notion that every woman is, metaphorically at least, a housewife. To extend the point cited earlier from the writings of Charlotte Perkins Gilman, having a full-time domestic slave not only makes a man an unwitting tyrant at home, but it makes it difficult for him to see other women as autonomous equals. In business settings men ask female peers to make coffee, take notes at meetings, handle social niceties for the entire group. On college faculties of 20 professors, for instance, it is not uncommon for the two or three women to plan receptions for visiting scholars, arrange refreshments for special meeings, circulate a card to be signed for the secretary's birthday, send flowers to the bereaved colleague. If women refuse to perform these functions, they usually go undone, unless wives or secretaries are drafted at the last minute. It is not that men are incapable of stopping by a bakery for some sweet rolls or calling a florist. It is simply that these acts take a modicum of planning, and men are just not used to thinking of them. Women worry about "housework" at home and at work.

For centuries both men and women have tolerated this division of labor because the servile nature of cleaning up after someone else and of taking care of the trivial detail work of another person's life has been disguised by glorifying these tasks with a high spirituality. Cleanliness is next to Godliness, and women are the moral guardians of our homes and our souls. As an 1897 household economics book stated, "cleaning can never pass from women's hands...for to keep the world clean, this is the one great task for women."[145]

Only recently have large numbers of people begun to explore the notion that the tasks of maintaining a livable domestic environment and the tasks of creating a normal and ethical society are the responsibilities of every adult. The concept of androgyny, discovering the best of the traditional feminine and the traditionally masculine traits in each person, promises at long last to challenge the idea of the woman as Other. The differences among us as individuals are far greater than the differences between men as a group and women as a group. Women as a group are no longer content to be relegated to the domestic role, and concomitantly, the physical isolation of home from other aspects of society is less satisfactory than ever.

NOTES

1. Eva Figes, *Patriarchal Attitudes* (New York: Stein and Day, 1970); Shulamith Firestone, *The Dialectic of Sex* (New York: William Morrow, 1970); Kate Millett, *Sexual Politics* (Garden City, N.Y.: Doubleday, 1970).
2. Carol Andreas, *Sex and Caste in America* (Englewood Cliffs, N.J.: Prentice-Hall, 1971), p. 3.
3. Betty Friedan, *The Feminine Mystique* (New York: Dell, 1963), p. 27.
4. Susan Grumich, "Women in Limbo: Social Class and Life Cycle Perspectives of Feminine Roles" (M.A. thesis, San Jose State University, 1972). See also Bennett M. Berger, *Working-Class Suburb* (Berkeley: University of California Press, 1971).
5. Margaret Mead, *Male and Female* (New York: William Morrow, 1949).
6. Frederich Engels, "The Monogamous Family," in *Up Against the Wall, Mother...*, ed. Elsie Adams and Mary Louise Briscoe (Beverly Hills, Calif.: Glencoe Press, 1971), p. 269.
7. Edward Westermarck, *The History of Human Marriage* (New York: The Allerton Book Company, 1922).
8. William O'Neill, ed., *The Woman's Movement: Feminism in the United States and England* (Chicago: Quadrangle Paperbacks, 1969), p. 16.
9. Phillippe Aries, *Centuries of Childhood: A Social History of Family Life* (New York: Alfred A.Knopf, 1962).
10. O'Neill, *Woman's Movement*, p. 17.
11. Ibid.
12. Connie Brown and Jane Seitz, "'You've Come a Long Way, Baby': Historical Perspectives," in *Sisterhood is Powerful: An Anthology of Writings from the Women's Liberation Movement*, ed. Robin Morgan (New York: Vintage Books, 1970), p. 6.
13. Tamara K. Hareven, ed., *Family and Kin in Urban Communities, 1700–1930* (New York: New Viewpoints, 1977), p. 3.
14. Ibid.
15. Christopher Lasch, "Family as Haven in Heartless World," *Salmagundi* 34 (Fall 1976): 44.
16. Beverly Jones, "The Dynamics of Marriage and Motherhood," in Morgan, *Sisterhood*, p. 52.
17. Margaret Fuller, "Women in the Nineteenth Century," in *Feminism: The Essential Historical Writings*, ed. Miriam Schneir (New York: Vintage Books, 1972), p. 64.
18. Jean-Jacques Rousseau, *Emile* (London: J.M. Dent and Sons, 1974), p. 328.
19. William H. Whyte, Jr., *The Organization Man* (Garden City, N.Y.: Anchor Books, 1957), p. 287.
20. Helena Z. Lopata, *Occupation Housewife* (New York: Oxford University Press, 1971), p. 97.
21. Simone de Beauvoir, *The Second Sex* (New York: Alfred A. Knopf, 1953); Mary Wollstonecraft, "A Vindication of the Rights of Woman," in Schneir, *Feminism*, pp. 5–18;

Virginia Woolf, "A Room of One's Own," in Adams and Briscoe, *Up Against the Wall*, pp. 388–99.

22. Sheila Ballentyne, *Norma Jean the Termite Queen* (New York: Bantam Books, 1976), p. 124.

23. Clarice Stasz Stoll, *Female and Male Socialization, Social Roles, and Social Structure* (Dubuque, Iowa: Wm. C. Brown, 1974), p. 153.

24. Lopata, *Occupation Housewife*, p. 194; F. Ivan Nye and Lois Wladis Hoffman, *The Employed Mother in America* (Chicago: Rand McNally, 1963), p. 30.

25. Lopata, *Occupation Housewife*, pp. 30–32.

26. Ibid., pp. 142, 150–60.

27. Friedan, *Feminine Mystique*, p. 26; Jones, "Dynamics," p. 55.

28. Personal conversation.

29. Marya Mannes, "Pardon Me, My Mind is Showing," in Adams and Briscoe, *Up Against the Wall*, pp. 407–09.

30. Angus Campbell, Phillip E. Converse, Willard L. Rodgers, *The Quality of American Life: Perceptions, Evaluations, and Satisfactions* (New York: Russell Sage Foundation, 1976), p. 400.

31. Meredith Tax, "Woman and Her Mind: The Story of Daily Life," in *Female Liberation: History and Current Politics*, Roberta Salper, ed. (New York: Alfred A. Knopf, 1972), p. 230.

32. Myra Marx Ferree, "The Confused American Housewife," *Psychology Today* (September 1976), pp. 76ff.

33. Philip Slater, *The Pursuit of Loneliness: American Culture at the Breaking Point* (Boston: Beacon Press, 1970), p. 68.

34. Jones, "Dynamics," pp. 50–51.

35. Marilyn French, *The Woman's Room* (New York: Jove/HBJ Books, 1978), pp. 113–14.

36. Morgan, *Sisterhood*, p. 31.

37. Ibid., p. 33.

38. Jones, "Dynamics," p. 60.

39. Tax, "Woman and Her Mind," p. 230.

40. Ann Crittendon Scott, "The Value of Housework for Love or Money," *Ms.* (July 1972): 59.

41. Ferree. "Confused Housewife," p. 76.

42. John Kenneth Galbraith, "How the Economy Hangs on Her Apron Strings," *Ms.* (May 1974): 75.

43. Ibid., pp. 75, 77.

44. Cyra McFadden, *The Serial* (New York: Alfred A. Knopf, 1977), p. 8.

45. Susanna Torre, ed., *Women in American Architecture: A Historic and Contemporary Perspective* (New York: Whitney Library of Design, 1977), pp. 15–40.

46. Ibid.

47. Galbraith, "Apron Strings," p. 112.

48. McFadden, *Serial*, pp. 36–37.

49. Henrik Ibsen, *A Doll's House*, The Oxford Ibsen, vol. 5, James McFarlane ed. and trans. (London: Oxford University Press, 1961), pp. 202–05.

50. Sinclair Lewis, *Main Street* (New York: Harcourt, Brace and Howe, 1920), pp. 71–73.

51. A Redstocking Sister, "Consumerism and Women," in *Woman in Sexist Society*, ed. Vivian Gornick and Barbara K. Moran (New York: Basic Books, 1971), p. 664.

52. Galbraith, "Apron Strings," pp. 76–77.

53. French, *Woman's Room*, p. 278.

54. Engels, "Monogamous Family," p. 276.

55. Charlotte Perkins Gilman, "The Home: Its Work and Influence," in Salper, *Female Liberation*, p. 115.

56. French, *Woman's Room*, p. 111.

57. Judy Syfers, "I Want a Wife," *Ms.* (Spring 1972): 56.

58. Woolf, "A Room of One's Own."

59. Pat Mainardi, "The Politics of Housework," in Morgan, *Sisterhood*, p. 450.

60. Darryl and Sandra Bem, public speech, San Jose State University Women's Week, 1972 "The Power of a Nonconscious Ideology: Training a Woman to Know Her Place."

61. Jane O'Reilly, "The Housewife's Moment of Truth," *Ms.* (Spring 1972): 54–69.

62. Ballentyne, *Norma Jean*.

63. "The Grass is Always Greener Over the Septic Tank," television movie.

64. *Psychology Today* (November 1978): 44.

65. Lopata, *Occupation Housewife*, p. 177.

66. Andreas, *Sex and Caste*, p. 116.

67. Brown and Seitz, "You've Come a Long Way, Baby," p. 17.

68. Howard Hayghe, "Families and the Rise of Working Wives—An Overview," *Monthly Labor Review*, Ninety-nine (May 1976): 13.

69. Sheila Tobias and Lisa Anderson, "Whatever Happened to Rosie the Riveter?" *Ms.* (June 1973): 92.

70. Ibid., p. 93.

71. Ibid., p. 93; Rosalyn Baxendale, Linda Gordon, and Susan Reverby, eds., *America's Working Women* (New York: Random House, 1976), pp. 310–12.

72. Tobias and Anderson, "Rosie the Riveter," p. 93.

73. Ibid.

74. Ibid.

75. Hayghe, "Families and Working Wives," p. 13.

76. Geraldine Carro, "The Wage-Earning Mother," *Ladies Home Journal* (December 1978): 56.

77. Ibid.

78. David Olson, "The (New) Cost of Being a Woman," *Mother Jones* (January 1977): 14.

79. McCall, cited in Carro, "Wage-Earning Mother," p. 56.

80. Ibid., p. 164.

81. Ibid., p. 56.

82. Ferree, "Confused Housewife," p. 76.

83. Lois Wladis Hoffman, "The Decision to Work," in Nye and Hoffman, *Employed Mother*, p. 28.

84. Kathleen V. Ritter and Lowell E. Hargens, "Occupational Positions and Class Identifications of Married Working Women: A Test of the Asymmetry Hypothesis," *American Journal of Sociology* (January 1975): 934–47.

85. Robert Weiss and Nancy Samuelson, "Social Roles of American Women: Their Contribution to a Sense of Usefulness and Importance," *Marriage and Family Living* 20 (November, 1958): 358–66.

86. McCall, cited in Carro, "Wage-Earning Mother," p. 164.

87. Nye and Hoffman, *Employed Mother*, p. 291.

88. Ferree, "Confused Housewife;" Nye and Hoffman, *Employed Mother*; Alice Rossi, "The Roots of Ambivalence in American Women," *Readings in the Psychology of Women*, Judith W. Bardwick, ed. (New York: Harper and Row, 1972), pp. 119–31.

89. Ruth E. Hartley, "Some Implications of Current Changes in Sex Role Patterns," in *Readings in the Psychology of Women*, p. 121.

90. Campbell, Converse, and Rodgers, *Quality of American Life*, p. 401.

91. Alice Rossi, "The Roots of Ambivalence in American Women," in Bardwick, *Readings in the Psychology of Women*, p. 125.

92. Brown and Seitz, "You've Come a Long Way, Baby," p. 6.

93. Mary Rowe, cited in Robin Morgan, "The Changeless Need—A Conversation with Dorothy Dinnerstein," *Ms.* (August 1978): 92.

94. John Scanzoni, *Sexual Bargaining Power Politics in the American Marriage* (Englewood Cliffs, N.J.: Prentice-Hall, 1972), p. 40.

95. Robert O. Blood and Robert L. Hamblin, "The Effect of the Wife's Employment on the Family Power Structure," *Social Forces* thirty-six (May 1958): 347–52.

96. Carro, "Wage-Earning Mother," p. 59.

97. Ibid.

98. Darla Miller, "Most Men Still 'Kings' in San Jose Homes," San Jose *Mercury*, December 6, 1978.

99. Madelon Bedell, "Supermom," *Ms.* (May 1973): 84ff.

100. Rossi, "Roots of Ambivalence," p. 121; Nye, op. cit., pp. 190–214.

101. Carro, "Wage-Earning Mother," p. 59.

102. Blood, cited in Nye and Hoffman, *Employed Mother*, p. 289.

103. Rossi, "Roots of Ambivalence," p. 126.

104. Carole Holahan and Lucie Gilbert, "In Two Career Marriages, Happy Wives Aim Low," reported in *Psychology Today* (November 1978): 28–34.

105. Beverly Johnson McEaddy, "Women Who Head Families: A Socioeconomic Analysis," *Monthly Labor Review* (June 1976): 3.

106. Ibid.

107. Ibid.

108. Karen Hapgood and Judith Getzels, *Planning, Women, and Change* (Chicago: American Society of Planning Officials: Advisory Service, 1974), p. 13.

109. McEaddy, "Women Who Head Families," p. 6.

110. Ibid., p. 5.

111. Ibid., p. 3.

112. Ruth A. Brandwein, Carol A. Brown, Elizabeth Maury Fox, "Women and Children Last: The Social Situation of Divorced Mothers and Their Families," *Journal of Marriage and the Family* thirty-six (August 1974): 502.

113. Campbell, Converse, and Rodgers, *Quality of American Life*, p. 404.

114. Lucie H. Bequaert, *Single Women Alone and Together* (Boston: Beacon Press, 1976), p. xii.

115. Brandwein, Brown, and Fox, "Women and Children Last," p. 511.

116. Bequaert, *Single Women*.

117. Dennis Marsden, *Mothers Alone: Poverty and the Fatherless Family* (London: Allen Lane, The Penguin Press, 1969), p. 109.

118. Brandwein, Brown, and Fox, "Women and Children Last," p. 506.

119. Stephen Birmingham, *The Golden Dream: Suburbia in the 1970's* (New York: Harper and Row, 1978), pp. 156–57.

120. Bequaert, *Single Women*, p. 82.

121. Ibid., p. 80.

122. Marilyn Pray, "Planning and Women in the Suburban Setting," in Hapgood and Getzels, *Planning, Women, and Change*, p. 52.

123. Janet L. Abu-Lughod, "Designing a City for All," in Hapgood and Getzels, *Planning, Women, and Change*, p. 37.

124. Hapgood and Getzels, *Planning, Women, and Change*.

125. "Who is the Real Family?" *Ms.* (August 1978): 43.

126. Pray, "Planning and Women," p. 53.

127. Jane Holtz Kay, "The House that Woman Built," *Ms.* (July 1974): 93.

128. Doris Cole, *From Tipi to Skyscraper: A History of Women in Architecture* (Boston: i press, 1973), p. 49.

129. Cole, *From Tipi to Skyscraper*, p. 28–52; Torre, *Women in American Architecture*, pp. 15–40.

130. Susanna Torre, Cynthia Rock, and Gwendolyn Wright, "Rethinking Closets, Kitchens

and Other Forgotten Spaces," *Ms.* (December 1977): 55.

131. Ibid.

132. Ibid., p. 54.

133. Ibid.

134. Cole, *From Tipi to Skyscraper*; Torre, *Women in American Architecture*.

135. Linda Greenhouse, "These Wives Found Cure to Some of the Ills of Suburbia," New York *Times*, October 1, 1971.

136. Charlotte Temple, "Planning and the Married Woman with Children—A New Town Perspective," in Hapgood and Getzels, *Planning, Women, and Change*, p. 47; Pray, "Planning and Women," p. 54.

137. Birmingham, *Golden Dream*, pp. 155–56; Pray, "Planning and Women," p. 54.

138. Pray, "Planning and Women."

139. Sylvia Fava, "Beyond Suburbia," *Annals of the American Academy of Political Science* 422 (November 1975): 21.

140. Ira Levin, *The Stepford Wives* (New York: Random House, 1972).

141. Friedan, *Feminine Mystique*, p. 26.

142. Lopata, *Occupation Housewife*, p. 71.

143. Torre, *Women in American Architecture*, p. 16.

144. Brown and Seitz, "You've Come a Long Way, Baby," p. 13.

145. Torre, *Women in American Architecture*, p. 18.

3

A STUDY OF THE IMPACT OF THE SUBURBAN ENVIRONMENT ON WOMEN: THE CASE OF THE SAN JOSE METROPOLITAN AREA

In order to focus our discussions of suburbia and women, this chapter presents a case study of the satisfaction that women have with suburban environments in an urban region that has extensive residential development characteristic of recent national suburban patterns—the San Jose metropolitan area.

BACKGROUND

Our study views suburbia with respect to the role of the physical environment, social class, subcultural ties, and the familial life cycle in determining satisfaction with the suburbs as a place to live. The precise effects of the physical environment on human behavior have fascinated urbanists for more than a century.[1] Housing reformers and others have been quick to furnish evidence readily dramatizing the gravity of the social issues they endeavored to bring to public attention. Simple cause and effect relationships might easily be inferred by readers whose consciences and resources could be brought to bear on the pernicious effects of slum living, for example. Only relatively recently have efforts been rekindled to explore the man-environment relationship in a more systematic way. In addition to a new serial, *Environment and Behavior* (1968–), at least two other journals (*Annals of the American Academy of Political and Social Science* [May 1970]; *Journal of Social Issues* [October 1966]) have devoted entire issues to the impact of the physical environment on man and society, while the book literature has been enriched by at least two major anthologies[2] and one synthesis of past interpretations.[3]

Yet, however instrumental these primarily academic forums may be, the world of planning policy and implementation remains untouched, albeit concerned. As environmental psychologist Kenneth Craik has cautioned an urban planner readership, "With the advent of massive urban renewal programs and the creation of entire new communities, the relationship between planners and designers,...and the user-clients and inhabitant clients...has become increasingly attenuated and indirect. Some new, reliable, empirical means of providing the necessary information and understanding of client groups has become necessary."[4] His specific suggestion, an exploration of "the degree of association of individual response variables with variations in objective, physical characteristics," forms the basis of our investigation of eight suburban environments.

Within individual physical settings, the man-environment relationship may vary over time and in different social and functional juxtapositions. For example, site plan features have been found more influential during the early stages of residence and may yield over time to other factors, such as social homogeneity.[5] Yet, although the site plan may mediate friendship opportunities in terms of relative proximity,[6] in the longer run, it may actually discourage friendship and community feeling.[7] If so, then how would this relationship affect the debate among those who argue that there still exists a strong need for roots, community identification, and devotion to place[8]—and those of the opposite viewpoint?[9] How does site planning affect privacy, the absence of noise and distraction, and the performance of household maintenance? Or, on a larger scale, according to Parr, "the uniformity and predictability of milieu may conceivably have much more drastic effects upon behavior than the mere discouragement of rambling movement, particularly among the young."[10] Until we can control for the physical environment and isolate its impacts on selected variables, it is prudent to conclude that the environment does have sequential and overlapping effects on human behavior; the extent of some of these impacts will be addressed in our study.

Similarly, social class may affect one's relationship with the surrounding built environment. Americans have traditionally been reluctant to inter-mingle across class lines,[11] but perhaps the course of a relatively open and pluralistic society has negated this view. It has been argued that education is the only aspect of social class that closely relates to the housing decision of a consumer.[12] Yet, under today's extensive middle-class umbrella, which shelters not only its traditional white-collar tenants but an affluent blue-collar population as well, how important are the imperatives of class? Do the engineer (a technician), the university professor (an intellectual), and the supermarket produce manager (educationally "unskilled") belong to different classes despite their side-by-side housing and presumably similar family income? What individuals are more likely to choose "aesthetic" living situations or perceive them to be a more important expression of themselves? Are they all just "straight" Americans living in an environment resoundingly rejected by their bohemian offspring, who may also be professors, engineers, or manual laborers? Are the determinants of how an individual lives based less on his/her parentally created environment and more influenced by the random meeting of peers in the wider society of expanding social opportunities? And is the media-based, mass-produced non-culture of product standardization that aesthetically circumscribes suburbia the lingua franca of what people expect, if not want, from their physical environment? Perhaps there exists in a metropolitan community many subcultures which flourish in a pluralistic society regardless of its physical backdrop. These subcultures may not necessarily be spatial communities of interest comprising, for example, musician, ethnics, media people, migrants from a particular region of the country or nationality, intellectuals, narcotics purveyors or artists.

If the effects of culture, social class, and the physical environment still stir controversy, then those of life cycle may soothe troubled minds. For two decades there has been little argument that the raising of children in the most self-contained units possible is the most desirable manner in which to proceed.[13] Yet, if the suburbs work best, in theory, for families with children, do they offer sufficient privacy to balance out the relative ease of childrearing? Are the housing units sufficiently well-designed to accommodate the healthful coexistence of adults and children? According to Sommer, "Under crowded conditions, social norms for maintaining privacy partially substitute for the lack of physical devices."[14] How adequate are these physical devices in an environment designed, again in theory, for a familial existence? Further, as the building industry reconciles itself to the interminable spiraling of housing costs beyond the reach of eager consumers, the return of the basic, no-frills house at an affordable price poses a problem in design. If the $75,000 house of today provides a less than ideal environment, is it reasonable to expect the stripped-down model of tomorrow to do better (or even as well) without a major rethinking of the environmental internal to the house as well as the external site plan?

Is suburbia palatable beyond the veneer of success it projects, or are there fundamental limitations as well as essential disadvantages permeating suburban living? Is the quality of today's suburban lifestyle an objective worth pursuing on behalf of those who have been denied the keys to the Kingdom?

METHOD

So that we might begin to address some of the questions raised above, our study tries to measure levels of satisfaction with various dimensions of suburban life for women residing in a range of social and physical environments representative of much of American suburbia. The dimensions of suburban life examined are variables concerned with the satisfaction with some of the major aspects of the quality of urban life, such as housing and community services. We also attempt to determine and measure demographic and environmental characteristics (independent variables), such as education, income, housing density, and design features, that seem to be related to such levels of satisfaction (dependent variables). That is, we test relationships of variables that are expected (based on theories and previous research) to help explain the variations anticipated in levels of satisfaction with suburban life. We also conduct exploratory studies of aspects of the suburban environment, such as locational preferences of suburban residents.

In particular, our research attempts to examine the influence of four theory-related clusters of independent variables—social class, subcultural, life cycle, and environmental—on four sets of dependent quality of life variables—housing environment, community services, social patterns, psychological well-being. The research design indicating the variables used in our study is presented in Figure 3.1.

Questions concerning each variable or measures of satisfaction were devised and put into the form of a questionnaire schedule. As Appendix A indicates, questions related to these measures of satisfaction were designed to yield an ordinal satisfaction score in accordance with the widely used Likert-type scale, such as those employed by Lansing et al. in their study of satisfaction of planned residential environments,[15] Anderson et al. in their study of satisfaction of low and moderate cost housing,[16] and Zehner in his study of the quality of life in new communities.[17] Thus, a score can be obtained for the "personal and family privacy" variable by asking:

Is it hard to find a place to be by yourself in the house?

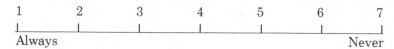

During Phase I of our study (Summer-Fall 1975), the questionnaire was constructed, pre-tested, and revised. In Phase II (1976), the questionnaire was administered to approximately 800 women residing in eight socially and economically matched, middle-income, suburban neighborhoods in the San Jose metropolitan area.

Dependent Variables

The dimensions of suburbia chosen for our study were intended to yield a comprehensive set of indexes for the satisfaction of suburban life—

FIGURE 3.1

Research Design

Independent Variables (IV):	*Dependent Variables* (DV):

a. *Social Class Influences*
  1. Income
  2. Education
  3. Occupational Status
 	
b. *Subcultural Influences*
  1. Ethnic Identity
  2. Regional Origin
  3. Length of Residency
 	
c. *Life Cycle Influences*
  1. Age
  2. Marital Status
  3. Number and Age of Children
 	
d. *Suburban Environmental Influences*
  1. Residential Density
  2. Household Distance from the Central City Center
  3. Age of Neighborhood
  4. Distance to Work
  5. Mean Neighborhood Income and Educational Levels
  6. Population Size of Political Unit
  7. Design and Site Plan Characteristics
	a. *Housing Environment*
	  1. Personal and Family Privacy
	  2. Size and arrangement of the Housing Unit and Lot
	  3. Economic and Functional responsibilities of home ownership
	  4. House and Neighborhood Appearance
	
	b. *Community Service*
	  1. Parks/open space
	  2. Schools
	  3. Police/security
	  4. Child Care
	  5. Transportation
	  6. Entertainment and Culture
	
	c. *Social Patterns*
	  1. Friendships
	  2. Group participation
	  3. Sense of belonging
	
	d. *Psychological Well-Being*
	  1. Fullness vs. Emptiness of Life
	  2. Receptivity towards the world
	  3. Social Respect
	  4. Personal Freedom
	  5. Sociability vs. Withdrawal
	  6. Companionship vs. Isolation
	  7. Work Satisfaction
	  8. Tranquility vs. Anxiety
	  9. Self Approving vs. Guilty
	  10. Self Confidence
	  11. Energy vs. Fatigue
	  12. Elation vs. Depression

Where

$$(DV)_i = a + b_j(IV)_j + b_k(IV)_k + \ldots$$

and

$(DV)_i$ = the $_ith$ Dependent Variable.

$(IV)_j$, $(IV)_k$ = the $_jth$ and $_kth$ Independent Variables.

a and b are coefficients

physical, social and psychological. While it appears that no broadly accepted theory about the quality of urban life exists,[18] the dimensions of suburban life were chosen for our study from conceptualizations about the quality of urban life most frequently generated by urban scholars.[19] As shown in Figure 3.1, these dimensions of suburban life were grouped into four clusters of dependent variables concerned with overall satisfaction with: housing environment, community services, social patterns, and psychological well-being. For example, the variables chosen as specific indexes of satisfaction with the housing environment are: personal and family privacy, size and arrangement of the housing unit and lot, economic and functional responsibilities of home ownership, and house and neighborhood appearance. In turn, each of these specific indexes of satisfaction is comprised of detailed measures of satisfaction, each related to a question in the questionnaire. As shown on Figure 3.2, the detailed measures associated with the specific index of "personal and family privacy" are concerned with unwanted visits, audio and visual privacy, and indoor and outdoor privacy. Since we are not certain with the relative importance of these measures, we weigh the scores of each of these measures equally in constructing the specific index of satisfaction of personal and family privacy and, in turn, weigh the specific indexes equally in building the overall index of satisfaction for the housing environment.

The other indexes of suburban life satisfaction were constructed in a similar manner with one exception: the specific indexes of psychological well-being were based on a particular scale which attempts to measure aspects of mental well-being considered to be most appropriate for our study of a non-pathological population—personal feeling scales, by Wessman and Ricks.[20] This scale is similar in content to the semantic differential scales Campbell, Converse, and Rodgers used in constructing their "index of general affect"[21] in their attempt to develop a qualitatively detailed way to measure overall life satisfaction or happiness. Our other measures of dimensions of the quality of suburban life, such as those for the housing environment, attempt to deal with an individual's satisfaction with a certain aspect of his/her life based on the conceptual model shown in Figure 3.3, which relates satisfaction of an attribute being assessed to the perception of that attribute and the standard against which the attribute is judged. In contrast, our scale for psychological well-being was designed primarily as a "Hedonic" scale to measure an individual's relative "happiness-unhappiness." While it has been argued that happiness measures are less stable than those for satisfaction due to short-term emotional fluctuations on which happiness measures are based,[22] our psychological scale was shown to be fairly stable over time.[23] We believe that the emotional oriented "happiness" measures reflect more deeply an indi-

FIGURE 3.2

Construction of Overall Index of Satisfaction

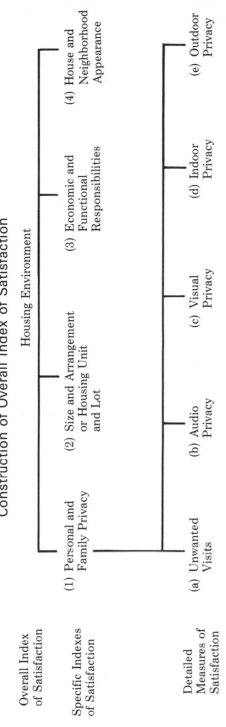

Overall Index
of Satisfaction

Specific Indexes
of Satisfaction

Detailed
Measures of
Satisfaction

Housing Environment

(1) Personal and
Family Privacy

(2) Size and Arrangement
or Housing Unit
and Lot

(3) Economic and
Functional
Responsibilities

(4) House and
Neighborhood
Appearance

(a) Unwanted
Visits

(b) Audio
Privacy

(c) Visual
Privacy

(d) Indoor
Privacy

(e) Outdoor
Privacy

where:

$$(1) = \frac{(a) + (b) + (c) + (d) + (e)}{5}$$

and:

$$\text{Housing Environment Score} = \frac{(1) + (2) + (3) + (4)}{4}$$

Source: Compiled by the authors.

FIGURE 3.3

Conceptual Model of Satisfaction

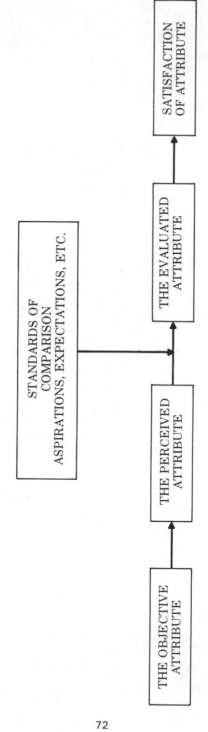

Source: Angus Campbell, Philip E. Converse, and Willard L. Rodgers *The Quality of American Life* (New York: Russell Sage Foundation, 1976), p. 13.

viduals inner sense of well-being than cognitive, judgmentally oriented "satisfaction" measures.[24]

These apparent differences between measures of happiness and satisfaction, may not make an overwhelming difference in our results as it was shown that global measures of happiness and satisfaction have a substantial overlap ($r = 0.50$) and that semantic differential scales similar in content to the ones we employ could have very similar correlations with measures of both happiness and satisfaction.[25] Thus, scales designed to estimate either levels of happiness or satisfaction measure similar attributes, and it is likely that our scale for psychological well-being will reflect both an individual's happiness and feelings about overall life satisfaction.

A complete presentation of the construction of all of our overall indexes of satisfaction is presented in Appendix B.

Independent Variables

Based on theories and previous research discussed earlier concerning the influences of social class, subculture, life cycle, and the environment, independent variables representing crucial demographic and environmental characteristics were chosen as the most likely explanations of changes in the satisfaction levels of dependent variables. These independent variables, which are presented in Figure 3.1, are grouped in four theory-related categories: social class influences, subcultural influences, life cycle influences, and suburban environmental influences. We present a discussion of the independent variables associated with each of these categories as well as their relationships with dependent variables.

However, because the literature that we review is often contradictory in its predictions and based on research conducted over a wide range of time and circumstances and because of the exploratory nature of our study, we do not feel justified in positing formal hypotheses. Rather, we state only general and tentative expectations of the relationships among the variables we examine.

Social Class Influences

It has been argued that the independent variables of income, education, and occupational status are related to social class influences which affect the satisfaction of dependent variables regardless of the residential environment.[26] Thus, a testing of these variables will be used to examine the validity of the social class theory.

Income. While it is clear that increases in family income purchase increments of housing quality, it has also been shown that such increases allow families to spend a smaller percentage of their income on housing.[27] Accordingly, higher-income families can use a greater percentage of their incomes to purchase other goods and services (e.g., collective goods, transportation, childcare, medical care, education) than lower-income households. In addition, there is evidence suggesting that increases in family income are positively associated with improved overall life satisfaction and mental health.[28] We therefore expected a positive relationship between family income and all dependent satisfaction variables.

Education. Studies have shown that households with high levels of education (years) are willing to spend more of their income on housing[29] and a planned residential environment rich in public facilities[30] than less-educated households with the same income. Thus, we could expect highly educated households to be found mostly in satisfying housing environments with access to superior public facilities, particularly schools.

However, since such households may have more sophisticated functional, social, and aesthetic tastes for housing, community facilities, and friendship patterns than those generally provided by the market in most relatively new suburban areas,[31] there could be considerable dissatisfaction with many aspects of their environments. If true, this in turn could lead to socialization problems and mental stress. Yet, a national study found that in general the most educated women have the greatest options in life for women, such as professional development, and that for married women who work there is a positive relationship between level of education and overall life satisfaction.[32] Given such findings, we anticipated that increases in the educational level of women will be associated positively with all dependent satisfaction variables.

Occupational Status. We could expect occupational level (e.g., professional, skilled operative, manual) to be highly correlated with years of education[33] and exclude it as a separate indicator of social class. However, we included occupational status in our examination of suburbia because of its potential relation to psychological well-being. Since there often exists a greater discrepancy between a woman's occupation and her level of education than that of a man,[34] it seems likely that an increase in woman's occupational status would have a more positive impact on her mental health than an increase in the years of education.[35] Indeed, studies have shown that employment status can have an important impact on overall life satisfaction for married women.[36] We therefore expected a positive relationship between occupational status and psychological well-being variables.

Subcultural Influences

Sometimes related to social class theory are subcultural influences concerned with ethnic or regional ties.[37] The theory to be examined here is that subcultural ties influence preferences and satisfaction of the suburban environment, independently.[38] In order to test this general expectation we examine the independent variables of ethnic identity, regional origin and length of residency.

Ethnic identity. There is considerable evidence indicating that households with strong ethnic ties, particularly if combined with working-class ties, often have a difficult time adjusting to the low density, low interaction level of a typical middle-class suburb.[39] It is our contention that a substantial portion of suburban population is comprised of "ex-ethnics"—individuals who are accepted and function in middle-class suburban life but who grew up in ethnically oriented neighborhoods and who miss the intensity and character of their ethnic youth.[40] If this is true, ex-ethnics may find many physical and social aspects of their suburban environments uncomfortable, dull, and generally unsatisfying. We expected such patterns of negative relationships to carry over into the realm of mental health and anticipated that ethnic identification will be negatively related to all dependent variables.

Regional Origin. Since the end of World War II, the San Jose Standard Metropolitan Statistical Area (SMSA) has been one of the most rapidly growing metropolitan regions in the nation. Most of this growth has been due to immigration of individuals from other regions to the San Jose suburbs. Hence much of suburbia in San Jose, and California in general, is inhabited by adults who spent their formative years in other regions.

In cases where the household head is from a large urban area where there is a high population density, the individual and family may develop greater social distance to the public, and social activities are likely to be more diverse and accessible to each household which interacts with some degree of sophistication.[41] However, in rural areas the number of people one meets is limited but the inclination to know them may be greater; society-at-large is probably not a significant factor, and the family will tend to be less sophisticated in dealing with social complexities and subcultural variety.[42] Therefore, it may be easier for individuals from large metropolitan areas to adjust to a new housing environment than for those from smaller communities.

In addition, it has been argued that women moving beyond commuting distance from their origins[43] to areas with unfamiliar density and social interaction patterns have substantial difficulties adjusting to a new environment.[44] We therefore expected that all satisfaction dependent variables would be positively related to the degree of urbanness (e.g., population size) of the community in which a woman spent her formative years and negatively related to the distance of that community from the San Jose metropolitan area.

Length of Residency. While it has been argued that some forms of loneliness (familial, existential, emotional) may not decrease easily with length of residence,[45] other studies have shown that mutual assistance among neighbors increase with the length of time a family has lived in one place.[46] This latter process may be especially true for residents having strong ethnic or subcultural ties.[47] It also seems likely that increased order and familiarity with the housing environment, community services, and friendship patterns generate more overall satisfaction with the passage of time.[48] Hence, we anticipated that length of residency will be positively related to all dependent variables.

Life Cycle Influences

The life cycle theory suggests that one's preferences and satisfactions with the housing environment are related mostly to the stage in one's life cycle rather than to the environment itself.[49] For example, households in the childrearing stage are expected to be more satisfied with low density, single-family housing in suburban areas than with high density residential environments.[50] The independent variables associated with life cycle, age, marital status, and number and age of children will be used to test this general conceptualization.

Age. It has been found that the younger the head of household, the more likely the purchase of the home has resulted in economic problems,[51] which in turn has been found the major cause of resident worries in newly established suburbs.[52] While some research indicates that women in the end of the childrearing life cycle (age group 35–50) are more likely to participate in the labor force,[53] enjoy more economic and psychic benefits than younger women with children, a considerable amount of evidence indicates that mental health declines with an increase in age for the total population structures.[4] We therefore expected that age will vary positively with satisfaction with the housing environment and negatively with satisfaction variables concerned with psychological well-being.

Marital Status. While it has been shown that many unmarried women achieve high levels of economic independence,[55] there is considerable evidence that women who are heads of households are likely to have substantially more problems than their married counterparts concerning income,[56] economic and functional responsibilities of homeownership,[57] mental health and social patterns,[58] and the enjoyment of community services.[59] Because of the extent of the problems associated with unattached women in what may be a couple-oriented suburban world, we expected that women who are heads of households will generally experience lower scores for all dependent satisfaction variables than will married women.

Number and Age of Children. Previous research has shown that the presence of children is directly related to neighboring and to participation in formal organizations.[60] In addition, there is evidence that the greater the number of children, the greater the degree of desire for low density housing;[61] and the older the children, the greater the degree of dissatisfaction with a low density environment.[62] At the same time, the increasing desire of women to participate in the labor force and other non-household-related activities[63] would suggest the opposite set of relationships: an increase in satisfaction with a decrease in the number of children and an increase in age of children.[64] Therefore, we anticipated that all dependent satisfaction variables will vary negatively with the number of children and positively with the mean age of all children.

Suburban Environmental Influences

Environmental deterministic theories suggest that the physical and social characteristics of the environment have considerable influence on the levels of satisfaction an individual has with that environment.[65] Despite evidence that might challenge this concept,[66] we will examine the significance of these environmental influences by testing variables associated with characteristics of the residential environment: residential density, household distance from the central city center, age of neighborhood, distance to work, mean neighborhood income and education levels, population size of political unit, and design and site plan characteristics. *Residential Density.* Housing satisfaction has been shown to vary inversely with residential density.[67] While conflicting findings exist about density,[68] it appears that the lower the density, the more life styles will tend to emphasize the role of the nuclear family[69] and the greater the degree of social participation.[70] Further, the lower the density the more likely one will find adaptive behavior based on specialized interests.[71] As density increases, it becomes more probable that a female head of household will be employed, have fewer children, be divorced or separated, be more mobile, engage in less neighboring, and engage in less community or civic activity.[72] In addition, as density increases, the more likely one will find restrictions on recreational and leisure activity.[73] Since low density housing is often a function of income and status,[74] we expect greater housing satisfaction as density decreases, and greater friendship and organizational participation for married women. Women who are heads of households who are often employed are likely to find these opportunities less advantageous and therefore a low density situation will probably be less satisfying for them. We anticipated that density will have a negative relationship with the dependent satisfaction variables concerned with the housing environment and social patterns for married women and the reverse relationship for women who are heads of households.

Household Distance from the Central City Center. It is clear that the central cities of our metropolitan areas are declining as regional employment foci.[75] Yet cities still remain dominant centers for our cultural, educational, and governmental activities as well as health and other important services. While it is true that these non-business activities have also decentralized, they tend to be relatively less dispersed throughout the lower density suburban areas.[76] Since it has been shown that women have less access to the automobile than do men[77] and the quality of public transportation in suburban areas is generally limited,[78] it seems likely that women living in outlying suburban areas would have more difficulty enjoying the community services of the central city as well as their social and psychological benefits than women who live in inlying neighborhoods.[79] We therefore expected that the household distance from the central city center (miles) will vary negatively with the satisfaction variables concerned with community services, social patterns, and psychological well-being.

Age of Neighborhood. People in established areas may have a clearer sense of social reality than those in newer areas, and women are most likely to be sensitive to this situation's impact.[80] It seems probable that older neighborhoods would find more cohesive and stable social organization in terms of the quantity and quality of friendships and in the choice of organizational affiliations. To the extent that older neighborhoods are likely to have residents with a greater average length of residency than those in newer developments, they should generate much of the physical, social, and psychological benefits attributed to individual length of residency.[81] We therefore anticipated that age of neighborhood will have a positive association with all dependent satisfaction variables.

Distance to Work. As documented by Meyer, Kain, and Wohl,[82] the journey to work is among the most important trips (as a percentage of all trips) emanating from households in virtually every metropolitan area of the nation. Indeed, employment location has been found to be the major force determining residential location for non-minority groups.[83] That is, once the employment location of the primary earner is established, a housing unit is found within the commuter-shed of that location. It has been argued that most families in the life cycle phase of childrearing prefer to consume more inexpensive land in outlying suburban areas in exchange for less accessibility—higher cost and time loss for commutation to work—than their inlying counterparts.[84] This appears to be the case even for individuals who both live and work in the suburbs.[85]

The question we would like to address is whether increases in commutation time affects the levels of satisfaction about aspects of the suburban environment. For example, it is known that the journey to work can often lengthen the work day by as much as 20 percent and therefore cut deeply into time otherwise spent on social and leisure activities[86] or conflict with home roles.[87] It has also been shown that longer journeys to work not only lessen overall satisfaction for a commuter but also for his or her spouse due to excessive time separation.[88] We therefore expected that the travel time to work of a woman and/or her spouse will vary negatively with her satisfaction with community services, social patterns, and psychological well-being.

Mean Neighborhood Income and Educational Levels. The mean income and educational level of a neighborhood is a decisive indicator of what the area's general preferences may be in terms of facilities and amenities as well as its ability to secure these goods. To the extent that an individual's income and education levels are at variance with the neighborhood means, it has been demonstrated that the individual's satisfaction with her/his housing situation may be diminished according to the magnitude of that variance.[89] Conversely, the greater the perceived homogeneity of residents in a neighborhood, the greater their participation is likely to be within the neighborhood.[90] When a person from a minority group ranks higher on these factors than does the community-at-large, Gans has found that this individual tends to take an active and influential role in community affairs in a manner far outweighing numerical representation. The rationale for this mode of behavior is that participation is a way of searching out friends.[91] Another motivation may be, according to Gans, that a minority group will often tend to buy in areas where their income and educational levels will be higher than the neighborhood means because they may wish to spend a lower percentage of their income on housing and they fear rejection by neighbors of similar income and educational levels.[92] On the other hand, if an individual falls below the neighborhood means on these items, dissatisfaction may result and may surface as resentment over these disequalities manifested in terms of variables which will tend to minimize the differences, for example, neighbors will be accused of "showing off."[93] Of course, if homogeneity is all-pervasive it may become more difficult to form social relationships based on more discriminate criteria.[94] It therefore seems likely that individuals whose education is significantly higher than that of the neighborhood mean (if it approaches 16 years) would have little basis for any great dissatisfaction; highly educated individuals are a minority in society benefiting from training that is generally related to a particular specialty. On the other hand, those with an educational level below that of the neighborhood mean would probably have different views on the quantity and quality of community services desired by that neighborhood and would be at a disadvantage in social intercourse, and these factors would have a negative impact on psychological factors. We expect that an income higher than the neighborhood mean would be of moderate importance; the individual would be free to leave at any time. A lower income would affect that individual's perception of desirable community services (limited by the level of taxation one could sustain); housing satisfaction would also be affected since the rising cost of maintenance and improvement would have a negative impact; friendships might be difficult due to lifestyle differences; and mental health may be adversely affected by the hard choices faced in terms of allocating very scarce resources to meet neighborhood norms. We therefore expected that as income and education decline below the neighborhood means there will be a substantial decline in all dependent satisfaction variables.

Population Size of Political Unit. While factors other than political have dictated massive shifts of population from central cities to the suburbs,[95] the net political effect of suburbanization has been the fragmentation and decentralization of governmental units.[96] This phenomenon favors those whose personal resources are sufficient to solve their own immediate problems[97] because the smaller the unit, the smaller a range of public goods that unit can furnish.[98] Thus, the suburbs provide the setting where particularistic goals and values may be vigorously pursued.[99] Expressed in economic terms, the higher the socioeconomic status of a unit of local government, the smaller its population is likely to be.[100] Further, it has been argued that political fragmentation is more efficient since each (relatively affluent) individual may choose and maximize the package of public services deemed most desirable.[101] Therefore, we expected that the population size of a political Unit will vary inversely with satisfaction on all community services variables.

Design and Site Plan Characteristics. Undifferentiated suburban tract housing developed by speculative merchant builders has come under fire from a number of sources for environmental and social reasons.[102] However, there are indications that the marketplace is also demonstrating the validity of these criticisms. As more Americans acquire a suburban background, two related trends are likely to emerge. First, those who have lived in the suburbs are more likely to want to continue to live there.[103] Second, these "suburbanized" individuals will probably tend to be more localized in their contacts.[104] It has been shown that this community-centered population is attracted to planned communities.[105] These individuals are generally upper middle-class seeking protection from unplanned change, physical as well as social, and access to shared facilities.[106]

For example, residents of Westlake Village, a planned community near Los Angeles of mixed housing types and densities, conform to the characteristics cited in the preceding discussion. Seventy-five percent lived previously in suburbs of Los Angeles or other large cities; only 4 percent came from central cities. The population is solidly upper middle-class in income ($22,000 median annual income in 1969) and occupation (college-educated professional and managerial). Previous amenities characteristic of suburban life (schools, social homogeneity) are taken for granted. Indeed, the chief concern of the residents of Westlake Village is a master plan which guarantees open space and environmental amenities which include, but do not stop at, recreational facilities.[107] Therefore, we expected that the greater the degree of planned characteristics in the site plan of a housing development, the greater the level of satisfaction on all dependent variables.

SUBJECTS AND SAMPLE

Using census tract and block statistics and preliminary field surveys, we identified eight middle and upper-middle class suburban neighborhoods (similar in terms of social and economic characteristics) which typify the range of suburban development in the San Jose metropolitan area (SMSA) and insure a substantial variation of most independent variables concerned with the environment. The social economic, and physical characteristics we employed to identify study neighborhoods were the independent variables (discussed above), such as years of school completed (for the population over 25 years old), annual household income ($10,000 to $40,000 in 1975), household distance from the central city center (miles), residential density (households per acre), and design and site plan characteristics (planned environments* vs. undifferentiated suburban development). Where feasible, data from the Special Census of the San Jose SMSA conducted in the spring of 1975 were incorporated in this selection process.[108]

Subjects for this study were women representatives of each neighborhood chosen randomly. As we are primarily interested in women in the childrearing life cycle, the study was limited to women between the ages of 20 and 50 who had at least one child of elementary school age living at home. Also, in order to avoid the initial adjustments associated with a new residential move, the study was restricted to women who had lived in their residence at least one year at the time of interview.

We interviewed women who represent a 5.4 percent sample, or approximately 100 of the households in each of the eight study neighborhoods.[109] Our total sample represents 825 households, or about 0.4 percent of the 195,000 households eligible** in the San Jose SMSA in 1975, that is,

---

*This includes a variety of planned environments, such as planned unit developments, condominium complexes, and other residential areas having special design and site plan characteristics (e.g., community facilities integrated into the overall site plan).

**These 195,000 households, or approximately 50 percent of the total of 392,400 households in the San Jose SMSA, were found eligible for our study using the criteria of income, age of female head, and children.

households which in 1975 had a female head between the ages of 20–50, had at least one child living at home, and had an estimated 1975 family income of at least $10,000, which represent the upper two-thirds of the 1975 family income distribution in the metropolitan area.

This study reports on the results from our interviews with women living in the following neighborhoods in 1976:

Neighborhood	Sample Size
1. Inlying single-family neighborhood in San Jose	105
2. Outlying single-family neighborhood in San Jose	100
3. Outlying planned unit developments in San Jose	97
4. Outlying condominiums in San Jose	101
5. Single-family neighborhood in Los Gatos	105
6. Condominiums in Los Gatos	103
7. Single-family neighborhood in Cupertino	109
8. Condominiums in Cupertino	105

As shown above, our sample was distributed spatially among four residential environments in the central city of San Jose, (Neighborhoods 1, 2, 3, 4), and four residential areas in nearby suburban communities of Los Gatos (Neighborhoods 6, 7) and Cupertino (Neighborhoods 7, 8). With the exception of Neighborhood 1, our inlying control neighborhood, which is 2.0 miles from the center of San Jose, all neighborhoods are approximately 8.0 miles* from the metropolitan center; and all neighborhoods have similar economic and social characteristics.** For quantitative and verbal description of each neighborhood, see Appendixes E, F, G, and H.

Table 3.1 reveals that with the possible exception of housing type (percent detached single-family),† our 1976 study samples of the central city and adjacent suburbs appear to be similar to the 1975 characteristics of middle-income families in those areas with respect to income, age of woman, marital status, size of household, and other household charac-

---

*For Neighborhoods 2 through 7, the mean household distance from the central city center ranged from 7.7 to 8.5 miles. See Appendix F.

**For all neighborhoods, the mean 1975 family income varied from $21,420 to $25,380, the mean level of education was at least high school graduation. See Appendix F.

†While the Housing Type (percent detached single-family) was considerably lower in our suburban sample than in the actual suburban population, this variance was virtually unavoidable. In order to have our sample approximate the percentage of multiple dwellings for total metropolitan area at the income, size, and tenure levels of our research, we needed, of course, to conduct our interviews where appropriate multiple dwellings exist—often in the adjacent suburbs.

TABLE 3.1

Comparison of Household Characteristics of Study Sample of Central City and Suburban Ring in the San Jose Metropolitan Area with Households Eligible for Study in Those Areas

Household Characteristics	Central City		Suburban Ring	
	1976 Study Sample (n = 403)	1975 Eligible Households Eligible for Study in the San Jose SMSA[a] (n = 79,000)	1976 Study Sample (n = 422)	1975 Eligible Households Eligible for Study in the San Jose SMSA[a] (n = 116,000)
Family income (1975)	23,000[b]	21,400[c]	23,400[b]	24,200[c]
Age of woman	33.7	32.9	35.6	34.1
Marital status (percent married)	90.1	87.3	80.7	79.8
Percent Caucasian	86.1	72.4[d] 88.9[f]	92.3	80.8[e] 92.3[f]
Persons per household	4.06	4.21	3.87	4.01
Monthly cost of household	282	271	303	277
Housing tenure (percent owner occupied)	93.5	85.7	88.3	86.6
Housing type (percent detached single-family)	75.0	62.1[d] 68.9[f]	50.5	56.0[e] 70.7[f]

[a]Households which had in 1975 a female head between the ages 20–50, had at least one child of elementary school age living at home, and had an estimated annual income of at least $10,000.

[b]1975 income reported during our field interviews held in 1976.

[c]Estimated 1975 mean household income from extrapolating 1965–74 income trends for households having an estimated 1975 income of $10,000 or more.

[d]Mean value for the entire household population in the central city of the San Jose SMSA.

[e]Mean value for the entire household population in the suburban ring of the San Jose SMSA.

[f]1975 mean value of census tracts from which study sample was drawn.

Source: Santa Clara County Planning Department, 1975 Countywide Census, Santa Clara County (1976).

FIGURE 3.4

Location of Study Neighborhoods

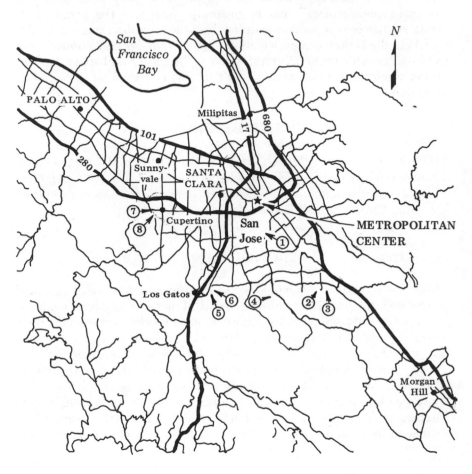

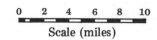

LEGEND:

1. Inlying S.F. (S.J.)
2. Outlying S.F. (S.J.)
3. Outlying PUD (S.J.)
4. Outlying Con (S.J.)
5. S.F. (L.G.)
6. Con (L.G.)
7. S.F. (Cup.)
8. Con (Cup.)

Scale (miles)

Source: California State Automobile Association.

teristics.* With regard to our total sample, Table 3.2 indicates that our study sample closely approximates the eligible households in the total San Jose metropolitan area** and is generally similar to the mean 1976 characteristics of comparable households in the suburban rings of all the SMSAs in the United States.† Thus, it appears that our study households have qualities which generally typify much of the middle and upper middle-income suburban environments in the San Jose metropolitan area and in the nation.

DATA COLLECTION

Data were collected through the use of a structured questionnaire administered by an interviewer in the home of each subject. Each personal interview was conducted by a trained woman graduate student from San Jose State University and lasted about one hour.

DATA ANALYSIS

After the data were collected, scores from questions concerning each variable were tabulated and transferred to IBM cards for statistical analysis by computer. First, simple correlation coefficients were computed in order to make a preliminary examination of the relationships between variables. This procedure also acted as a technique for screening out independent variables with marginal influences on dependent variables. Other statistical techniques, such as t-tests and analysis of variance were used to test differences between mean scores of subgroups of our study sample (for example, multi-family vs. single-family residents). Partial correlation coefficients were employed primarily to test for expected relationships

---

*In order to attain our objective of studying neighborhoods of equal population size, a greater proportion of the populations of Los Gatos (3.3 percent) and Cupertino (3.8 percent) are included in the total sample than those from San Jose (0.6 percent). To the extent that these two political units may have social, economic, and physical characteristics not typical of the San Jose metropolitan area, care should, of course, be taken in generalizing about the population (see Table 3.1). That is, one-half of our sample comes from two areas which are a much smaller proportion of the total SMSA. Turning this analysis around, however, there is a general correspondence in a broader sense in that San Jose constitutes about one-half of the population of the SMSA and other small communities (of which Los Gatos and Cupertino are examples) constitute the other half.

**Although the percent caucasian for our sample study of 89.2 was substantially higher than the mean value for the total San Jose SMSA of 79.2, it was quite similar to the mean value of the middle and upper middle-income census tracts from which our sample was drawn of 90.6.

† Households in the suburban rings of all SMSAs with at least one child less than 18-years-old living at home in 1976. Based on SMSA definitions of 1970.

TABLE 3.2

Comparison of Household Characteristics of Study Sample with Households Eligible for Study in the San Jose Metropolitan Area and in Suburban Rings of All Standard Metropolitan Statistical Areas in the United States

Household Characteristics	1976 Study Sample (n=825)	1975 Households Eligible for Study in the San Jose SMSA[a] (n=195,000)	1976 Comparable Suburban Households in all SMSAs[b] (n=12,700,000)
Family income (1975)	23,200[c]	22,500[d]	21,000[e]
Age of woman	34.7	33.5	34.2
Marital status (percent married)	85.4	83.5	80.5
Percent Caucasian	89.2	79.2[f] 90.6[g]	91.6
Persons per household	3.98	4.11	4.31
Monthly cost of household	290	273	256[h]
Housing tenure (percent owner occupied)	90.1	86.2	75.7
Housing type (percent detached single-family)	63.0	61.3[f] 69.8[g]	72.3

[a]Households which in 1975 had a female head between the ages 20–50, had at least one child of elementary school age living at home, and had an estimated 1975 annual income of at least $10,000.

[b]Households which in 1976 were in the suburban rings of all SMSA's (as defined in 1970) and had at least one child less than 18 years old living at home.

[c]1975 income reported during our field interviews held in 1976.

[d]Estimated 1975 mean household income from extrapolating 1965–74 income trends for households having an estimated 1975 income of $10,000 or more.

[e]1975 mean income for owner-occupied households.

[f]Mean value for the entire household population for the San Jose SMSA.

[g]1975 mean value of census tracts from which study sample was drawn.

[h]1975 mean value from a national survey of 23 typical SMSAs.

Sources: All San Jose SMSA data from Santa Clara County Department, *1975 Countywide Census, Santa Clara County* (1976). Data for suburban rings of all U.S. SMSAs from: U.S., Department of Commerce, Bureau of the Census, *Consumer Income: Household Money Income in 1975 By Housing Tenure and Residence for the United States, Regions, Divisions and States* (Washington, D.C.: Government Printing Office, 1977); except "age of woman" data from U.S., Department of Commerce, Bureau of the Census, *Household and Family Characteristics* (Washington, D.C.:, Government Printing Office, 1977); and except "monthy cost of household" and "housing type" data from U.S., Department of Commerce, Bureau of the Census, *Annual Housing Survey: 1975 Summary of Housing Characteristics for Selected Metropolitan Areas* (Washington, D.C.: Government Printing Office, 1978).

between independent and dependent variables in the entire sample.[*] In some cases, multiple regression analysis was used to test the combined impact of the independent variables expected to influence each dependent variable.

Because of the exploratory nature of our study, we are using only tentative expectations of the relationships among the variables examined, and two tailed t-tests of significance seem most appropriate for our study. We recognize, of course, the social science convention of obtaining a confidence level of at least 0.95 ($p<0.05$) before granting any theoretical importance to the relationships uncovered. However, in order to call the attention of the reader to potentially important areas for future research, we report our results with a somewhat lower confidence level of 0.90 ($p<0.10$).

NOTES

1. Jacob Riis, *How the Other Half Lives* (New York: Hill and Wang, 1957); Roy Lubove, *The Progressives and the Slums* (Pittsburgh, Penn.: University of Pittsburgh Press, 1962).

2. See for example, Rudolf H. Moos and Paul M. Insel, eds., *Issues in Human Ecology: Human Milieus* (Palo Alto, Calif.: National Press Books, 1973); and Harold Proshansky et al., eds. *Environmental Psychology: People and Their Settings* (New York: Holt, Rinehart and Winston, 1976).

3. Examples are William Michelson, *Man and His Urban Environment* (Reading, Mass.: Addison-Wesley, 1976); and J. Douglas Porteous, *Environment and Behavior: Planning and Everyday Urban Life* (Reading, Mass.: Addison-Wesley, 1977).

4. Kenneth H. Craik, "The Comprehension of the Everyday Physical Environment," *Journal of the American Institute of Planners* 34 (January 1968): 29–37.

5. Robert Gutman, "Site Planning and Social Behavior," *Journal of Social Issues* 22 (Winter 1966): 103–15.

6. Robert K. Merton, "Social Psychology of Housing," in *Current Trends in Social Psychology*, ed. Wayne Dennis et al. (Pittsburgh, Penn.: University of Pittsburgh Press, 1951), pp. 163–217; Leon Festinger et al., *Social Pressures in Informal Groups* (Stanford, Calif.: Stanford University Press, 1951); and William H. Whyte, *The Organization Man* (Garden City, N.Y.: Anchor Books, 1957).

7. Robert Sommer, "Man's Proximate Environment", *Journal of Social Issues* 22 (1966): 59–70.

8. Erving Goffman, *The Presentation of Self in Everyday Life* (New York: Doubleday, 1959); Allen Wheelis, *The Quest for Identity* (New York: Norton, 1958).

9. Melvin Webber, "The Urban Place and the Nonplace Urban Realm," *Explorations into Urban Structure*, ed. Melvin Webber et al. (Philadelphia: University of Pennsylvania Press, 1964), pp. 79–173; Richard L. Meier, *A Communications Theory of Urban Growth* (Cambridge, Mass.: MIT Press, 1962).

10. A. E. Parr, "Psychological Aspects of Urbanology," *Journal of Social Issues* 22 (1966): 39–45.

11. Herbert J. Gans, *The Levittowners* (New York: Vintage Books, 1967).

---

[*]The independent variables used in our partial correlation analysis are shown in Appendix C: all of section a and b; c1 and d3, 4 and 5. Because of the almost binary nature of the other independent variables, they were examined with t-tests or analysis of variance.

12. Charles Tilly, "Occupational Rank and Grade of Residence in a Metropolis," *American Journal of Sociology* 67 (1961): 323–30.

13. Whyte, *Organization Man*; Gans, *Levittowners*.

14. Robert Somner, *Personal Space: The Behavioral Basis of Design* (Englewood Cliffs, N.J.: Prentice-Hall, 1969).

15. John B. Lansing et al., *Planned Residential Environments* (Ann Arbor: University of Michigan Press, 1970).

16. James R. Anderson et al., "Resident's Satisfaction: Criteria for the Evaluation of Housing for Low and Moderate Income Families" (paper delivered at the American Institute of Planners Conference, Denver, October 1974).

17. Robert B. Zehner, *Indicators of the Quality of Life in the New Communities* (Cambridge, Mass.: Ballinger, 1977).

18. Angus Campbell, Philip E. Converse, and Willard L. Rodgers, *The Quality of American Life: Perceptions, Evaluations, and Satisfactions* (New York: Russell Sage Foundation, 1976); Environmental Protection Agency, *The Quality of Life Concept* (Washington, D.C.: Environmental Protection Agency, 1973); Henry J. Schmandt and Warner Bloomberg, Jr., eds. *The Quality of Urban Life*, (Beverly Hills, Calif.: Sage, 1969).

19. William R. Ewald, Jr., ed., *Environment for Man* (Bloomington: Indiana University Press, 1967), pp. 3–109; Claude S. Fischer and Robert Max Jackson, "Suburbs, Networks and Attitudes," in *The Changing Face of the Suburbs*, ed. Barry Schwartz (Chicago: University of Chicago Press, 1963), pp. 279–307; Charles Haar ed., *The President's Task Force on Suburban Problems* (Cambridge, Mass.: Ballinger, 1974); William Michelson, *Environmental Choice, Human Behavior, and Residential Satisfaction* (New York: Oxford University Press, 1977); Harvey S. Perloff, "A Framework for Dealing with the Urban Environment: An Introductory Statement," in *The Quality of the Urban Environment* (Baltimore, Md.: Johns Hopkins Press, 1969), pp. 3–31; Schmandt and Bloomberg, *Quality of Urban Life*; Nestor E. Terleckyi, *Improvements in the Quality of Life: Estimates of Possibilities in the United States* (Washington, D.C.: National Planning Association, 1975); Zehner, *Quality of Life*.

20. Alden E. Wessman and David F. Ricks, *Mood and Personality* (New York: Holt, Rinehart and Winston, 1966).

21. Campbell, Converse, and Rodgers, *Quality of American Life*.

22. Zehner, *Quality of Life*, p. 9.

23. Wessman and Ricks, *Mood and Personality*, p. 247.

24. Ibid.

25. Campbell, Converse, and Rodgers, *Quality of American Life*.

26. Mark Baldassare and Claude S. Fischer, "Suburban Life: Powerlessness and Need for Affiliation," *Urban Affairs Quarterly* 10 (1975): 314–26; Gans, *Levittowners*; Harvey Marshall, "Suburban Life Styles: A Contribution to the Debate," in *The Urbanization of the Suburbs*, ed. Louis H. Masotti and Jeffrey K. Hadden (Beverly Hills, Calif.: Sage, 1973), pp. 123–48.

27. Sherman Maisel and Louis Winnick, "Family Housing Expenditures: Illusive Laws and Intrusive Variances," in *Urban Housing*, ed. William L.C. Wheaton et al. (New York: Free Press, 1966), pp. 139–53.

28. Campbell, Converse, and Rodgers, *Quality of American Life;* Gans, *Levittowners*; Thomas A. C. Rennie et al., *Mental Health in the Metropolis* (New York: McGraw-Hill, 1962); William Rushing, "Two Patterns in the Relationship Between Social Class and Mental Hospitalization," *American Sociological Review* 34 (1969): 533–41.

29. Arnold Feldman and Charles Tilly, "The Interaction of Social and Physical Space," *American Sociological Review* 25 (1966): 877–84.

30. Lansing et al., *Planned Environments*.

31. Wendell Bell and Marian Boat, "Urban Neighborhoods and Informal Social Relations," *American Journal of Sociology* 62 (1957): 391–98; William Michelson, "Environmental Change," Centre for Urban and Community Studies Research Paper, no. 60, October 1973.

32. Campbell, Converse, and Rodgers, *Quality of American Life*.

33. Michelson, *Man and Urban Environment*.

34. Cynthia Epstein, *Woman's Place* (Berkeley: University of California Press, 1970); Juanita Kreps, *Sex in the Market Place* (Baltimore, Md.: Johns Hopkins Press, 1971).

35. Walter R. Gove and Jeannette F. Tudor, "Adult Sex Roles and Mental Illness," in *Changing Women in a Changing Society*, ed. Joan Huber (Chicago: University of Chicago Press, 1973), pp. 50–73.

36. Campbell, Converse, and Rodgers, *Quality of American Life*; James D. Wright, "Are Working Women Really More Satisfied?" *Journal of Marriage and the Family* 40 (1978): 301–14.

37. Herbert J. Gans, *The Urban Villagers* (New York: Free Press of Glencoe, 1962); Gans, *Levittowners*.

38. Michelson, *Man and Urban Environment*.

39. Gans, *Levittowners*; Michelson, *Environmental Choice*.

40. Nathan Glazer and Daniel P. Moynihan, *Beyond the Melting Pot* (Cambridge, Mass.: MIT Press, 1963); Nathan Kantrowitz, "Ethnic and Racial Segregation in the New York Metropolis, 1960," *American Journal of Sociology* 74 (1969): 685–95; Michael Novak, "How American Are You If Your Grandparents Came from Serbia in 1888?" in the *Rediscovery of Ethnicity: Its Implications for Culture and Politics in America*, ed. Sallie Te Selle (New York: Harper and Row, 1973), pp. 1–20.

41. Derk de Jonge, "Some Notes on Sociological Research in the Field of Housing," mimeo, Delft University of Technology, 1967.

42. Claude S. Fischer, "Toward a Subcultural Theory of Urbanism," *American Journal of Sociology* 80 (1975): 1319–41; de Jonge, "Sociological Research in Housing."

43. Gans, *Levittowners*.

44. Michelson, *Environmental Choice*.

45. Gans, *Levittowners*; Clark E. Moustakas, *Loneliness and Love* (Englewood Cliffs, N.J.: Prentice-Hall, 1972); Robert S. Weiss et al., *Loneliness* (Cambridge, Mass.: MIT Press, 1973).

46. Norman Schulman, "Mutual Aid and Neighboring Patterns: The Lower Town Study," *Anthropoligica* 9 (1967): 51–60; E. Pfeil, "The Pattern of Neighboring Relations in Dortmund-Nordstadt," in *Readings in Urban Sociology* ed. R.E. Pahl (London: Pergamon Press, 1968), pp. 136–58.

47. Gans, *Levittowners*.

48. Baldassare and Fischer, "Suburban Life"; Michelson, *Environmental Choice*.

49. Baldassare and Fischer, "Suburban Life"; Michelson, *Environmental Choice*.

50. Porteous, *Environment and Behavior*.

51. S.D. Clark, *The Suburban Society* (Toronto: University of Toronto Press, 1966).

52. Gans, *Levittowners*.

53. Karen Hapgood and Judith Getzels, eds., *Planning, Women and Change* (Chicago: American Society of Planning Officials, 1974), pp. 1–32; Campbell, Converse, and Rodgers, *Quality of American Life*.

54. See, for example, Robert N. Butler and Myrna I. Lewis, *Aging and Mental Health* (St. Louis: C.V. Mosby, 1977); and Rennie et al., *Mental Health in the Metropolis*.

55. Elizabeth M. Havens, "Women, Work and Wedlock: A Note on Female Marital Patterns in the United States," in *Changing Women in a Changing Society*, ed. Joan Huber (Chicago: University of Chicago press, 1973, pp. 213–19.

56. U.S., Bureau of the Census, "Household Income in 1972 and Selected Social and Economic Characteristics of Households Series," series p-60, 80 (1972); Campbell, Converse, and Rodgers, *Quality of American Life*.

57. Hapgood and Getzels, *Planning, Women, and Change*.

58. Economic and Social Opportunities, Inc., *Female Heads of Household and Poverty in Santa Clara County* (San Jose, Calif.: Economic and Social Opportunities, 1974).

59. Marilyn M. Pray, "Planning and Women in the Suburban Setting," in Hapgood and Getzels, *Planning, Women and Change*, pp. 51–56.

60. Scott Greer, "The Family in Suburbia," in *The Urbanization of the Suburbs*, Louis H. Masotti and Jeffrey K. Hadden (Beverly Hills, Calif.: Sage, 1973), pp. 149–70.

61. Michelson, *Man and Urban Environment*.

62. Ibid.

63. Melanie Freitas, "Women in Suburbia," (Planning Report, Urban and Regional Planning Department, San Jose State University, 1974).

64. Hapgood and Getzels, *Planning, Women, and Change*; Economic and Social Opportunities, Inc. *Female Heads of Household*; Campbell, Converse and Rodgers, *Quality of American Life*, pp. 406–09.

65. See, for example, Michelson, *Man and Urban Environment*; Humphrey Osmund, "Some Psychiatric Aspects of Design," in *Who Designs America?*, ed. Laurence B. Holland (Garden City, N.Y.: Anchor Books, 1966), pp. 281–318; Donald N. Rothblatt, "Improving the Design of Urban Housing," in *Urban Housing*, ed. Vasily Kouskoulas (Detroit, Mich.: National Science Foundation, 1973), pp. 149–54; Henry Sanoff, "Neighborhood Satisfaction: A Study of User Assessments of Low Income Residential Environment," in *Proceedings of the Second Inernational Symposium on Lower-Cost Housing Problems,* ed. Oktal Ural (St. Louis: University of Missouri-Rolla, 1972), pp. 119–24; and Zehner, *Quality of Life.*

66. See Gans, *Levittowners*; Nathan Glazer, "Slum Dwellings Do Not Make a Slum," *New York Times Magazine* (November 21, 1965): 55; and Daniel M. Wilner et al., *The Housing Environment and Family Life* (Baltimore, Md., Johns Hopkins Press, 1962).

67. Lansing et al., *Planned Environments*.

68. Myrna M. Weissman and Eugene S. Paykel, "Moving and Depression in Women," in Weiss, *Loneliness*, p. 154–64.

69. Michelson, *Man and Urban Environment*.

70. Donald N. Rothblatt, "Housing and Human Needs," *Town Planning Review* 42 (1971): 130–44; and Aida K. Tomeh, "Informal Group Participation and Residential Patterns," *American Journal of Sociology* 70 (1964): 28–35.

71. Michelson, *Man and Urban Environment*.

72. John Raven, "Sociological Evidence on Housing (2: The Home Environment)," *The* Oxford University Press, 1972); and Eshref Shevky and Wendell Bell, *Social Area Analysis* (Stanford, Calif.: Stanford University Press, 1955).

73. John Raven, "Sociological Evidence on Housing (2: The Home Environment," *The Architectural Review* 142 (1967): 236ff.

74. Michelson, *Environmental Choice*.

75. John F. Kain, "The Distribution and Movement of Jobs and Industry," in *The Metropolitan Enigma,* ed. James O. Wilson (Washington, D.C.: U.S. Chamber of Commerce, 1967), pp. 1–31.

76. Pray, "Planning and Women."

77. Phyllis Kaniss and Barbara Robins, "The Transportation Needs of Women," in Hapgood and Getzels *Planning, Women and Change*, pp. 63–70.

78. John R. Meyer, "Urban Transportation," in *The Metropolitan Enigma*, ed. James O. Wilson (Washington, D.C.: U.S. Chamber of Commerce, 1967), pp. 34–75.

79. Michelson, *Environmental Choice*; Porteous, *Environment and Behavior*.

80. Clark, *Suburban Society*.

81. Baldassare and Fischer, "Suburban Life"; Michelson, *Environmental Choice*.

82. John R. Meyer, John F. Kain, and Martin Wohl, *The Urban Transportation Problem* (Cambridge: Harvard University Press, 1965).

83. John F. Kain, "The Journey to Work as a Determinant of Residential Location," in *Urban Analysis*, ed. Alfred N. Page and Warren R. Segfried (Glenview, Ill.: Scott, Foresman, 1970), pp. 207–26.

84. William Alonso, "A Theory of the Urban Land Market," in *Readings in Urban Economics*, ed. Matthew Edel and Jerome Rothenberg (New York: Macmillan, 1972), pp. 104–11.

85. Kain, "Journey to Work."

86. See Howard S. Lapin, *Structuring the Journey to Work* (Philadelphia: University of Pennsylvania Press, 1964); John Wolforth, "The Journey to Work," in *Internal Structure of the City*, ed. Larry S. Bourne (New York: Oxford University Press, 1971), pp. 240–47; and Harvey Marshall, "Suburban Life Styles: A Contribution to the Debate," in *The Urbanization of the Suburbs*, eds. Louis H. Masotti and Jeffrey K. Hadden (Beverly Hills, Ca.: Sage, 1973), pp. 123–48.

87. Julie A. Erickson, "An Analysis of the Journey to Work for Women," *Social Problems* 24 (1977): 428–35.

88. Clark, *Suburban Society*.

89. Gans, *Levittowners;* Robert Gutman, "Population Mobility in the American Middle Class," in *The Urban Condition,* ed. Leonard J. Duhl (New York: Basic Books, 1963), pp. 172–83.

90. Aida K. Tomeh, "Empirical Considerations on the Problem of Social Integration," *Sociological Inquiry* 39 (1969): 65–76.

91. Herbert J. Gans, "Effects of the Move from City to Suburb," in Duhl, *Urban Condition*, pp. 184–98.

92. Gans, *Levittowners*.

93. Ibid.

94. Clark, *Suburban Society*.

95. Gans, *Levittowners*; Baldassare and Fischer, "Suburban Life."

96. Robert C. Wood, *1400 Governments* (Cambridge: Harvard University Press, 1961); Robert L. Lineberry and Ira Sharksansky, *Urban Politics and Public Policy* (New York: Harper and Row, 1971).

97. Oliver P. Williams, *Metropolitan Political Analysis* (New York: Free Press, 1971).

98. Robert L. Bish, *The Public Economy of Metropolitan Areas* (Chicago: Markham, 1971); Henry J. Schmandt and G. Stephens, "Measuring Municipal Output," *National Tax Journal* 6 (1960): 369–75.

99. Robert C. Wood, *Suburbia: Its People and Their Politics* (Boston: Houghton-Mifflin, 1958).

100. Louis H. Masotti and D. Bowen, "Communities and Budgets: The Sociology of Municipal Expenditures," *Urban Affairs Quarterly* 1 (1965): 38–58; Bryan T. Downes, "Suburban Differentiation and Municipal Policy Choices," in *Community Structure and Decision-Making*, ed. Terry N. Clark (San Francisco: Chandler, 1968), pp. 243–67.

101. Robert L. Bish and Hugh O. Nourse, *Urban Economics and Policy Analysis* (New York: McGraw-Hill, 1975); C.M. Liebout, "A Pure Theory of Local Expenditures," in *Readings in Urban Economics*, ed. Matthew Edel and Jerome Rothenberg (New York: Macmillan, 1972), pp. 513–23.

102. Edward P. Eichler and Marshall Kaplan, *The Community Builders* (Berkeley: University of California Press, 1967); William H. Whyte, *The Last Landscape* (New York: Doubleday, 1969).

103. Joseph Zelan, "Does Suburbia Make a Difference?" in *Urbanism in World Perspective,* ed. Sylvia F. Fava (New York: Crowell, 1968), pp. 401–08.

104. Sylvia F. Fava, "Beyond Suburbia," *Annals of the American Academy of Political and Social Science* 422 (1975): 10–24.

105. Michelson, *Man and Urban Environment*; Carl Werthman et al., *Planning and the Purchase Decision: Why People Buy in Planned Communities* (Berkeley: University of California Press, 1965).

106. Lansing et al., *Planned Environments*; Michelson, *Environmental Choice*.

107. Francine Rabinovitz and James Lamare, "After Suburbia, What?" in *Los Angeles: Viability and Prospects for Metropolitan Leadership*, ed. Werner Z. Hirsch (New York: Praeger, 1971), pp. 169–206.

108. See Santa Clara County Planning Department, *1975 Countywide Census, Santa Clara County* (1976).

109. The mean number of occupied households in each census tract in the San Jose SMSA was 1,870. Ibid.

4

FINDINGS AND CONCLUSIONS

This chapter presents our findings and conclusions of the San Jose study described previously. Our findings and conclusions deal with the comparative influence of the four categories of independent variables—social class, subcultural, life cycle, and suburban environmental—on levels of satisfaction in four realms of the quality of life—housing environment, community services, friendship patterns, and psychological well-being. For each independent variable we state our expectations and findings and discuss their implications.

SOCIAL CLASS INFLUENCES

Income

Expectations

Income will vary positively with all dependent satisfaction variables.

Findings

Our data only partially supports this contention (see Table 4.1). As expected, there is a strong positive relationship between income and the overall index of satisfaction with the housing environment ($p < 0.010$). Striking within this measure is the strong linkage between income and satisfaction with homeownership responsibilities ($p < 0.005$). This variable

TABLE 4.1

Relationships between Family Income and Indexes of Satisfaction

Satisfaction Index	Partial Correlation Coefficient[a] (n=825)
a. Housing environment	0.0971[d]
Privacy	−0.0004
House and Lot	0.0243
Homeownership Responsibilities	0.1518[e]
Appearance	0.0559
b. Community services	0.0186
Parks	−0.0868[c]
Schools	0.0093
Security	0.1120[e]
Child Care	−0.0303
Transportation	0.1054[e]
Entertainment and Culture	−0.0660[b]
Social patterns	0.0552
Friendships	0.0422
Group activities	0.0488
Sense of belonging	0.0411
Psychological well-being	−0.0130
Fullness vs. emptiness of life	0.0423
Receptivity towards the world	0.0191
Social respect	−0.0452
Personal freedom	0.0173
Sociability	−0.0536
Companionship	−0.0330
Work satisfaction	−0.0679[b]
Tranquility vs. anxiety	0.0524
Self approving vs. guilty	−0.0497
Self confidence	−0.0357
Energy vs. fatigue	−0.0651[b]
Elation vs. depression	0.0014

[a]two-tailed t-test for all correlations yields $p > 0.100$ unless otherwise noted
[b]t-test for this correlation yields $p < 0.100$
[c]t-test for this correlation yields $p < 0.050$
[d]t-test for this correlation yields $p < 0.010$
[e]t-test for this correlation yields $p < 0.005$
Source: Compiled by the authors.

includes not only financial considerations but the expenditure of time as well.

With respect to community services, our expectation is again borne out, although here the indications are somewhat mixed. While the overall positive relationship between income and community services is not significant, satisfaction with security and transportation (both show $p < 0.005$) most definitely is. However, two additional components, parks ($p < 0.050$) and entertainment and culture ($p < 0.100$) both demonstrated a negative relationship with income. Social patterns fail to reveal statistical support for our expectations. Most measures of psychological well-being show a weak negative relationship with respect to income. The overall index of satisfaction is not significant, and only two specific indexes—work satisfaction and energy vs. fatigue—warrant interest ($p < 0.100$).

Discussion

Although income is clearly an important resource, it is not the permeating factor for middle and upper middle-income families it was expected to be. Indeed, in various measures this independent variable often operates contrary to our expectations. In the area of psychological well-being, income varied inversely with two specific indexes, work satisfaction ($p < 0.100$) and energy vs fatigue ($p < 0.100$). Is it possible that respondents might trade off an increment of income for more qualitative returns, say, in leisure time? Is inflation nibbling away at the margin of extra work incentives? Also operating contrary to our expectations is the general area of social patterns. Here no relationship with our independent variable prevails.

With respect to community services, income provides mixed results for what we had anticipated. For the specific indexes of transportation and security, the factor of income operated as expected ($p < 0.005$ for both). Economic resources could be brought to bear in the area of security; for example, burglar alarms or automatic garage door openers, and thus the capability of investing in such devices would clearly reflect affluence. Transportation may be viewed the same way. The economics of automobile ownership, operation, and maintenance clearly favors the family with more resources. However, an inverse relationship to two less overtly materialistic variables clouds the picture: satisfaction with parks ($p < 0.050$) and with entertainment and culture ($p < 0.100$).

With respect to the latter, the explanation is rather straightforward. Although the statistical evidence for our total sample population is not decisive, when it is split into San Jose residents vs. those of Cupertino and Los Gatos combined, the picture comes into clearer focus. As will be shown later in this chapter, the mean entertainment and culture satisfaction score for San Jose residents is 4.9937, while that for those of Cupertino/Los Gatos is 5.95 (see Table 4.30). This difference of almost a full point is significant at the $p < 0.005$ level. What accounts for such a difference? San Jose's population of about 600,000 sprawls over an area of 140 square miles. Facilities and opportunities of all kinds are widely dispersed. Cupertino and Los Gatos, on the other hand, are much more compact geographically, and each contains less than one-twentieth of San Jose's population. Further, each community's cultural opportunities are quite centralized and highly accessible to the suburban population. As indicated later in this chapter, other specific indexes of satisfaction with community services as well as the overall index emphasize the difference between San Jose and Cupertino/Los Gatos.

The negative relationship between income and satisfaction with parks can also be explained. Because half of our sample resides within the open space-starved City of San Jose, it is not surprising that a negative relationship exists between the income and parks variables ($p < 0.050$). (In contrast, Los Gatos and Cupertino respondents, residents of the other two municipalities in this study, show no significant statistical relationship here.) Not surprisingly, parks are a major political issue in this community whose citizens relish, among other things, its mild climate. The space in which to recreate (especially for those with the time, desire, and accoutrements) is not there. Because the city grew so rapidly and, in doing so, vigorously courted development interests, open space has always been a low priority land use. Qualitatively, then, many residents tend to be dissatisfied. In quantitative, more materialistic terms, the situation is more favorable. Nowhere is this better illustrated than in the area of the housing environment. In this most material and central of concerns, the evidence for our expectations is substantial. In the overall index of satisfaction with the housing environment, what we had anticipated is strongly upheld ($p < 0.010$), and this evidence is still clearer in the positive variation of income with satisfaction with homeownership responsibilities ($p < 0.005$). Thus, income is a strong barometer in areas of greatest materialistic impact. But, when concerns that fall into the social and psychological realms of life are scrutinized, one could say that there are clouds on the horizon. If, as in San Jose, the public sector did not (and now, following California's Proposition 13, cannot)[1] provide such amenities, then, in the future, the void is waiting to be filled by the private sector, assuming sufficient economic demands can be generated.

Education

Expectations

A woman's level of education will vary positively with all dependent satisfaction variables.

TABLE 4.2

Relationships between Woman's Education and Indexes of Satisfaction

Satisfaction Index	Partial Correlation Coefficient[a] (n=825)
Housing environment	0.0327
Privacy	−0.0342
House and lot	0.0001
Homeownership responsibilities	−0.0110
Appearance	0.0954[d]
Community services	0.1020[e]
Parks	−0.0212
Schools	0.0850[c]
Security	0.1442[e]
Child Care	0.0433
Transportation	0.0303
Entertainment and culture	0.0580[b]
Social patterns	0.0705[c]
Friendships	0.0358
Group activities	0.0805[c]
Sense of belonging	0.0880[c]
Psychological well-being	0.0625[b]
Fullness vs. emptiness of life	0.0876[c]
Receptivity towards the world	0.0730[c]
Social respect	0.0797[c]
Personal freedom	−0.0375
Sociability	−0.0240
Companionship	0.0730[c]
Work satisfaction	0.0678[b]
Tranquility vs. anxiety	0.0592[b]
Self approving vs. guilty	−0.0021
Self confidence	0.0198
Energy vs. fatigue	0.0510
Elation vs. depression	0.0450

[a]two-tailed t-test for all correlations yields $p > 0.100$ unless otherwise noted
[b]t-test for this correlation yields $p < 0.100$
[c]t-test for this correlation yields $p < 0.050$
[d]t-test for this correlation yields $p < 0.010$
[e]t-test for this correlation yields $p < 0.005$
Source: compiled by the authors.

Findings

Our data demonstrates in general the validity of these expectations, as shown in Table 4.2. All four groups of dependent variables show some positive relationship with the level of a woman's education. With respect to the overall index of satisfaction with housing environment, the relationship is insignificant, but perhaps one of the most abstract indexes of satisfaction, the appearance of the housing environment, bears out our expectations ($p < 0.010$). Other than its value as an objective measure of years of schooling and thus the securing of a particular certificate, education seems to share this variable's somewhat ephemeral character. With respect to the community services, the linkage is even more compelling. The relationship is extremely strong with regard to the overall index of satisfaction specific indexes; schools ($p < 0.050$), security ($p < 0.005$) and entertainment and culture ($p < 0.100$) add additional reinforcement to our expectations. Social patterns maintain this consistency. The overall index of satisfaction ($p < 0.050$) and two of three specific indexes perform according to what we had anticipated ($p < 0.050$). Although as a group, the overall index of satisfaction with psychological well-being is only significant at the 0.100 level, six specific indexes are supportive, four at the level of $p < 0.050$ (fullness vs. emptiness of life, receptivity towards the world, social respect, and companionship) and two at the level of $p < 0.100$ (work satisfaction and tranquility vs. anxiety). Thus, education appears to be a variable of great permeability with an impact on diverse spheres of human existence.

Discussion

The clear-cut trend as demonstrated in the preceding section indicates that education provides qualitative if not quantitative benefits to the general population. In order to illuminate these benefits to a greater degree, we have split our sample population into two groups, those who have gone no further than high school and those who have at least some college background (see Table 4.3 for a comparison of mean scores). As can be seen, those with a higher increment of education tend to be more satisfied in an impressive array of variables. In the area of psychological well-being, the mean score difference in the overall index of satisfaction is quite significant ($p < 0.010$) as it is with four of the twelve specific indexes. Indeed, three of these (receptivity towards the world, work satisfaction, and self-confidence) are even more strongly delineated ($p < 0.005$). An additional four— fullness vs. emptiness of life, sociability, companionship, and elation vs. depression—are also of interest ($p < 0.050$). Education, then, does make an impact on feelings of psychological well-being.

TABLE 4.3

Mean Scores of Indexes of Satisfaction for Women with High School Educations and College Backgrounds

Satisfaction Index	Satisfaction Scores[a]	
	High School (n=209)	College (n=616)
Housing environment	5.57	5.60
Privacy	5.85	5.81
House and lot	5.66	5.53
Homeownership responsibilities	5.08	5.26[b]
Appearance	5.70	5.78
Community services	4.97	5.15[d]
Parks	4.86	5.01
Schools	5.02	5.23[b]
Security	4.94	5.34[e]
Child care	4.15	4.19
Transportation	5.40	5.42
Entertainment	5.23	5.58[e]
Social patterns	5.18	5.37[c]
Friendships	5.51	5.70[c]
Group activities	4.95	5.35[e]
Sense of belonging	5.00	5.05
Psychological well-being	6.71	7.08[d]
Fullness vs. emptiness of life	6.93	7.20[c]
Receptivity towards the world	6.70	7.09[e]
Social respect	7.38	7.72
Personal freedom	6.60	7.00
Sociability	6.82	7.10[c]
Companionship	7.36	7.60[c]
Work satisfaction	6.91	7.55[e]
Tranquility vs. anxiety	6.12	6.32[b]
Self approving vs. guilty	6.64	6.79
Self confidence	6.74	7.28[e]
Energy vs. fatigue	6.29	6.61[d]
Elation vs. depression	6.51	6.73[c]

[a] two-tailed t-test for all score differences yields $p > 0.100$ unless otherwise noted

[b] t-test for score difference yields $p < 0.100$

[c] t-test for score difference yields $p < 0.050$

[d] t-test for score difference yields $p < 0.010$

[e] t-test for score difference yields $p < 0.005$

Source: Compiled by the authors.

Satisfaction with social patterns is also influenced by one's level of education. Both the overall index of satisfaction and the specific index of friendships satisfaction are differentiated by educational background ($p < 0.050$), and satisfaction with group activities supports our expectations even more strongly ($p < 0.005$). With respect to community services, again level of education proves itself to be a factor. Those with college backgrounds score higher on the overall index of satisfaction ($p < 0.010$) and even more strongly on two specific indexes, security and entertainment and culture (both $p < 0.005$). Three exdexes show no statistical differentiation and one (schools) is weakly related ($p < 0.100$). The only overall index of satisfaction that is not significantly linked to educational level is housing environment. Only one specific index, homeownership responsibilities ($p < 0.100$), shows even a marginal score difference.

Thus, by this aggregation of two distinct groups of educational attainment, it seems clear that this independent variable exercises an important influence on the quality of women's lives as evidenced by these findings.

Occupational Status

Expectation

A positive relationship exists between a woman's occupational status and psychological well-being variables.

Findings

The tabulations of this variable do not provide strong support for our expectations (see Table 4.4). Unexpectedly, none of the specific indexes of psychological well-being had a significant relationship to occupational status, except social respect with a weak negative association ($p < 0.100$). Also unexpectedly, the overall index of satisfaction with the housing environment had a positive linkage with occupational status at the 0.010 level. Here, the specific indexes of homeownership responsibilities and appearance were the underlying positive relationships with occupational status ($p < 0.050$, 0.005 respectively).

As expected, there are no significant associations between the overall indexes of satisfaction with community services or social patterns and occupational status. However, there is a mild positive linkage between group activities and occupational status ($p < 0.100$); and more detailed analysis indicates that these group activities are quite extensive for working women outside of their immediate neighborhood ($p < 0.005$).

TABLE 4.4

Relationships between Woman's Occupation and Indexes of Satisfaction

Satisfaction Index	Partial Correlation Coefficient[a] (n=825)
Housing environment	0.0926[d]
Privacy	0.0421
House and lot	0.0268
Homeownership responsibilities	0.0713[c]
Appearance	0.1227[e]
Community services	0.0276
Parks	0.0061
Schools	0.0473
Security	0.0396
Child care	−0.0359
Transportation	0.0013
Entertainment and culture	−0.0041
Social patterns	0.0484
Friendships	0.0337
Group activities	0.0632[b]
Sense of belonging	0.0064
Psychological well-being	−0.0139
Fullness vs. emptiness of life	−0.0344
Receptivity towards the world	−0.0226
Social respect	−0.0625[b]
Personal freedom	0.0207
Sociability	0.0244
Companionship	−0.0336
Work satisfaction	−0.0261
Tranquility vs. anxiety	0.0260
Self approving vs. guilty	−0.0373
Self confidence	0.0013
Energy vs. fatigue	0.0304
Elation vs. depression	0.0093

[a]two-tailed t-test for all correlations yields p > 0.100 unless otherwise noted

[b]t-test for this correlation yields p < 0.100

[c]t-test for this correlation yields p < 0.050

[d]t-test for this correlation yields p < 0.010

[e]t-test for this correlation yields p < 0.005

Source: Compiled by the authors.

Discussion

Pursuing the question of occupational status further, we have aggregated mean satisfaction scores by employment status: women who do not work outside the home ("non-working") and those who do work outside the home ("working"). As Table 4.5 indicates, our expectations are partially upheld. Women who work outside the home are all, in our subjective categorization, of higher occupational status than those who do not work outside the home ("housewives"). We find that working women are more satisfied on two specific indexes of psychological well-being, as per our expectation. These indexes, self-approving vs. guilty and self-confidence, show a statistically significant difference between scores, but neither one is particularly strong ($p<0.050$ and $p<0.100$, respectively).

Our findings from Table 4.4 indicated that women in the highest occupational echelons found the greatest satisfaction with their housing environment. Such findings cannot be explained by the greater financial resources of high employment status women since income was held constant during our partial correlation analysis. As will be discussed later in this chapter, a more likely explanation is that working women, especially women in the highest occupational levels (professional and managerial) often chose relatively supportive housing environments (e.g., planned condominiums) than do non-working women. Thus, 47 percent of working women in our sample live in multiple dwellings compared to 27 percent of the non-working women.

We find from Table 4.5 that the non-working women score higher on overall housing satisfaction than do their average working counterparts, based largely on their higher satisfaction with homeowner responsibilities ($p<0.050$). Since the average working woman comes from a household with a family income not significantly higher than that of the non-working woman, our findings suggest she is often working to supplement the income of a spouse with a modest income or is a single woman supporting herself (23 percent of our sample of working women were single family heads). Also, as practically all the non-working women are married (95 percent of our non-working sample), it seems likely that they would have more time to assist in the household maintenance activities than their working counterparts.

The same forces of time and accessibility may also be underlying the somewhat higher sense of belonging experienced by the non-working women ($p<0.100$). Indeed, our previous analysis suggests that working women are more likely to be involved in group activities outside their immediate neighborhoods than their non-working counterparts.

In summary, then, a woman's occupational status does not appear to be a major influence in our study. While the average working woman seems to be

TABLE 4.5

Mean Scores of Indexes of Satisfaction for Women's Occupational Status

Satisfaction Index	Satisfaction Scores[a]	
	Non working (n=405)	Working (n=420)
Housing environment	5.64[b]	5.54
Privacy	5.85	5.80
House and lot	5.61	5.52
Homeownership responsibilities	5.33[c]	5.10
Appearance	5.79	5.74
Community services	5.10	5.10
Parks	4.97	4.98
Schools	5.19	5.16
Security	5.26	5.22
Child care	4.18	4.20
Transportation	5.40	5.42
Entertainment	5.48	5.49
Social patterns	5.35	5.30
Friendships	5.64	5.68
Group activities	5.22	5.29
Sense of belonging	5.13[b]	4.95
Psychological well-being	6.92	7.07
Fullness vs. emptiness of life	7.15	7.12
Receptivity towards the world	6.92	7.06
Social respect	7.44	7.83
Personal freedom	6.76	7.04
Sociability	7.06	6.99
Companionship	7.49	7.58
Work satisfaction	7.23	7.53
Tranquility vs. anxiety	6.28	6.27
Self approving vs. guilty	6.65	6.85[c]
Self confidence	7.02	7.27[d]
Energy vs. fatigue	6.48	6.58
Elation vs. depression	6.68	6.67

[a]two-tailed t-test for all score differences yields p > 0.100 unless otherwise noted

[b]t-test for score difference yields p < 0.100

[c]t-test for score difference yields p < 0.050

[d]t-test for score difference yields p < 0.010

[e]t-test for score difference yields p < 0.005

Source: Compiled by the authors.

involved in the larger world beyond her neighborhood and reaps some psychological benefits from these outside activities, she also appears to pay for these outside activities with lower satisfaction of housing and socialization within her neighborhood.

SUBCULTURAL INFLUENCES

Ethnic Identity

Expectation

Ethnic identity will vary inversely with all dependent variables.

Findings

In general, our data does not support this contention (see Table 4.6). Variables associated with the housing environment display a slight negative trend and thus weakly uphold our initial presumption. The overall index of satisfaction in this area is insignificant. However, two of the four variables in this area support our anticipation, but only one, the appearance of the housing environment ($p < 0.050$) warrants statistical interest.

Moving on to the community services sector, the generally weak support for our expectations continues. The negative anticipated trend seems to arise most tellingly in the score for our transportation variable ($p < 0.050$). A similar pattern holds with our social patterns variables. Of the three specific indexes within social patterns only one supports our contention with any degree of statistical significance. The score on the group activities variable relates inversely with ethnic identity ($p < 0.050$). However, when we arrive at our group of psychological well-being variables, the situation changes decisively from modest support of our expectations to clear refutation. Both the overall satisfaction index and ten of twelve specific indexes demonstrate strong statistical affinities which sharply cast doubt on our expectations. Not only is the global score highly significant ($p < 0.005$), but equally so are five of the ten components. Of the other five, four are almost as compelling ($p < 0.050$), and one certainly does not depart greatly from the overall pattern ($p < 0.100$).

Discussion

While strong feelings of ethnic and/or cultural identity are not widespread in our sample (only 21.7 percent, or 176 out of a total of 813 who

TABLE 4.6

Relationships between Ethnic Identity and Indexes of Satisfaction

Satisfaction Index	Partial Correlation Coefficient[a] (n=825)
Housing environment	−0.0325
Privacy	0.0051
House and lot	0.0128
Homeownership responsibilities	−0.0145
Appearance	−0.0839[c]
Community services	−0.0199
Parks	−0.0309
Schools	−0.0044
Security	0.0431
Child care	−0.0158
Transportation	−0.0716[c]
Entertainment and culture	−0.0527
Social patterns	−0.0524
Friendships	0.0265
Group activities	−0.0705[c]
Sense of belonging	−0.0063
Psychological well-being	0.1228[e]
Fullness vs. emptiness of life	0.0361
Receptivity towards the world	0.1320[e]
Social respect	0.1036[e]
Personal freedom	0.0743[c]
Sociability	0.0898[e]
Companionship	0.1137[e]
Work satisfaction	0.0668[b]
Tranquility vs. anxiety	0.0837[c]
Self approving vs. guilty	0.1015[e]
Self confidence	0.0902[c]
Energy vs. fatigue	0.1292[e]
Elation vs. depression	0.0300

[a]two-tailed t-test for all correlations yields $p > 0.100$ unless otherwise noted

[b]t-test for this correlation yields $p < 0.100$

[c]t-test for this correlation yields $p < 0.050$

[d]t-test for this correlation yields $p < 0.010$

[e]t-test for this correlation yields $p < 0.005$

Source: Compiled by the authors.

responded to this question), those who do identify with a particular group appear to have refuted at least some of our expectations. In particular, we believed that feelings aligned with our overall index of psychological well-being would be adversely affected by a strong feeling of ethnic identity. To the contrary, the scores indicated that ethnic identity is quite positively linked with both the general and many specific indexes in this area. As Glazer and Moynihan's classic study of New York City ethnicity indicates, indentification with one's heritage in a world "beyond the melting pot" appears to be a positive force in the lives of our respondents.[2] Obviously, strong feelings of ethnic and/or cultural identity are a factor to be reckoned with in a socially heterogenous society and call attention to the subtle and hidden imperatives of these feelings. However, in more tangible areas of inquiry our expectations are realized. With respect to the housing environment, the specific index of the house and neighborhood appearance confirmed our anticipation of an inverse relationship ($p < 0.050$) (see Table 4.6). The spare, bland image of many suburban neighborhoods may be quite different from the intensity of the housing environments that many of these people experienced at an earlier time in their lives. The specific index of transportation was also a source of evidence for our belief of an inverse relationship between ethnicity and all dependent variables. It could be argued that the generally low-density setting that characterizes the San Jose metropolitan area serves as an impediment to an efficient transportation system, especially for individuals who come from older, inlying, ethnic neighborhoods well serviced by public transportation.

In order to explore the concept of ethnic identity further, we have compiled Table 4.7, which compares those with weak or no such identity with those who registered strong feelings. It appears that incomes are not higher for "non" or "weak" ethnics, though the difference is not significant. With regard to transportation "strong" ethnics, both men and women, have a longer journey to work both in time and distance although *only the distances* are statistically significant. As can be seen, "strong" ethnic women travel more than 3.5 additional miles to work than "weak" ethnic women ($p < 0.010$), and with the men, the distance is longer, by a nearly equal increment ($p < 0.050$). Perhaps this is another reason for the inverse relationship between ethnicity and the specific index of satisfaction with transportation.

As is shown in Table 4.6, in the area of social patterns our expectations continue to hold up, as ethnics tend to be less satisfied with group activities ($p < 0.050$). Returning to Table 4.7, we can examine in greater detail the nature of their social relationships. As expected, it appears that respondents with a strong ethnic identity experience less rich interactions close to home. This indeed may be their preference. They have fewer acquaintances and neighborly contacts within the proximate residential environment.

TABLE 4.7

Mean Satisfaction Scores for Selected Variables by Respondent's Strength of Ethnic Identity[f]

| | Satisfaction Scores[a] | |
| | Weak Identity (n=717) | Strong Identity (n=96) |
Variable		
Income (1975)	$21,800	$24,300
Number of cars	1.90	1.97
Use public transit per week	0.41	0.36
Length of residency (years)	3.22	3.64
Journey to work		
Woman		
Miles	4.23	6.92[d]
Time (minutes)	8.64	10.73
Man		
Miles	12.15	15.38[c]
Time (minutes)	21.76	22.50
Speaking acquaintances (in neighborhood)	24.39[e]	15.45
Neighbors to discuss general interest topics	9.34[c]	6.88
Neighbors to borrow from	4.44[e]	3.28
Neighbors to aid in crisis	4.89[e]	3.27
Neighbors to aid in projects	2.60[b]	2.06
Close friends one hour away	4.94	7.32[b]
Strength of involvement with		
Religious groups	2.58	3.11[c]
Political organizations	1.63	1.97[b]
Informal groups outside neighborhood	2.70	3.53[e]
Action groups outside neighborhood	1.73	2.63[e]
Social organizations outside neighborhood	1.86	2.72[e]
Other organized groups	1.95	2.52[e]

[a]two-tailed t-test for all score differences yields $p > 0.100$ unless otherwise noted

[b]t-test for score differences yields $p < 0.100$

[c]t-test for score differences yields $p < 0.050$

[d]t-test for score differences yields $p < 0.010$

[e]t-test for score differences yields $p < 0.005$

[f]Based on the question, "Do you identify with any ethnic or cultural group?" (see questionnaire, Appendix A). A "non" or "weak" identity is a score of 1–4; a "strong" identity is a score of 5–7.

Source: Table compiled by the authors.

When we view five variables illustrating this situation, three show decisive differences (p<0.005), which place strong ethnics at somewhat of a disadvantage. However, when non-spatial activities are considered (e.g., religious and political organizations and groups outside the neighborhood) strong ethnics show a much greater degree of involvement. If they are less satisfied with group activities, it is evidently because of the distance factor in their non-spatial character. This accords with what is observed about California lifestyles and urban development. That is, spatial factors may be assuming less relevance in postwar urbanization than they held in earlier periods.[3]

In summary, then, ethnicity promises to be a provocative subject for research in California. Will there be an interpretation for newly urbanizing communities to counterpose the work of Glazer and Moynihan in New York, with its contrasting and more spatially oriented ethnic demarcations?

Regional Origin

Expectation

All satisfaction variables will be positively related to the degree of urbanness (population size) of the community in which a respondent spent her formative years and negatively related to the distance of that community from the San Jose area.

Findings

With respect to the population size of the community of origin, our results provide some support for what we had anticipated. Table 4.8 illustrates these findings and differs from our other data presentations in three ways. First, note that the vertical columns juxtapose communities of origin by their degree of urbanness but only those which provide statistically useful information (when p<0.100). Thus, suburban-urban comparisons are omitted. Second, because no significant relationships exist with respect to our overall index of satisfaction and specific indexes of satisfaction in the area of psychological well-being, those variables have been deleted. Third, the actual presentation of the data itself will include only those mean scores which lend themselves to a statistically relevant analysis. Thus, any scores that result in p<0.100 will be so designated.

It is clear that respondents from the least urban of origins, those from rural areas, exhibit the lowest levels of satisfaction. Although there are no significant relationships that pertain to the overall index of satisfaction with the housing environment, two of its four specific indexes are of statistical interest. Respondents with urban origins were more satisfied with the specific index of privacy ($p < 0.100$) than those of rural background. Rural respondents also fare less well than those of small town background in the area of house and lot satisfaction ($p < 0.050$). The pattern of statistically significant scores that demonstrates that respondents of rural background tend to be least satisfied continues in the area of community services. In both the overall index of satisfaction and satisfaction with the security, respondents from rural areas fare the worst. Small town and suburban respondents show significantly higher scores in the overall satisfaction index (both $p < 0.050$) and in the specific index of security ($p < 0.010$). In addition, urban respondents also score higher in this latter area ($p < 0.100$). The pattern holds when social pattern variables are considered. The specific index of satisfaction with friendships shows rural backgrounds to be the least satisfied when juxtaposed with the other three levels of urbanness. Respondents from small towns fared better ($p < 0.050$), as did those from suburban and urban backgrounds ($p < 0.100$ for both). Thus, it is in conformance with our expectations that respondents from rural backgrounds will tend to be the least satisfied with their current suburban situations.

But what of juxtapositions between respondents of small town backgrounds versus those from suburban and urban backgrounds? Here the evidence departs from our expectations. There are two specific indexes (house and lot, and sense of belonging) that show statistically relevant results for small town-suburban comparisons. In both, scores for women from small town backgrounds are higher ($p < 0.100$ and $p < 0.050$, respectively). Similarly, on the one specific index where a statistically significant relationship exists between our small town and urban-origin populations, satisfaction with entertainment and culture, respondents from a small town background fared a little bit better ($p < 0.100$). With respect to comparisons between women from suburban and urban backgrounds there were, as previously stated, no statistically relevant comparisons to be made.

The question pertaining to the distance of one's location of origin has yielded results that provide weak support for our expectations (see Table 4.9). Variables pertaining to the housing environment support our expectations. Not only is the global score in line with what we had anticipated ($p < 0.050$), but so is the appearance of the housing environment ($p < 0.100$). Running counter to this, however, is satisfaction with house and lot, which shows an unexpected positive relationship ($p < 0.050$). With respect to community services, there is a general show of support for our contention, but only the satisfaction with childcare variable shows statistical significance ($p < 0.050$). The group of variables under the general heading of social patterns continues this trend. Although only one variable, friend-

TABLE 4.8

Mean Scores of Indexes of Satisfaction for Degree of Urbanness

Mean Satisfaction Scores[a]

Satisfaction Index	Rural– (n=78)	Small Town (n=286)	Rural– (n=78)	Suburban (n=268)	Rural– (n=78)	Urban (n=191)	Small Town– (n=286)	Suburban (n=268)	Small Town– (n=286)	Urban (n=191)
Housing environment		a		a		a		a		a
Privacy		a		a	5.69	5.91[b]		a		a
House and lot	5.34	5.67[c]		a		a	5.67[b]	5.49		a
Homeownership responsibilities		a		a		a		a		a
Appearance		a		a		a		a		a
Community services	4.91	5.13[c]	4.91	5.15[c]		a		a		a
Parks		a		a		a		a		a
Schools		a		a		a		a		a
Security	4.87	5.32[d]	4.87	5.33[d]	4.87	5.19[b]		a		a
Child care		a		a		a		a		a
Transportation		a		a		a		a		a

	Entertainment and culture	Social patterns	Friendships	Group activities
Entertainment and culture				
Social patterns	5.39[a]			
Friendships	5.71[c]	5.39[a]		
Group activities	5.66[b]	5.39[a]	5.69[b]	
Sense of belonging	5.17[c]	4.90[a]	5.59[b]	5.34[a]

[a] two-tailed t-test for all score differences yields $p > 0.100$ unless otherwise noted

[b] t-test for score difference yields $p < 0.100$

[c] t-test for score difference yields $p < 0.050$

[d] t-test for score difference yields $p < 0.010$

[e] t-test for score difference yields $p < 0.005$

Source: Compiled by the authors.

TABLE 4.9

Relationships between Location of Origin and Indexes of Satisfaction

Satisfaction Index	Partial Correlation Coefficient[a] (n=825)
Housing environment	−0.0780[c]
Privacy	−0.0347
House and lot	0.0811[c]
Homeownership responsibilities	−0.0329
Appearance	−0.0594[b]
Community services	−0.0333
Parks	−0.0300
Schools	−0.0194
Security	0.0104
Child care	−0.0730[c]
Transportation	−0.0222
Entertainment and culture	−0.0035
Social patterns	−0.0406
Friendships	−0.0612[b]
Group activities	−0.0178
Sense of belonging	−0.0240
Psychological well-being	0.0459
Fullness vs. emptiness of life	−0.0081
Receptivity towards the world	0.0952[d]
Social respect	0.0270
Personal freedom	0.0140
Sociability	0.0184
Companionship	0.0467
Work satisfaction	0.0447
Tranquility vs. anxiety	−0.0184
Self approving vs. guilty	0.0170
Self confidence	0.0420
Energy vs. fatigue	0.0489
Elation vs. depression	−0.0305

[a]two-tailed t-test for all correlations yields $p > 0.100$ unless otherwise noted

[b]t-test for this correlation yields $p < 0.100$

[c]t-test for this correlation yields $p < 0.050$

[d]t-test for this correlation yields $p < 0.010$

[e]t-test for this correlation yields $p < 0.005$

Source: Compiled by the authors.

ships, shows marginal statistical significance ($p < 0.100$), the consistent inverse relationship between these dependent variables and locational origins lends a degree of credence to our expectations. Less successful in fulfilling our presumptions is the cluster of specific psychological well-being indexes. Not only do these fail to show a compelling statistical relationship with the distance of our respondents' locations of origin, but one index, receptivity towards the world varies positively ($p < 0.010$), that is, contrary to our expectations.

Discussion

It is clear that respondents from rural areas are notably less satisfied with many aspects of their lives than are those from more urbanized origins. Measures of satisfaction with security and with friendships are the most telling. Concern with rising rates of criminal behavior is pandemic in many metropolitan areas, especially as the social and economic characteristics of suburban populations continue to broaden. Perhaps rurally raised respondents are experiencing more difficulty in adapting to both the positive and negative aspects of the urbanization of the suburbs. They are also less satisfied with the friendships they have experienced. Thus, respondents from rural backgrounds tend to feel less secure materially but also perhaps less secure socially as well. On the other hand, there is no solid evidence that the increasing urbanness of one's origins produces greater levels of satisfaction once the rural population is excluded. As indicated, there are no statistically significant relationships between respondents of suburban and urban backgrounds. With limited opportunities to evaluate small town versus suburban and urban backgrounds, the evidence, albeit limited, suggests that small town backgrounds tend to produce greater levels of satisfaction. Is it a matter of the expectations that coalesce during one's formative years? The limitations imposed by small town life are well known, although Americans today rate the qualities of such an environment rather highly as many recent opinion polls have shown.[4] Perhaps what renders this trend less surprising is the fact that our sample population contains a plurality from a small town background, 34.8 percent; with 32.6 percent from suburbs, 23.2 percent from large cities and 9.5 percent from rural areas. Perhaps suburban life is the ideal compromise for those seeking small town ambience while at the same time having access to metropolitan economic opportunities.

Insofar as the distance of one's origins from the San Jose area is concerned, the sheer mileage as the crow flies alone may not be the best source of a productive inquiry. Perhaps more important is the ease and/or travel time involved in making a return trip to one's roots. It may be much easier to fly to a major Eastern metropolitan area than it would be to reach a smaller community one-third or one-half the distance away. An airline connection to Wichita, Des Moines, or Amarillo may be a far greater ordeal than transportation to the Northeast.

In an attempt to gain a more finely honed perspective on the question of the distance of one's origins from the San Jose metropolitan area, we have compiled two additional tables (4.10 and 4.11) which split our sample population into two groups, one less than one day's drive (up to 500 miles) from San Jose, the other more than one day's drive (over 500 miles). Table 4.10 compares satisfaction scores by our respondents' community of origin, while Table 4.11 compares scores by our respondents' community of residence prior to moving to the San Jose area. It can be seen that the distance of one's community of origin is the more decisive factor in our expectations. While the general area of the housing environment has produced no strong statistical relationships, respondents from communities less than 500 miles from the San Jose area score higher on two specific indexes of satisfaction with community services, childcare, and transportation (p<0.050 for both). Not only does the group of more proximate origins have a greater number of friends an hour away (5.9 vs. 4.4, p<0.050) but it contrasts markedly with the statistic pertaining to close friends further than an hour away. The more proximate group has 6.3 of these, while those of more distant origins have almost twice as many in this category, 11.1 (p<0.005). Only one specific index of psychological well-being, elation vs. depression (p<0.050) (which favors those of proximate origin) was of relevance in this comparison. Thus, the distance of one's origins is most relevant to social patterns satisfaction and to two specific indexes in our community services cluster of variables.

Distance of prior residence from San Jose does not reveal any clear pattern. Perhaps the rate of mobility in society emphasizes the importance of "roots," for, when we are birds of passage, of what importance is our most recent nest? Therefore, those more proximate to their "roots" appear to confirm partially our expectations, with an emphasis on more rewarding social relations.

Length of Residency

Expectation

The length of residency will be positively related to all dependent satisfaction variables.

TABLE 4.10

Mean Scores of Indexes of Satisfaction for Distance of Community of Origin from the San Jose Metropolitan Area

Satisfaction Index	Satisfaction Scores[a]	
	500 Miles or Less (n=485)	501 Miles or More (n=329)
Housing environment	5.62	5.53
Privacy	5.85	5.78
House and lot	5.62[b]	5.45
Homeownership responsibilities	5.22	5.20
Appearance	5.81	5.69
Community services	5.13	5.06
Parks	4.98	4.97
Schools	5.18	5.18
Security	5.21	5.29
Child care	4.28[c]	4.04
Transportation	5.48[c]	5.29
Entertainment	5.45	5.53
Social patterns	5.38[c]	5.23
Friendships	5.73[c]	5.53
Group activities	5.29	5.20
Sense of belonging	5.10	4.95
Psychological well-being	7.01	6.96
Fullness vs. emptiness of life	7.17	7.06
Receptivity towards the world	6.97	7.01
Social respect	7.75	7.46
Personal freedom	6.94	6.80
Sociability	7.04	6.99
Companionship	7.49	7.60
Work satisfaction	7.38	6.41
Tranquility vs. anxiety	6.27	6.27
Self approving vs. guilty	6.79	6.69
Self confidence	7.17	7.08
Energy vs. fatigue	6.55	6.51
Elation vs. depression	6.75[c]	6.56

[a]two-tailed t-test for all score differences yields $p > 0.100$ unless otherwise noted
[b]t-test for score difference yields $p < 0.100$
[c]t-test for score difference yields $p < 0.050$
[d]t-test for score difference yields $p < 0.010$
[e]t-test for score difference yields $p < 0.005$
Source: Compiled by the authors.

TABLE 4.11

Mean Scores of Indexes of Satisfaction for Distance of Community of Prior Residence from the San Jose Metropolitan Area

Satisfaction Index	Satisfaction Scores[a]	
	500 Miles or Less (n=718)	501 Miles or More (n=94)
Housing environment	5.60	5.52
Privacy	5.84	5.70
House and lot	5.57	5.50
Homeownership responsibilities	5.22	5.26
Appearance	5.79	5.60
Community services	5.12	5.00
Parks	4.95	5.11
Schools	5.19	5.11
Security	5.25	5.22
Child care	4.22	3.98
Transportation	5.46[c]	5.16
Entertainment	5.46	5.80[c]
Social patterns	5.35	5.18
Friendships	5.67	5.55
Group activities	5.28	5.12
Sense of belonging	5.06	4.93
Psychological well-being	7.00	6.97
Fullness vs. emptiness of life	7.12	7.29
Receptivity towards the world	7.01	6.91
Social respect	7.67	7.36
Personal freedom	6.90	6.96
Sociability	7.06[b]	6.80
Companionship	7.52	7.63
Work satisfaction	7.39	7.40
Tranquility vs. anxiety	6.27	6.33
Self approving vs. guilty	6.77	6.65
Self confidence	7.17	6.97
Energy vs. fatigue	6.54	6.53
Elation vs. depression	6.67	6.73

[a]two-tailed t-test for all differences yields $p > 0.100$ unless otherwise noted
[b]t-test for score difference yields $p < 0.100$
[c]t-test for score difference yields $p < 0.050$
[d]t-test for score difference yields $p < 0.010$
[e]t-test for score difference yields $p < 0.005$
Source: compiled by authors.

Findings

With respect to the housing environment our results do not support this expectation (see Table 4.12). The overall trend is negative with one specific index, appearance of housing environment, showing an inverse relationship ($p < 0.100$). Our community services cluster of variables reverses this trend somewhat, but only one, satisfaction with transportation, conforms to what we had anticipated ($p < 0.005$). The area that shows the strongest support for our expectations is that of social patterns. Both the overall index of satisfaction and the specific index of friendships are statistically significant ($p < 0.050$), while the sense of belonging variable is a further source of support ($p < 0.005$). The psychological well-being cluster of variables as a group shows virtually no relationship to length of residency. The only measure of statistical relevance within the twleve specific indexes under discussion is an unexpected inverse relationship between length of residency and work satisfaction ($p < 0.100$). Thus, social patterns is the only cluster of variables that seems to support our contentions.

Discussion

Does familiarity breed contempt? Or, are expectations inevitably subject to downward revision or disappointment? These questions appear to be mildly operative in the case of the housing environment. The inverse relationship between the index of satisfaction with the appearance of the housing environment and length of residency is a signal. Perhaps the major source of dissatisfaction with the passage of time is with the symbolic properties of the house and neighborhood. Is the character of suburbia a factor here? Although the age of the dwelling unit inevitably will result in increased maintenance responsibilities, the negative scores on this item were not significant. Perhaps, then, the discontent that accumulates over time is not strongly focused. On the other hand, social patterns do show strong support for our supposition. This is clearly a matter of common sense for no matter how satisfactory or unsatisfactory a living environment, close friends will be made with the passage of time. One's sense of belonging makes the strongest statement of this phenomenon. Yet, why were there no strong correlations in the psychological well-being cluster of variables?

LIFE CYCLE INFLUENCES

Age

Expectation

Age will vary positively with satisfaction with the housing environment and negatively with psychological well-being.

TABLE 4.12

Relationship between Length of Residency and Indexes of Satisfaction

Satisfaction Index	Partial Correlation Coefficient[a] (n=825)
Housing environment	−0.0462
Privacy	−0.0548
House and lot	0.0026
Homeownership responsibilities	−0.0226
Appearance	−0.0626[b]
Community services	0.0051
Parks	−0.0218
Schools	0.0093
Security	−0.0543
Child care	0.0260
Transportation	0.1183[e]
Entertainment and culture	0.0393
Social patterns	0.0722[c]
Friendships	0.0718[c]
Group activities	−0.0280
Sense of belonging	0.1251[e]
Psychological well-being	0.0008
Fullness vs. emptiness of life	0.0529
Receptivity towards the world	0.0460
Social respect	−0.0241
Personal freedom	0.0029
Sociability	−0.0309
Companionship	−0.0512
Work satisfaction	−0.0607[b]
Tranquility vs. anxiety	0.0234
Self approving vs. guilty	0.0146
Self confidence	0.0127
Energy vs. fatigue	−0.0130
Elation vs. depression	0.0369

[a]two-tailed t-test for all correlations yields $p > 0.100$ unless otherwise noted
[b]t-test for this correlation yields $p < 0.100$
[c]t-test for this correlation yields $p < 0.050$
[d]t-test for this correlation yields $p < 0.010$
[e]t-test for this correlation yields $p < 0.005$
Source: Compiled by the authors.

Findings

As Table 4.13 indicates, our survey did confirm the general expectations. None of the relationships between women's age and community services satisfaction or social patterns satisfaction were significant. However, the predicted relationships between age, satisfaction with housing environment, and psychological well-being did occur. The positive relationship between age and satisfaction with the housing environment seems to be a function of the aesthetic considerations of satisfaction with house and lot design and the feeling that one's neighborhood is a valid symbol of one's tastes. The other two specific indexes of satisfaction, satisfaction with privacy and homeownership responsibilities did not correlate significantly with age.

All but two of the specific indexes comprising the psychological well-being index (receptivity towards the world and companionship) were found to correlate negatively with a woman's age. The weakest of the significant correlations ($p < 0.100$) were for items dealing with personal freedom, work satisfaction, tranquility vs. anxiety and self-approval vs. guilt. The strongest correlations ($p < 0.005$) were found between age and low scores on self-confidence and depression. Based on the strong partial correlation coefficients for the overall satisfaction indexes of the housing environment and psychological well-being ($p < 0.005$), we may say with some confidence that as women become older they become more satisfied with their homes and neighborhoods and less content in their personal psychological lives.

Discussion

A woman who is older has had more time to settle in the sort of neighborhood that she would like to live in and to decorate her house and landscape her lot according to her preference. This rather simple explanation of the findings is the most satisfactory that we are able to suggest. Responsibilities of homeownership do not seem to vary according to age, but rather a woman's satisfaction with how her home, lot, and neighborhood look and how well they fit her needs. Since income was held constant in the calculation of the partial correlation coefficients, the increased satisfaction of older women with their housing environment cannot be attributed to the financial ability to purchase the sort of home and accessories that they prefer. Women who are older apparently like their housing environment better than younger women regardless of the length of time they have had to get the house in order. There is some evidence that material expectations lower with age.[5] Perhaps as women age they come to appreciate convenience and familiarity over opulence. In Chapter Two we discussed the

TABLE 4.13

Relationship between Woman's Age and Indexes of Satisfaction

Satisfaction Index	Partial Correlation Coefficient[a] (n=825)
Housing environment	0.1063[e]
Privacy	0.0421
House and lot	0.0659[b]
Homeownership responsibilities	0.0355
Appearance	0.1568[e]
Community services	−0.0352
Parks	−0.0102
Schools	−0.0525
Security	−0.0128
Child care	−0.0410
Transportation	0.0156
Entertainment and culture	−0.0336
Social patterns	−0.0539
Friendships	−0.0522
Group activities	−0.0391
Sense of belonging	−0.0479
Psychological well-being	−0.1190[e]
Fullness vs. emptiness of life	−0.0851[c]
Receptivity towards the world	−0.0340
Social respect	−0.0822[c]
Personal freedom	−0.0888[c]
Sociability	−0.0645[b]
Companionship	−0.0426
Work satisfaction	−0.0689[b]
Tranquility vs. anxiety	−0.0651[b]
Self approving vs. guilty	−0.0633[b]
Self confidence	−0.1094[e]
Energy vs. fatigue	−0.0909[c]
Elation vs. depression	−0.1084[e]

[a]two-tailed t-test for all correlations yields p > 0.100 unless otherwise noted

[b]t-test for this correlation yields p < 0.100

[c]t-test for this correlation yields p < 0.050

[d]t-test for this correlation yields p < 0.010

[e]t-test for this correlation yields p < 0.005

Source: Compiled by the author.

concept of a woman being married to her home. Lopata's research cited there suggested that it was at a somewhat late period in a woman's life cycle that her relationship with her home took on prime importance.[6] Rodgers, Campbell, and Converse confirm that older married women and widows "like housework" more than any other life cycle group.[7]

The negative scores on the various indexes of psychological well-being are not surprising. Much of the literature has suggested that ours is a youth-oriented culture and that women in particular have been socialized to have negative reactions to aging. Still, considering the youthfulness of our sample (age 20 to 50 with a mean of 34.7), we were not prepared for the very strong association of age with lower scores on nearly every specific index of psychological well-being. One possible explanation that we considered was that one particular age group, perhaps the oldest women in our sample, had scored drastically lower than the other groups. We divided the women into six age ranges and compared the means of these groups on dependent variables. One-way analysis of variance did not reveal any significant differences among the various age groups. Therefore, we can conclude that the relationships existing between women's age and our dependent variables operate fairly consistently across the entire range of ages from 20 to 50.

Marital Status

Expectation

Married women will have higher scores on all dependent satisfaction measures than will unmarried women.

Findings

Our findings strongly support the presumption, based on the review of the literature, that suburbia is a less congenial environment for single and divorced women than for married women. In all four of the overall indexes of satisfaction married women scored significantly higher. An examination of the specific indexes of satisfaction gives some insight into the nature of the differences in satisfaction related to marital status.

As Table 4.14 indicates, the lower satisfaction with the housing environment is explained almost entirely by the fact that unmarried women found homeownership responsibilities much more difficult than married women ($p < 0.005$). Maintenance responsibilities were more burdensome to the unmarried ($p < 0.050$), but the most dramatic difference is found in the

TABLE 4.14

Mean Scores of Indexes of Satisfaction for Marital Status

Satisfaction Index	Satisfaction Scores[a]	
	Married (n=705)	Unmarried (n=120)
Housing environment	5.62[c]	5.40
Privacy	5.84	5.72
House and lot	5.58	5.49
Homeownership responsibilities	5.31[e]	4.63
Appearance	5.77	5.75
Community services	5.13[b]	4.98
Parks	4.96	5.03
Schools	5.18	5.15
Security	5.20	5.12
Child care	4.23[c]	3.92
Transportation	5.46[c]	5.18
Entertainment	5.50	5.40
Social patterns	5.39[e]	4.96
Friendships	5.68	5.53
Group activities	5.37[e]	4.90
Sense of belonging	5.13[e]	4.51
Psychological well-being	6.97[c]	6.77
Fullness vs. emptiness of life	7.16[e]	6.63
Receptivity towards the world	6.96	6.80
Social respect	7.50	7.38
Personal freedom	6.74	6.80
Sociability	7.06[b]	6.83
Companionship	7.56	6.34
Work satisfaction	7.33	7.22
Tranquility vs. anxiety	6.32[d]	5.93
Self approving vs. guilty	6.74	6.63
Self confidence	7.10	6.99
Energy vs. fatigue	6.51	6.30
Elation vs. depression	6.70[c]	6.40

[a]two-tailed t-test for all score differences yields $p > 0.100$ unless otherwise noted
[b]t-test for score difference yields $p < 0.100$
[c]t-test for score difference yields $p < 0.050$
[d]t-test for score difference yields $p < 0.010$
[e]t-test for score difference yields $p < 0.005$
Source: compiled by the authors.

difficulties of the financial responsibilities of homeownership. Nearly a full scale point separated the average married woman (5.26) and the average unmarried woman (4.30)—significant at the 0.001 level. Married women were more satisfied than single women with community services. Although unmarried women rated lower satisfaction on every specific index except parks, the two specific indexes of satisfaction that show statistically significant differences between the two groups are satisfaction with child care and transportation ($p < 0.050$ for both).

Social patterns in suburbia were also more satisfying for married women than unmarried women ($p < 0.005$). The married group found opportunities for group activities more satisfactory and also expressed a much stronger sense of belonging in their neighborhoods ($p < 0.005$). In fact the friendship patterns for unmarried women were much different than those of married women, especially in their immediate neighborhoods, as will be discussed later. However, the degree of *satisfaction* with friendships did not differ significantly between the two groups.

Married women reported a greater overall sense of psychological well-being at the 0.050 level. The four specific indexes of satisfaction that contribute to this difference were fullness vs. emptiness of life ($p < 0.005$), sociability ($p < 0.100$), tranquility vs. anxiety ($p < 0.010$) and elation vs. depression ($p < 0.050$). The remaining specific indexes of psychological well-being registered no differences between the groups.

These findings provide strong support for the position expressed by many observers that the physical and social environment of suburbia is more supportive of married women than of single and divorced women.

Discussion

The differences between married and unmarried women's satisfaction with the housing environment and with community services can be attributed largely, if not exclusively, to economic factors. The unmarried woman's income from all sources averaged in the $14,000 to $16,000 range, while family income for married women in this sample averaged between $22,000 and $24,000. Eighty-two percent of the unmarried women were employed as compared to 46 percent of the married women. The former group tend to work at jobs commensurate with their education (1.06 of the occupation/education ratio) while married women tend to be under-employed (0.76 on the occupation/education ratio). The unmarried women are apparently required to work to their full capacity in order to live in the kinds of homes included in our sample. Although renters were a small proportion of our sample (9.1 percent), single women were much more likely to rent homes than were married women (22 percent as opposed to 7 percent). Thus, even in our largely middle to upper middle-class sample, the financial problems of the unmarried woman are well documented. She does like her suburban home and neighborhood. She is pleased with the appearance of her home and neighborhood. But she finds the financial responsibilities of homeownership extremely difficult, and without a partner to help with maintenance or to help hire gardners and housekeepers she also finds the maintenance responsibilities burdensome. (Only 4 percent of divorced women hire help with their housework according to one study.)[8] The differences between the married and unmarried women's satisfaction with transportation and childcare services can no doubt be attributed as well to the difficulties single women experience in financing these services.

The lower satisfaction of the unmarried women with the social patterns of suburbia is best understood by examining the actual differences in friendship patterns and group participation. Table 4.15 reveals that married women have many more casual acquaintances in their neighborhoods, more people that they can chat with, borrow from, count on for aid in emergencies in home repair projects. When it comes to discussion of personal problems, however, married and unmarried alike have between one and two neighbors with whom they perceive that level of intimacy. When asked how many close friends they have in their neighborhoods, in the San Jose Area, within an hour of their home, and farther away, married and unmarried women reported the same numbers.

Group participation scores reflected a similar pattern. Unmarried women were not as involved in informal groups, action groups, or groups related to their children's activities in the neighborhood as were married women. Beyond the neighborhood, however, marital status is not related to the level of involvement in political organization, informal social groups, action groups, or other organized groups. Married women were more involved in religious groups. These differences might be a product of the time demands made on unmarried parents; extra childcare and maintenance responsibilities and the larger commutation time of single women (to be reported later) may well cut down the time available for socializing. Another implication of these findings is that there may well be some social discrimination against single women in suburbia as the literature has suggested. Unmarried women are not unsociable, and they are not opposed to joining groups, as their participation outside the neighborhood indicates. They are sociable, though relatively unhappy with the opportunities for group involvement in their neighborhoods and with their much lower sense of identification with the neighborhood.

It appears that single women who live in suburbia are able to fill their most important needs for friendship and belonging through relationships and group involvement outside their neighborhood environment and through one or two close friendships closer to home. They are aware of and

TABLE 4.15

Mean Scores of Indexes of Satisfaction for Marital Status and Selected Factors of Friendships and Group Involvement

	Mean Scores[a]	
Variable	Married (n=705)	Unmarried (n=120)
Number of speaking aquaintances in neighborhood	23.73[e]	16.40
Neighbors to discuss topics of general interest	9.40[e]	7.00
Neighbors to borrow from	4.44[c]	3.45
Neighbors to aid in crises	4.85[b]	3.61
Neighbors to aid in projects	2.59[c]	1.88
Neighbors to discuss personal problems	1.59	1.56
Close friends in neighborhood	2.37	2.11
Close friends in San Jose Area	8.75	8.52
Close friends one hour away	5.33	4.45
Close friends farther away	13.60	16.61
Satisfaction neighborhood friends	5.67	5.49
Neighborhood informal groups	2.15[c]	1.75
Neighborhood action projects	2.26[e]	1.68
Children's activity groups	3.63[e]	2.85
Religious groups	2.75[e]	2.03
Political organizations	1.69	1.53
Outside informal groups	2.77	2.97
Outside action groups	1.86	1.84
Outside social organization	1.92	2.14
Other organized groups	2.00	2.10
Satisfaction with group opportunities in neighborhood	5.17[e]	4.63
Satisfaction with group opportunities in San Jose Area	5.45	5.21
Identification with neighborhood	4.76[e]	4.01
Satisfaction with neighborhood identification	5.49[e]	5.01

[a]two-tailed t-test for all score differences yields $p > 0.100$ unless otherwise noted
[b]t-test for score difference yields $p < 0.100$
[c]t-test for score difference yields $p < 0.050$
[d]t-test for score difference yields $p < 0.010$
[e]t-test for score difference yields $p < 0.005$
Source: compiled by the authors.

somewhat troubled by their lack of casual neighborly contact with a variety of people. They feel that they do not really belong to the neighborhood in a social sense. They would like to have more involvement in neighborhood groups, and it would be interesting to know if their dissatisfaction springs from the absence of the type of groups they would prefer or from a sense of unwelcomeness in present groups.

Although married women scored higher than unmarried women on the overall index of psychological well-being and on four of the specific indexes, it is difficult to discern any pattern as to why these four indexes differentiated between the two groups, while eight others did not (see Table 4.14). Three of the four, fullness vs. emptiness of life, tranquility vs. anxiety, and elation vs. depression, may be considered the most global of the measures. The fourth significant factor, sociability, might be explained in terms of the above discussion of neighboring patterns. The fact that another measure, companionship, showed no relationship to marital status offers some support for our suggestion that unmarried women may have satisfying friendships but unsatisfying neighborhood acquaintanceships.

Number and Age of Children

Expectation

All dependent satisfaction indexes will vary negatively with the number of children and positively with the age of children.

Findings

The number of children did vary negatively with many of the satisfaction indexes, but only the relationships with satisfaction with the housing environment were statistically significant as shown in Table 4.16. Here the overall satisfaction index showed a strong negative relationship with a greater number of children (p<0.005). Each of the specific indexes of satisfaction dealing with privacy, house and lot satisfaction, home-ownership responsibilities, and appearance also showed a negative relationship to the number of children in the household.

The average age of children showed the predicted relationship on only one of the four overall indexes of satisfaction, psychological well-being, (p<0.050). Table 4.17 shows that this score is influenced by a strong relationship between the woman's feeling of personal freedom (p<0.005) and the average age of her children and moderate relationships (p<0.100) between their ages and her feelings of fullness of life, social respect, self-

TABLE 4.16

Relationships between Number of Children and Indexes of Satisfaction

Satisfaction Index	Partial Correlation Coefficient[a] (n=825)
Housing environment	−0.1522[e]
Privacy	−0.1143[e]
House and lot	−0.1117[e]
Homeownership responsibilities	−0.1125[e]
Appearance	−0.0788[c]
Community services	−0.0190
Parks	−0.0400
Schools	0.0285
Security	0.0027
Child care	−0.0138
Transportation	−0.0566
Entertainment and culture	−0.0456
Social patterns	0.0018
Friendships	0.0018
Group activities	−0.0057
Sense of belonging	0.0097
Psychological well-being	0.0097
Fullness vs. emptiness of life	0.0426
Receptivity towards the world	0.0325
Social respect	−0.0172
Personal freedom	−0.0109
Sociability	0.0188
Companionship	0.0034
Work satisfaction	−0.0225
Tranquility vs. anxiety	0.0014
Self approving vs. guilty	−0.0052
Self confidence	0.0002
Energy vs. fatigue	0.0221
Elation vs. depression	0.0488

[a]two-tailed t-test for all correlations yields $p > 0.100$ unless otherwise noted
[b]t-test for this correlation yields $p < 0.100$
[c]t-test for this correlation yields $p < 0.050$
[d]t-test for this correlation yields $p < 0.010$
[e]t-test for this correlation yields $p < 0.005$
Source: compiled by the authors.

TABLE 4.17

Relationships between Average Age of Children and Indexes of Satisfaction

Satisfaction Index	Partial Correlation Coefficient[a] (n=825)
Housing environment	−0.0218
Privacy	0.0304
House and lot	0.0476
Homeownership responsibilities	−0.0630[b]
Appearance	−0.0754[c]
Community services	−0.0250
Parks	0.0181
Schools	0.0203
Security	0.0340
Child care	−0.0527
Transportation	−0.0406
Entertainment and culture	0.0315
Social patterns	0.0053
Friendships	0.0209
Group activities	0.0364
Sense of belonging	−0.0218
Psychological well-being	0.0817[c]
Fullness vs. emptiness of life	0.0654[b]
Receptivity towards the world	0.0436
Social respect	0.0649[b]
Personal freedom	0.1036[e]
Sociability	0.0429
Companionship	0.0519
Work Satisfaction	−0.0078
Tranquility vs. anxiety	0.0125
Self approving vs. guilty	0.0659[b]
Self confidence	0.0327
Energy vs. fatigue	0.0629[b]
Elation vs. depression	0.0591[b]

[a] two-tailed t-test for all correlations yields $p > 0.100$ unless otherwise noted

[b] t-test for this correlation yields $p < 0.100$

[c] t-test for this correlation yields $p < 0.050$

[d] t-test for this correlation yields $p < 0.010$

[e] t-test for this correlation yields $p < 0.005$

Source: compiled by the authors.

approval, energy, and elation. The only other significant relationships revealed on this table run counter to our expectations. Two of the specific indexes of satisfaction with the housing environment, responsibilities of homeownership and appearance of the housing environment related negatively to the average age of children.

In summary, our expectations regarding number and age of children were only partially confirmed. Number of children varied negatively only with satisfaction with the housing environment, and average age of children varied positively only with measures of psychological well-being.

Discussion

The failure of number and age of children to predict as many dimensions of satisfaction as we had expected might be explained by the generally small size of the families in our sample. In line with a general trend among middle-class households, the participants in our survey had rather small families, averaging 2.1 children. Participation in the study required at least one child, and our frequency data shows only a small proportion of large families (five or more children). Thus, the range of family size may not have been great enough to reflect subtle differences in the impact of this variable. For this sample at least, it appears that while larger families may make one's home seem more inadequate, they do not affect one's satisfaction with the community in general, social patterns, or personal satisfaction in life.

Average age of children correlates quite predictably with certain aspects of psychological well-being, such as freedom vs. constraint and energy vs. fatigue. As the review of literature underscores, the years that women are responsible for infants and toddlers are difficult years in many respects. In an effort to understand why these effects did not also show themselves in other areas of a woman's satisfaction, we conducted some ad hoc analyses of the data. Recognizing the potential fallacies attendant upon the use of average age of child as an indicator of various factors in the mother's life, we recoded the data according to the age of the youngest child. Only one partial correlation coefficient showed a significant relation between the age of the youngest child and satisfaction. The older one's youngest child the less satisfied one tends to be with the schools in the neighborhood. Surprisingly, an analysis of variance did not reveal any significant differences on the satisfaction indexes between mothers whose youngest child was preschool age and mothers whose youngest child fell into other age brackets. This secondary analysis revealed one curious characteristic of our data. While the mean age of children in our sample was 8.5 and the mean age of the youngest child in each household was 6.8, the modal age of the youngest child was one year. Seventy-nine mothers of one-year-old children participated in the study. It is doubtful that nearly one of ten mothers of a school-age child in the general population has a child one-year-old or younger. Possibly these women were more likely to be at home when our interviewers called or more likely to grant an interview in order to speak to another adult. Of course, the failure of our analysis to discover any major differences in satisfaction scores related to age of youngest child discredits the notion of the isolated and unhappy mother of a small child. Thus, it appears that knowing the average age of a woman's children will not tell us as much about her general satisfaction as we had expected, but it will tell us more than knowing the age of her youngest child.

SUBURBAN ENVIRONMENTAL INFLUENCES

Residential Density

Expectation

Density will have negative relationships with dependent satisfaction variables concerned with the housing environment and social patterns for married women and the reverse relationships for women who are heads of households.

Findings

Our data partially support our expectation. Using our sample of married women and comparing multi-family areas (14.5 units per net residential acre average) with single-family neighborhoods (6.1 units per acre average), Table 4.18 indicates that density has the unexpected positive relationships with the overall satisfaction with the housing environment ($p < 0.005$) and community services ($p < 0.005$). The positive relationship between density and overall satisfaction of the housing environment centered around the relatively high satisfaction with homeowner responsibilities (time and money) that residents of higher density areas expressed. The desirability of density with regard to community services was based on the higher satisfaction expressed for the site and management characteristics of condominiums (park, security, and cultural and entertainment activities) compared to that for single-family areas.

The inconclusive finding about the relationship of density and social patterns for married women was the result of two off-setting superiorities: a higher satisfaction of group participation among high-density residents, and a greater sense of belonging for single-family residents. As expected, the scores of psychological well-being were inconclusive.

TABLE 4.18

Mean Scores of Indexes of Satisfaction for Married Women in Multi-Family and Single Family Housing

Satisfaction Index	Satisfaction Scores[a]	
	Multi-Family (n=231)	Single-Family (n=471)
Housing environment	5.79[e]	5.54
Privacy	5.81	5.85
House and lot	5.55	5.59
Homeownership responsibilities	5.99[e]	4.99
Appearance	5.80	5.75
Community services	5.28[e]	5.05
Parks	5.11[c]	4.89
Schools	5.17	5.19
Security	5.69[e]	5.05
Child care	4.30	4.19
Transportation	5.42	5.47
Entertainment	5.75[e]	5.38
Social patterns	5.37	5.40
Friendships	5.69	5.68
Group activities	5.50[c]	5.23
Sense of belonging	4.91	5.23[d]
Psychological well-being	7.00	6.96
Fullness vs. emptiness of life	7.12	7.18
Receptivity towards the world	7.00	6.94
Social respect	7.46	7.52
Personal freedom	6.85	6.70
Sociability	7.12	7.03
Companionship	7.57	7.56
Work satisfaction	7.19	7.40
Tranquility vs. anxiety	6.40	6.28
Self approving vs. guilty	6.75	6.74
Self confidence	7.09	7.12
Energy vs. fatigue	6.56	6.49
Elation vs. depression	6.69	6.70

[a] two-tailed t-test for all score differences yields $p > 0.100$ unless otherwise noted
[b] t-test for score difference yields $p < 0.100$
[c] t-test for score difference yields $p < 0.050$
[d] t-test for score difference yields $p < 0.010$
[e] t-test for score difference yields $p < 0.005$
Source: compiled by the authors.

TABLE 4.19

Mean Scores of Indexes of Satisfaction for Unmarried Women in Multi-Family and Single Family Housing

Satisfaction Index	Satisfaction Scores[a]	
	Multi-Family (n=78)	Single Family (n=43)
Housing environment	5.52[c]	5.12
Privacy	5.74	5.74
House and lot	5.42	5.60
Homeownership responsibilities	5.05[e]	3.78
Appearance	5.87	5.49
Community services	5.07[b]	4.77
Parks	5.06	4.95
Schools	5.26	4.91
Security	5.29[c]	4.81
Child care	3.89	4.01
Transportation	5.27	5.00
Entertainment	5.45	5.31
Social patterns	4.94	4.95
Friendships	5.40	5.66
Group activities	5.00	4.65
Sense of belonging	4.45	4.65
Psychological well-being	7.38	6.68
Fullness vs. emptiness of life	7.14	6.65
Receptivity towards the world	7.45	6.70
Social respect	8.96	7.42
Personal freedom	8.38	6.71
Sociability	6.86	6.74
Companionship	7.49	7.24
Work satisfaction	8.19	6.88
Tranquility vs. anxiety	6.13	5.70
Self approving vs. guilty	6.91	6.67
Self confidence	7.50	7.05
Energy vs. fatigue	6.86	6.21
Elation vs. depression	6.69	6.26

[a]two-tailed t-test for all score differences yields $p > 0.100$ unless otherwise noted
[b]t-test for score difference yields $p < 0.100$
[c]t-test for score difference yields $p < 0.050$
[d]t-test for score difference yields $p < 0.010$
[e]t-test for score difference yields $p < 0.005$
Source: compiled by the authors.

   With regard to unmarried women, Table 4.19 shows that the data yielded
the expected positive relationships between density and the overall
satisfaction with the housing environment ($p<0.050$) as well as with
community services ($p<0.100$). Also, similar to the findings for married
women, the data show inconclusive relationships between density and the
overall satisfaction of social patterns and psychological well-being. Not
only were the findings for unmarried women about the relationships
between density and all overall satisfaction measures similar to those for
married women, but the underlying factors for these relationships were also
similar. For example, it appears that the primary reason for the positive
linkage between density and the housing environment was also the
relatively easier time women living in high density housing had in dealing
with homeownership responsibilities.

Discussion

   It appears that higher density housing areas not only work better for
unmarried women than do single-family neighborhoods, but are also more
rewarding environments for married women with small children. Indeed, as
Table 4.20 indicates, married women had significantly higher scores

TABLE 4.20
Mean Scores of Overall Indexes of Satisfaction for
Marital Status and Density

		Marital Status	
Density	Overall Indexes of Satisfaction	Married (n=704)	Unmarried (n=121)
Multi-family housing (n=309)	Housing environment	5.79^c	5.52
	Community services	5.28^c	5.07
	Social patterns	5.37^e	4.94
	Psychological well-being	7.00	7.38
		(n=231)	(n=78)
Single family housing (n=516)	Housing environment	5.55^e	5.16
	Community services	5.02^c	4.82
	Social patterns	5.38^d	4.99
	Psychological well-being	6.97	6.69
		(n=473)	(n=43)

[a] two-tailed t-test for all correlations yields $p > 0.100$ unless otherwise noted
[b] t-test for score difference yields $p < 0.100$
[c] t-test for score difference yields $p < 0.050$
[d] t-test for score difference yields $p < 0.010$
[e] t-test for score difference yields $p < 0.005$
Source: compiled by the authors.

(p<0.050) for three overall satisfaction indexes than their unmarried counterparts in both single-family and multi-family housing.

If we extend our analysis to consider the relationships of employment status and density we find a similar pattern to that found for marital status. As Table 4.21 reveals, the overall satisfaction scores for the housing environment and community services were significantly higher for both working (p<0.010) and non-working (p<0.050) women living in multi-family units compared to their counterparts in single-family housing. And these differences were based on specific indexes of satisfaction similar to those found for marital status.

Finally, if we examine the relationships of density and age of housing shown on Table 4.22, we find once again the desirability of the multi-family housing units emerging with respect to the housing environment

TABLE 4.21

Mean Scores of Overall Indexes of Satisfaction for Employment Status and Density

Employment Status	Overall Indexes of Satisfaction[a]	Density	
		Multi-Family Housing (n=306)	Single Family Housing (n=513)
Non-working (n=399)	Housing environment	5.79[c]	5.59
	Community services	5.26[c]	5.04
	Social patterns	5.36	5.35
	Psychological well-being	6.98	6.89
		(n=111)	(n=288)
Working (n=420)	Housing environment	5.69[e]	5.40
	Community services	5.21[d]	5.01
	Social patterns	5.22	5.38
	Psychological well-being	7.17	6.98
		(n=195)	(n=255)

[a]two-tailed t-test for all score differences yields p > 0.100 unless otherwise noted
[b]t-test for score difference yields p < 0.100
[c]t-test for score difference yields p < 0.050
[d]t-test for score difference yields p < 0.010
[e]t-test for score difference yields p < 0.005
Source: compiled by the authors.

TABLE 4.22
Mean Scores of Overall Indexes of Satisfaction for Density
by Age of Housing

Age of House (Years)	Overall Indexes of Satisfaction[a]	Density	
		Multi-Family Housing (n=299)	Single-Family Housing (n=503)
1–3 (n=206)	Housing environment	5.76[c]	5.39
	Community services	5.20[b]	4.97
	Social patterns	5.28	5.07
	Psychological well-being	7.21	6.86
		(n=157)	(n=49)
4–6 (n=246)	Housing environment	5.67[e]	5.37
	Community services	5.23[e]	4.66
	Social patterns	5.23	5.22
	Psychological well-being	6.98	6.90
		(n=140)	(n=106)
7–17 (n=181)	Housing environment	5.71	5.34
	Community services	5.53	5.05
	Social patterns	5.88	5.28
	Psychological well-being	7.56	6.82
		(n=4)	(n=177)
18 + (n=182)	Housing environment	5.15	5.78
	Community services	4.81	5.19
	Social patterns	4.33	5.61
	Psychological well-being	6.42	7.10
		(n=1)	(n=181)

[a]two-tailed t-test for all score differences yields $p > 0.100$ unless otherwise noted
[b]t-test for score difference yields $p < 0.100$
[c]t-test for score difference yields $p < 0.050$
[d]t-test for score difference yields $p < 0.010$
[e]t-test for score difference yields $p < 0.005$
Source: compiled by the authors.

(p<0.050) and community services (p<0.100). Thus, our findings strongly suggest that multi-family areas provide more efficient and better organized housing environments and a more supportive set of community services for all women with children than do single-family housing areas.

Household Distance from the Central City Center

Expectation

Household distance from the central city center (miles) varies negatively with the satisfaction variables concerned with community services, social patterns, and psychological well-being.

Findings

This expectation is supported strongly by our data. Comparing an inlying single-family neighborhood (about two miles from the city center) with an outlying single-family area (approximately eight miles from the city center), Table 4.23 indicates a negative relationship between household distance from the central city center and all overall indexes of satisfaction ($p<0.050$). As anticipated, the satisfaction with community services was especially high for the inlying area residents ($p<0.005$) and for transportation services in particular ($p<0.005$) due to their relatively greater proximity to the city center. Other specific indices of satisfaction which, as expected, indicated significantly higher scores ($p<0.050$) for the inlying area are sense of belonging, fullness of life, receptivity towards the world, and companionships.

Unanticipated was the relatively high satisfaction with the housing environment reported by inlying area residents based primarily on the design aspects of the house and lot and appearance (all $p<0.005$).

Discussion

It is, of course, possible that some of the satisfaction expressed by residents in the inlying area was due to the overall aesthetic qualities of that area since it is an older, established, tree-lined, residential neighborhood with a relatively strong physical and social identity compared to the newer outlying area. Yet, when we use some control of our sample with respect to age of housing, the across-the-board superiority of the inlying neighborhood held up, with the exception of psychological well-being scores (see Table 4.24).

Thus, despite the highly decentralized pattern of shopping, entertainment, and cultural facilities in the San Jose area, our findings suggest that the accessibility to the central city center available to inlying neighborhood residents provides them with many physical and social benefits which residents in outlying areas do not receive. These results

TABLE 4.23

Mean Scores of Indexes of Satisfaction for Inlying and Outlying Single-Family Housing Neighborhoods in San Jose

	Satisfaction Scores[a]	
Satisfaction Index	Inlying Area (n=103)	Outlying Area (n=100)
Housing environment	5.91[e]	5.32
Privacy	6.21	5.66
House and lot	6.02[e]	5.41
Homeownership responsibilities	4.90	4.82
Appearance	6.52[e]	5.32
Community services	5.07[e]	4.45
Parks	5.60[e]	3.71
Schools	4.75	4.83
Security	5.08[c]	4.55
Child care	4.42[c]	4.04
Transportation	5.47[e]	4.83
Entertainment	5.06	4.98
Social patterns	5.67[c]	5.33
Friendships	5.92	5.72
Group activities	5.41	5.11
Sense of belonging	5.60[c]	5.07
Psychological well-being	7.13[c]	6.84
Fullness vs. emptiness of life	7.34[c]	6.94
Receptivity towards the world	7.05[c]	6.73
Social respect	7.58	7.55
Personal freedom	6.69	6.48
Sociability	7.13	7.00
Companionship	7.90[c]	7.51
Work satisfaction	7.75	7.36
Tranquility vs. anxiety	6.49[c]	6.01
Self approving vs. guilty	6.93	6.72
Self confidence	7.18	7.05
Energy vs. fatigue	6.63[d]	6.15
Elation vs. depression	6.89[b]	6.56

[a]two-tailed t-test for all score differences yields $p > 0.100$ unless otherwise noted
[b]t-test for score difference yields $p < 0.100$
[c]t-test for score difference yields $p < 0.050$
[d]t-test for score difference yields $p < 0.010$
[e]t-test for score difference yields $p < 0.005$
Source: compiled by the authors.

TABLE 4.24

Mean Scores of Overall Indexes of Satisfaction for Inlying and Outlying Neighborhoods in San Jose for Housing Seven Years Old and Older

Residential Area	Overall Indexes of Satisfaction			
	Housing Environment	Community Services	Social Patterns	Psychological Well-Being
Inlying (n=105)	5.91	5.07	5.67	7.13
Outlying (n=36)	5.43	4.50	5.33	6.84
Range of possible scores	1.00–7.00	1.00–7.00	1.00–7.00	1.00–10.00
T-test probability that difference is due to chance	0.010	0.007	0.050	0.200

Note: Mean scores of satisfaction indexes are computed as the weighted average scores of the variables comprising each index as shown in appendix B.
Source: compiled by the authors.

corroborate the findings of others that women living in outlying suburban areas experience difficulties related to accessibility for such activities as employment[9] and, when not socially involved locally, residents of these outlying areas tend to be more isolated than their central city counterparts.[10] Perhaps as a metropolitan area grows geographically and becomes more suburban in character its population becomes increasingly localized and regionally isolated in nature.

Age of Neighborhood

Expectation

Age of neighborhood will have a positive association with all dependent satisfaction variables.

Findings

Our findings generally support this expectation. As Table 4.25 indicates, our partial correlation analysis shows a positive relationship between age of neighborhood (as measured by age of house) and the overall indexes of satisfaction with the housing environment ($p < 0.100$), social patterns ($p < 0.050$), and psychological well-being ($p < 0.100$). With the exception of the negative relationship with satisfaction of homeowners' responsibilities ($p < 0.005$), age of neighborhood varied positively with all the other specific indexes of satisfaction with the housing environment at the 0.005 level.

The social success of the older housing environments was based primarily on the positive relationships between age of neighborhood and satisfaction with friendships ($p < 0.050$) and sense of belonging ($p < 0.005$). Also, the positive linkage of the older neighborhoods to psychological well-being was primarily socially oriented, as indicated by the positive relationships between the age of neighborhood and social respect and companionship at the 0.050 level. Apart from the positive relationship with satisfaction of parks ($p < 0.005$), the age of neighborhood had no significant linkages with community facilities.

Discussion

While the older neighborhoods seem to have the disadvantage of housing with a high incidence of maintenance responsibilities, these housing environments are still considered more desirable than newer areas because of the satisfaction they create in privacy, arrangement and design of house and lot, and overall appearance. More importantly, the older neighbor-

TABLE 4.25

Relationships between Age of Neighborhood and Indexes of Satisfaction

Satisfaction Index	Partial Correlation Coefficient[a] (n=825)
Housing environment	0.0594[b]
Privacy	0.1076[e]
House and lot	0.1127[e]
Homeownership responsibilities	−0.1990[e]
Appearance	0.1718[e]
Community services	0.0185
Parks	0.1325[e]
Schools	0.0008
Security	−0.0128
Child care	−0.0111
Transportation	−0.0129
Entertainment and culture	−0.0402
Social patterns	0.0841[c]
Friendships	0.0760[c]
Group activities	0.0104
Sense of belonging	0.1034[e]
Psychological well-being	0.0571[b]
Fullness vs. emptiness of life	0.0634[b]
Receptivity towards the world	0.0505
Social respect	0.0711[c]
Personal freedom	−0.0587[b]
Sociability	−0.0212
Companionship	0.0769[c]
Work satisfaction	0.0753[c]
Tranquility vs. anxiety	0.0295
Self approving vs. guilty	0.0598[b]
Self confidence	0.0559[b]
Energy vs. fatigue	0.0423
Elation vs. depression	0.0462

[a]two-tailed t-test for all correlations yields $p > 0.100$ unless otherwise noted
[b]t-test for this correlation yields $p < 0.100$
[c]t-test for this correlation yields $p < 0.050$
[d]t-test for this correlation yields $p < 0.010$
[e]t-test for this correlation yields $p < 0.005$
Source: compiled by the authors.

hoods seem to provide a more cohesive, stable, and supportive social and psychological network for their residents than do new residential areas. Apparently, people are willing to tolerate the annoying maintenance costs of older housing and possible social constraints in order to receive the aesthetic, social, and psychological benefits of living in established neighborhoods. Perhaps the older residential areas, with their tree-lined streets, traditional housing appearance, and varied age population structure, create the image and feeling of continuity in an era of rapid change and great household mobility.

Distance to Work

Expectation

Travel time to work for a woman and/or her spouse will vary negatively with her satisfaction with community services, social patterns, and psychological well-being.

Findings

This expectation was partially support by our data. The partial correlations on Table 4.26 indicate that woman's travel time to work varies negatively with only one overall index of satisfaction, social patterns ($p < 0.050$), mostly because of the apparently detrimental impacts of long journeys to work on satisfaction with friendships and group activities ($p < 0.050$). With the exception of the negative linkages to the specific indexes of psychological well-being of fullness of life and sociability ($p < 0.100$ and $p < 0.050$, respectively), woman's travel time to work had no other significant relationships with measures of woman's satisfaction.

More in keeping with our expectation were the negative relationships that man's travel time to work has with the overall indexes of satisfaction with community services ($p < 0.050$) and social patterns ($p < 0.100$), shown on Table 4.27. The dissatisfaction with community services was related to the negative scores for transportation ($p < 0.050$) and entertainment and culture ($p < 0.100$); while the social dissatisfaction was based on the negative value of sense of belonging. The slight dissatisfaction of psychological well-being were similar to those found with respect to woman's travel time.

Unexpectedly, man's travel time to work was also negatively associated with the overall satisfaction with the housing environment ($p < 0.050$), based primarily on the dissatisfaction indicated for homeownership responsibilities ($p < 0.010$).

TABLE 4.26

Relationships between Woman's Travel Time to Work and Indexes of Satisfaction

Satisfaction Index	Partial Correlation Coefficient[a] (n=825)
Housing environment	−0.0054
Privacy	−0.0012
House and lot	−0.0235
Homeownership responsibilities	−0.0023
Appearance	0.0082
Community services	0.0220
Parks	−0.0272
Schools	0.0514
Security	−0.0015
Child care	−0.0218
Transportation	−0.0327
Entertainment and culture	0.0101
Social patterns	−0.0795[c]
Friendships	−0.0720
Group activities	−0.0803[c]
Sense of belonging	−0.0299
Psychological well-being	−0.0410
Fullness vs. emptiness of life	−0.0643[c]
Receptivity towards the world	−0.0096
Social respect	−0.0321
Personal freedom	−0.0448
Sociability	−0.0847[c]
Companionship	0.0205
Work satisfaction	−0.0547
Tranquility vs. anxiety	−0.0269
Self approving vs. guilty	−0.0347
Self confidence	0.0237
Energy vs. fatigue	0.0045
Elation vs. depression	−0.0195

[a] two-tailed t-test for all correlations yields $p > 0.100$ unless otherwise noted
[b] t-test for this correlation yields $p < 0.100$
[c] t-test for this correlation yields $p < 0.050$
[d] t-test for this correlation yields $p < 0.010$
[e] t-test for this correlation yields $p < 0.005$
Source: compiled by the authors.

TABLE 4.27

Relationships between Man's Travel Time to Work and Indexes of Satisfaction

Satisfaction Index	Partial Correlation Coefficient[a] (n=825)
Housing environment	−0.0766[c]
Privacy	−0.0388
House and lot	−0.0221
Homeownership responsibilities	−0.0932[d]
Appearance	−0.0508
Community services	−0.0691[c]
Parks	−0.0389
Schools	−0.0661
Security	−0.0265
Child care	0.0026
Transportation	−0.0790[c]
Entertainment and culture	−0.0612[b]
Social patterns	−0.0614[b]
Friendships	−0.0197
Group activities	−0.0441
Sense of belonging	−0.0602[b]
Psychological well-being	−0.0277
Fullness vs. emptiness of life	−0.0572[b]
Receptivity towards the world	−0.0336
Social respect	0.0216
Personal freedom	0.0310
Sociability	−0.0369
Companionship	−0.0631[b]
Work satisfaction	0.0038
Tranquility vs. anxiety	0.0385
Self approving vs. guilty	−0.0294
Self confidence	0.0423
Energy vs. fatigue	−0.0396
Elation vs. depression	−0.0275

[a] two-tailed t-test for all correlations yields $p > 0.100$ unless otherwise noted
[b] t-test for this correlation yields $p < 0.100$
[c] t-test for this correlation yields $p < 0.050$
[d] t-test for this correlation yields $p < 0.010$
[e] t-test for this correlation yields $p < 0.005$
Source: compiled by the authors.

Discussion

The fact that man's travel time has a greater overall negative impact on woman's satisfaction than woman's travel time may reflect certain female-male dependencies based on traditional household role structures. For example, the negative relationship of man's travel time and woman's satisfaction with the housing environment is based largely on dissatisfaction with homeownership responsibilities—activities which involve home maintenance work, which traditionally has been considered man's work and which may not be completed because of man's excessive time away from home while commuting to and from work. The same process may be functioning with the woman's enjoyment of community services being dependent on the man's availability to serve as an escort for her to partake in those services, such as entertainment and culture.

It seems that while a long commutation time for men has a substantially broad negative impact on women, increased women's travel time has mostly a negative social effect on women. These differential effects of commutation time of women and men may be related to differences in middle-class, male-female social roles, which seem to encourage the woman's dependence on the presence of a man for her satisfaction with housing and community services.

Mean Neighborhood Income and Educational Levels

Expectation

As income and education decline below the neighborhood means there will be a substantial decline in all dependent satisfaction variables.

Findings

Our data supports this expectation with considerable force. As expected, Table 4.28 reveals that the ratio of family income to the mean neighborhood family income is positively correlated with overall satisfaction with housing environment ($p < 0.005$) and community services ($p < 0.050$), as well as with the specific indexes of satisfaction with social patterns (such as friendships, $p < 0.100$) and psychological well-being (such as fullness of life, $p < 0.010$). As shown in Table 4.29, the ratio of women's education to the mean neighborhood woman's education has positive relationships with the overall satisfaction with community services ($p < 0.050$) and social patterns ($p < 0.050$), as well as with several specific indexes of satisfaction with

TABLE 4.28

Relationships between Ratio of Family Income to Mean Neighborhood Family Income and Indexes of Satisfaction

Satisfaction Index	Partial Correlation Coefficient[a] (n=825)
Housing environment	0.1084[e]
Privacy	0.0478[b]
House and lot	0.0725[c]
Homeownership responsibilities	0.1580[e]
Appearance	0.0014
Community services	0.0800[c]
Parks	0.0015
Schools	0.0060
Security	0.0951[d]
Child care	0.0747[c]
Transportation	0.0849[c]
Entertainment and culture	−0.0090
Social patterns	0.0364
Friendships	0.0676[b]
Group activities	0.0316
Sense of belonging	−0.0069
Psychological well-being	−0.0307
Fullness vs. emptiness of life	0.0963[d]
Receptivity towards the world	0.0386
Social respect	−0.0117
Personal freedom	0.0499
Sociability	−0.0223
Companionship	0.0315
Work satisfaction	0.0315
Tranquility vs. anxiety	0.0574[b]
Self approving vs. guilty	−0.0148
Self confidence	−0.0088
Energy vs. fatigue	0.0213
Elation vs. depression	−0.0142

[a]two-tailed t-test for all correlations yields $p > 0.100$ unless otherwise noted
[b]t-test for this correlation yields $p < 0.100$
[c]t-test for this correlation yields $p < 0.050$
[d]t-test for this correlation yields $p < 0.010$
[e]t-test for this correlation yields $p < 0.005$
Source: compiled by the authors.

TABLE 4.29

Relationships between Ratio of Woman's Education to Mean Neighborhood Woman's Education and Indexes of Satisfaction

Satisfaction Index	Partial Correlation Coefficient[a] (n=825)
Housing environment	−0.0171
Privacy	0.0153
House and lot	−0.0652[b]
Homeownership responsibilities	0.0193
Appearance	−0.0159
Community services	0.0782[c]
Parks	0.0163
Schools	0.0672[b]
Security	0.1532[e]
Child care	−0.0296
Transportation	−0.0196
Entertainment and culture	0.0962[d]
Social patterns	0.0896[c]
Friendships	0.0652[b]
Group activities	0.1149[e]
Sense of belonging	0.0204
Psychological well-being	0.0343
Fullness vs. emptiness of life	0.0491
Receptivity towards the world	0.1036[e]
Social respect	0.0619[b]
Personal freedom	−0.0352
Sociability	0.0626[b]
Companionship	0.0558
Work satisfaction	0.0930[d]
Tranquility vs. anxiety	0.0412
Self approving vs. guilty	−0.0305
Self confidence	0.0717[c]
Energy vs. fatigue	0.0551
Elation vs. depression	0.0322

[a] two-tailed t-test for all correlations yields $p > 0.100$ unless otherwise noted

[b] t-test for this correlation yields $p < 0.100$

[c] t-test for this correlation yields $p < 0.050$

[d] t-test for this correlation yields $p < 0.010$

[e] t-test for this correlation yields $p < 0.005$

Source: compiled by the authors.

psychological well-being, such as receptivity towards the world and self-confidence, at the 0.005 and 0.050 levels, respectively. The only negative finding was the weak relationship between woman's education and satisfaction with house and lot ($p < 0.100$).

Discussion

While satisfaction generally increases with increases in both the relative family income and women's education, it seems that income primarily influences satisfaction of a physical nature (such as with housing), and education relates more toward social satisfaction. These findings seem to reinforce our earlier findings concerned with income and education, which suggest that increases in income mostly improve a woman's ability to consume goods and services, while increases in her relative education provide her with greater social and psychological opportunities and rewards both within the residential neighborhood and the work world beyond. Indeed, our perusal of the multiple regression analysis (which we chose not to report in this study due to its low explanatory power) indicates that woman's education is the independent variable that explains the most variance in the overall satisfaction with community services, friendship patterns, and psychological well-being.

Population Size of Political Unit

Expectation

The population size of a political unit will vary inversely with satisfaction on all community services variables.

Findings

This expectation was strongly supported by our data. A comparison of four central city neighborhoods in San Jose (1975 population = 551,400) with the four suburban neighborhoods in Los Gatos (1975 population = 23,900) and Cupertino (1975 population = 22,000) shows a significant difference in scores of overall satisfaction with community services at the 0.005 level favoring the smaller suburban communities (see Table 4.30). Indeed, the suburban communities had significantly higher scores for all specific indexes of community services ($p < 0.050$), as well as for community-related specific indexes of satisfaction for social patterns (like

TABLE 4.30

Mean Scores of Indexes of Satisfaction for Central City and Suburbs

Satisfaction Index	Satisfaction Scores[a]	
	Central City (n=403)	Suburbs (n=422)
Housing environment	5.62	5.56
Privacy	5.87	5.77
House and lot	5.61	5.52
Homeownership responsibilities	5.21	5.22
Appearance	5.81	5.72
Community services	4.88	5.28[e]
Parks	4.69	5.23[e]
Schools	4.95	5.38[e]
Security	4.98	5.48[e]
Child care	4.30	4.09[c]
Transportation	5.25	5.57[e]
Entertainment	4.99	5.95[e]
Social patterns	5.27	5.37
Friendships	5.60	5.71
Group activities	5.11	5.39[e]
Sense of belonging	5.07	5.01
Psychological well-being	6.94	6.94
Fullness vs. emptiness of life	7.05	7.12
Receptivity towards the world	6.88	6.99[b]
Social respect	7.45	7.51
Personal freedom	6.77	6.73
Sociability	7.03	7.03
Companionship	7.59	7.47
Work satisfaction	7.41[b]	7.22
Tranquility vs. anxiety	6.29	6.34
Self approving vs. guilty	6.74	6.70
Self confidence	7.10	7.08
Energy vs. fatigue	6.45	6.51
Elation vs. depression	6.66	6.65

[a]two-tailed t-test for all score differences yields $p > 0.100$ unless otherwise noted
[b]t-test for score difference yields $p < 0.100$
[c]t-test for score difference yields $p < 0.050$
[d]t-test for score difference yields $p < 0.010$
[e]t-test for score difference yields $p < 0.005$
Source: compiled by the authors.

group activities, $p<0.005$), and for psychological well-being (such as receptivity towards the world, $p<0.100$).

Even when controlling for age of housing, as shown, for example, on Table 4.31, we find that the suburban communities consistently have higher scores of overall satisfaction with community services ($p<0.050$) and to a lesser extent with social patterns. The central city only excelled with respect to the overall satisfaction with the housing environment in the older housing categories probably due to the highly desirable appearance of the older San Jose neighborhoods.

Discussion

It appears that residents of political units with smaller and more homogeneous populations have more satisfaction from community services than residents of larger political units. While the 1975 family incomes were not significantly different between the upper middle-class residents of the central city and suburbs in our study, the average 1975 suburban household income was in fact substantially higher than that for the central city ($19,400 and $15,000, respectively). Thus, the high satisfaction with community services experienced by households in the smaller political units not only may reflect their homogeneity of public service preferences but may also indicate that their almost uniformly high levels of income enable them to realize their preferences. Although the financial requirement for supporting suburban public services would not be a problem for most of the middle and upper middle-income households in our study, it would probably be a formidable obstacle to many central city families with average incomes and a desire to exercise suburban-like preferences for community services.

Our findings also suggest that the superiority of smaller units for community service satisfaction may be related to the more participatory nature of smaller-unit residents as reflected in their intense involvement in group activities. This participation, in turn, is likely to provide residents of small communities with a relatively greater control over and satisfaction with public services in their community. Perhaps, as indicated in other studies, this vigorous participation is a means of providing local political control as a means of generally preserving community sovereignty within the metropolitan area.[11]

Yet, other findings of our study using exploratory variables concerned with locational preferences suggest a possible decline over time in the importance of community services with regard to overall residential satisfaction. As Appendix G indicates, of the eight neighborhoods studied, three showed a high degree of congruence between "reasons for present

TABLE 4.31

Mean Scores of Overall Indexes of Satisfaction for
Central City and Suburbs, by Age of Housing

Age of House (Years)	Overall Indexes of Satisfaction[a]	Central City (n=391)	Suburbs (n=401)
1–3 (n=206)	Housing environment	5.54	5.79[b]
	Community services	4.90	5.35[e]
	Social patterns	5.07	5.38[c]
	Psychological well-being	7.39	6.89
		(n=100)	(n=106)
4–6 (n=246)	Housing environment	5.48	5.63
	Community services	4.75	5.28[e]
	Social patterns	5.05	5.44[e]
	Psychological well-being	6.85	7.06
		(n=141)	(n=105)
7–17 (n=181)	Housing environment	5.57[b]	5.25
	Community services	4.71	5.19[d]
	Social patterns	5.40	5.25
	Psychological well-being	6.86	6.82
		(n=57)	(n=124)
18+ (n=182)	Housing environment	5.90[c]	5.61
	Community serviceas	5.08	5.30[c]
	Social patterns	5.68	5.51
	Psychological well-being	7.12	7.05
		(n=103)	(n=79)

[a]two-tailed t-test for all score differences yields $p > 0.100$ unless otherwise noted
[b]t-test for score difference yields $p < 0.100$
[c]t-test for score difference yields $p < 0.050$
[d]t-test for score difference yields $p < 0.010$
[e]t-test for score difference yields $p < 0.005$
Source: compiled by the authors.

location" and "reasons for satisfaction of present home" (inlying single-family in San Jose, outlying single-family in San Jose, outlying condominium in San Jose). For the latter two, housing cost and design appear to be the essence for the initial location decision and ensuing satisfaction. In the inlying area, housing design and neighborhood appearance were in the forefront. In all four San Jose neighborhoods, housing considerations were pre-eminent both before and after the purchase. Only in the outlying planned unit development did respondents list a non-housing consideration in their reasons for locating (schools), and this was not a factor in subsequent satisfaction. In San Jose, expectations were based on the housing product and appear to have been well satisfied.

Turning to the four suburban neighborhoods, non-housing factors were all pre-eminent in the purchase decision. In the Cupertino single-family area, housing cost was listed as a secondary purchase factor. Do initial reasons for location share a congruence with subsequent satisfaction? The verdict is mixed. Respondents in the Cupertino condominiums and Los Gatos single-family houses may find their expectations to have been met with respect to schools. Other reasons appear to be modified by experience. Appearance of neighborhood was at best a secondary factor in locating and maintains that position when evaluated after the move. Convenience to work disappears in retrospect, as every area but one does not seem to enjoy much of an advantage with respect to proximity; the inlying area of San Jose is by far the best situated in this question, although respondents did not list it as a factor in their reasons for locating or present satisfaction. A similar pattern to the Cupertino condominiums holds for respondents from the single-family neighborhood of Los Gatos.

Community services considerations lead the reasons for locating as expressed by residents of the Los Gatos condominiums, but they are not a factor in present satisfaction with their home. The house design is overwhelmingly dominant when the living situation is evaluated. Although housing costs were an important influence for locating on the part of respondents in Cupertino's single-family neighborhood, locational aspects (schools, work, shopping) lend a locational coloring to their purchase decision. Yet, house design emerges as their primary reason for current satisfaction with the dwelling unit, although work and shopping persist; schools, however, appear not to have met expectations.

It seems that the initial housing choice was based on a split between the preferences of central city residents, who focused on home characteristics, such as housing cost, and suburban residents, who stressed public services such as schools. Yet, it was also shown that current satisfaction with their living environment was based primarily on housing design characteristics. These findings suggest that over time environmentally closer influences, such as housing considerations, may take precedence over more distant neighborhood qualities. It also appears that the households that were initially self-selected into neighborhoods by using measurable, strictly functional criteria, were probably conditioned over time by their environments and other influences into using more personal qualitative design criteria in expressing current satisfaction. These findings appear to support generally Michelson's concept that residential satisfaction may reflect not only a mix of self-selection and the behavioral patterns emerging from environmental situations but also the degree of congruence between a current situation and long-range environmental aspirations.[12]

Design and Site Plan Characteristics

Expectation

The greater the degree of planned characteristics in the site plan of a housing development, the greater the level of satisfaction on all dependent variables.

Findings

Our data partially support our expectation. Using a comparison of planned areas (comprising planned unit developments of single-family homes and planned multi-family condominiums) to less planned areas (made up of conventional, single-family, suburban neighborhoods), Table 4.32 indicates a significantly higher overall satisfaction with the housing environment ($p < 0.010$) and community services ($p < 0.050$) for the planned areas, and more overall satisfaction with social patterns for the less planned neighborhoods ($p < 0.050$). Our data yielded inconclusive results for overall psychological well-being. The desirability of the planned areas was based on the specific satisfactions of homeownership responsibilities for the housing environment and sense of security for community services, both significant at the 0.005 level; while the unexpected superiority of the less planned areas centered around specific satisfactions of friendships ($p < 0.010$) and sense of belonging ($p < 0.005$) for social patterns. The inconclusive finding concerning the influence of planned environments on psychological well-being results from two compensating relationships: the higher satisfaction of personal freedom for residents of planned areas ($p < 0.005$); and greater fullness of life for less planned area residents ($p < 0.010$).

If we attempt to control for age of housing, we find on Table 4.33 that planned areas maintain their relative superiority in terms of overall satisfaction with the housing environment and community services. However, the relative desirability of the less planned areas with respect to overall satisfaction with social patterns seem to be negated. That is, it appears that overall satisfaction with social patterns is more a function of age of housing than of planned characteristics of the residential area.

If we compare two neighborhoods adjacent to one another in the same

TABLE 4.32

Mean Scores of Indexes of Satisfaction for Planned and Les Planned Areas

Satisfaction Index	Satisfaction Scores[a]	
	Planned Areas (n=406)	Less Planned Areas (n=419)
Housing environment	5.67[d]	5.51
Privacy	5.78	5.85
House and lot	5.51	5.62
Homeownership responsibilities	5.63[e]	4.81
Appearance	5.77	5.76
Community services	5.16[c]	5.04
Parks	4.98	4.96
Schools	5.21	5.14
Security	5.45[e]	5.04
Child care	4.24	4.12
Transportation	5.42	5.41
Entertainment	5.52	5.45
Social patterns	5.23	5.41[c]
Friendships	5.55	5.76[d]
Group activities	5.32	5.19
Sense of belonging	4.82	5.25[e]
Psychological well-being	6.94	6.93
Fullness vs. emptiness of life	6.98	7.18[c]
Receptivity towards the world	6.94	6.94
Social respect	7.45	7.51
Personal freedom	6.91[e]	6.59
Sociability	7.06	6.99
Companionship	7.54	7.52
Work satisfaction	7.28	7.35
Tranquility vs. anxiety	6.32	6.21
Self approving vs. guilty	6.68	6.77
Self confidence	7.10	7.08
Energy vs. fatigue	6.53	6.42
Elation vs. depression	6.64	6.66

[a]two-tailed t-test for all score differences yields $p > 0.100$ unless otherwise noted
[b]t-test for score difference yields $p < 0.100$
[c]t-test for score difference yields $p < 0.050$
[d]t-test for score difference yields $p < 0.010$
[e]t-test for score difference yields $p < 0.005$
Source: compiled by the authors.

TABLE 4.33

Mean Scores of Overall Indexes of Satisfaction for Planned and Less Planned Areas by Age of Housing

Age of House (Years)	Overall Indexes of Satisfaction[a]	Planned Areas (n=394)	Less Planned Areas (n=408)
1–3 (n=206)	Housing environment	5.68	5.56
	Community services	5.14	5.13
	Social patterns	5.22	5.38
	Psychological well-being	7.15	6.81
		(n=196)	(n=10)
4–6 (n=246)	Housing environment	5.65[c]	5.23
	Community services	5.18[e]	4.45
	Social patterns	5.20	5.29
	Psychological well-being	6.99	6.82
		(n=181)	(n=65)
7–17 (n=181)	Housing environment	5.72[b]	5.30
	Community services	5.12	5.05
	Social patterns	5.63	5.25
	Psychological well-being	6.97	6.82
		(n=21)	(n=160)
18+ (n=182)	Housing environment	5.15	5.78
	Community services	4.81	5.19
	Social patterns	4.33	5.61
	Psychological well-being	6.42	7.10
		(n=1)	(n=181)

[a]two-tailed t-test for all score differences yields $p > 0.100$ unless otherwise noted
[b]t-test for score difference yields $p < 0.100$
[c]t-test for score difference yields $p < 0.050$
[d]t-test for score difference yields $p < 0.010$
[e]t-test for score difference yields $p < 0.005$
Source: compiled by the authors.

city built during the same time period with similar housing except that one area is a planned development while the other is a less planned conventional environment, we can extend our analysis further and attempt to control for density, size of political unit, distance from the central city center, and age of housing. Using this comparison we find on Table 4.34 that the planned area continues to maintain a substantial advantage in

TABLE 4.34

Mean Scores of Indexes of Satisfaction for Planned and Less Planned Single Family Neighborhoods in San Jose

Satisfaction Index	Satisfaction Scores[a]	
	Planned Area (n=97)	Less Planned Area (n=103)
Housing environment	5.51	5.32
Privacy	5.78	5.66
House and lot	5.49	5.41
Homeownership responsibilities	5.27[c]	4.82
Appearance	5.59	5.40
Community services	4.95[e]	4.45
Parks	4.59[e]	3.71
Schools	5.28[c]	4.83
Security	5.00[c]	4.55
Child care	4.41[c]	4.04
Transportation	5.53[e]	4.83
Entertainment	5.04	4.98
Social patterns	5.14	5.33
Friendships	5.32	5.72[c]
Group activities	5.13	5.11
Sense of belonging	4.89	5.07
Psychological well-being	6.93	6.84
Fullness vs. emptiness of life	6.94	6.94
Receptivity towards the world	6.86	6.73
Social respect	7.48	7.55
Personal freedom	7.14[d]	6.48
Sociability	7.08	7.00
Companionship	7.59	7.51
Work satisfaction	7.39	7.36
Tranquility vs. anxiety	6.34	6.01
Self approving vs. guilty	6.58	6.72
Self confidence	7.26	7.05
Energy vs. fatigue	6.60[c]	6.15
Elation vs. depression	6.65	6.56

[a]two-tailed t-test for all score differences yields p > 0.100 unless otherwise noted
[b]t-test for score difference yields p < 0.100
[c]t-test for score difference yields p < 0.050
[d]t-test for score difference yields p < 0.010
[e]t-test for score difference yields p < 0.005
Source: compiled by the authors.

terms of overall satisfaction with only community services (p<0.005). Indeed the planned area excells in five of the six specific indexes of satisfaction with community services. Also, the planned area maintains its superiority with respect to other specific indexes of satisfaction with the housing environment (like homeownership responsibilities, p<0.050). And the less planned area maintained its desirability regarding the specific satisfaction of friendships (p<0.050).

Discussion

It seems that planned areas provide more efficient and rewarding housing environments and community services than do less planned areas. However, depending on the specific design and social composition, planned areas may be less socially rewarding with respect to friendships than are less planned, conventional single-family areas. An explanation for the relatively low social interaction in the planned areas is that a higher percentage of women in these areas are employed outside the household (64 percent in planned areas and 44 percent in less planned areas) and work at jobs that have significantly greater status (demands) and commutation times (p<0.007 and p<0.001, respectively) than their counterparts in the less planned developments. It seems likely that the women in the planned environments simply have less time and energy for socializing.

Thus, our findings suggest a possible self-selection process related to the satisfaction of planned areas. Because the planned areas provide housing and services which are more supportive and less demanding of women with children than are less planned environments, the planned areas attract women with greater demands on their time and energy, working women with relatively high status (or demanding) jobs, which, in turn, decrease the opportunities for friendship formation within the planned areas.

Also, our findings indicate that with the possible exception of positive feelings of personal freedom (probably because of the relative ease of living in planned environments), the planned areas had little or no association with psychological well-being variables. Thus, as found in other recent studies,[13] while planned environments seem to make positive contributions toward satisfaction with housing and community services, such environments appear to have only a modest positive influence on the broader realms of life satisfaction concerned with social and psychological well-being.

SUMMARY

In this section we discuss the comparative influence of our clusters of independent variables on the global aspects of the quality of life indexes:

FIGURE 4.1

Comparative Influence of Independent Variable Categories on Overall Housing Environment Satisfaction

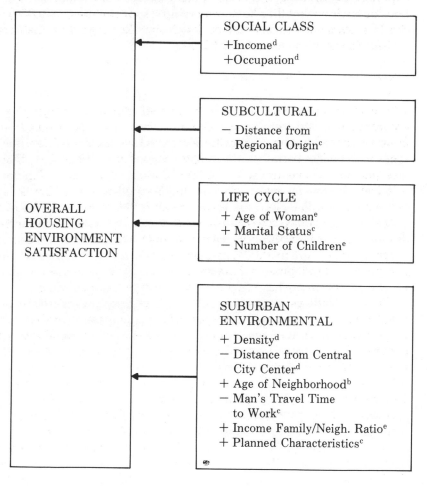

Source: compiled by the authors.

housing environment, community services, social patterns, and psychological well-being. As mentioned previously, we chose not to use our multiple regression analysis in our study for estimating the relative importance of the independent variables, due to its low explanatory power (less than 10 percent). Instead, we present a comparative analysis of the overall findings of our study. As Figure 4.1 indicates, there seems to be a balance between environmental and combined social influences on overall housing environment satisfaction. Table 4.35 reveals that all influence clusters had about a 70 percent success rate of significant independent variables at the 0.100 level, with the exception of subcultural influences. It appears that life cycle was the most important set of social influences, and suburban environmental factors represented the single most influential set of independent variables. The variables with the greatest interaction with overall housing satisfaction are marital status, number of children, and income.

When we examine the overall community services satisfaction on Figure 4.2, it appears that the suburban environmental cluster becomes the overwhelmingly dominant set of influences, and subcultural influences decline to zero. Indeed, if we delete the variables significant at the 0.100

TABLE 4.35

Comparative Success Rate of Influence of Independent Variable Categories

| Overall Index of Satisfaction | Percent Significant[a] Independent Variables in each category | | | |
	Social Class	Subcultural	Life Cycle	Suburban Environmental
Housing environment	67 67[b]	25 25[b]	75 75[b]	67 56[b]
Community services	33 33[b]	0 0[b]	25 0[b]	78 78[b]
Social patterns	33 33[b]	25 25[b]	25 25[b]	56 45[b]
Psychological well-being	33 0[b]	25 25[b]	75 75[b]	11 0[b]

[a]Percentage independent variables found significant at the 0.100 level unless otherwise noted.

[b]Percentage independent variables found significant at the 0.050 level.

Source: compiled by the authors.

FIGURE 4.2

Comparative Influence of Independent Variable Categories on Overall Community Services Satisfaction

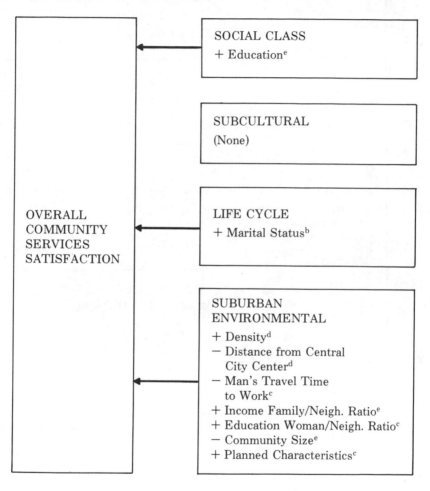

Source: compiled by the authors.

FIGURE 4.3

Comparative Influence of Independent Variable Categories on Overall Social Patterns Satisfaction

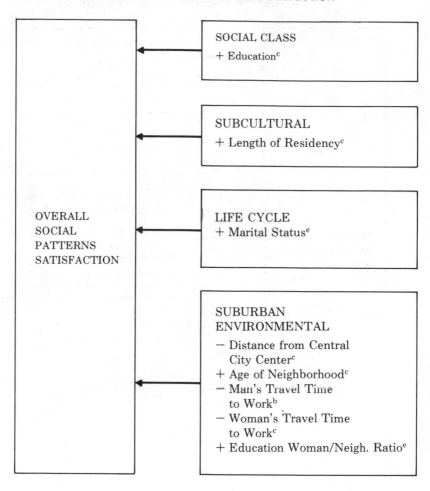

Source: compiled by the authors.

FIGURE 4.4

Comparative Influence of Independent Variable Categories on Overall Psychological Well-Being

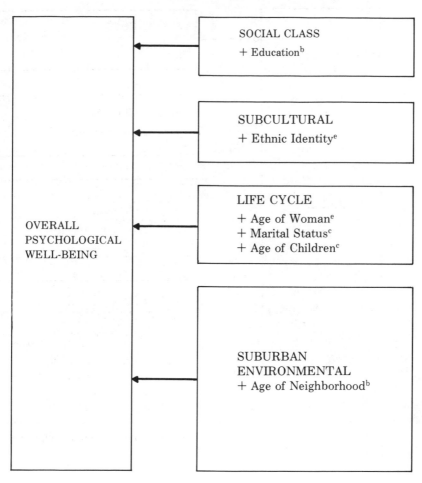

SOCIAL CLASS

+ Education[b]

SUBCULTURAL

+ Ethnic Identity[e]

LIFE CYCLE

+ Age of Woman[e]
+ Marital Status[c]
+ Age of Children[c]

OVERALL PSYCHOLOGICAL WELL-BEING

SUBURBAN ENVIRONMENTAL
+ Age of Neighborhood[b]

Legend

[b]t-test yields p $<$ 0.100
[c]t-test yields p $<$ 0.050
[d]t-test yields p $<$ 0.010
[e]t-test yields p $<$ 0.005

Source: compiled by the authors.

level, woman's education remains the only social influence on community service satisfaction. Other important single variables with high correlations are the environmental variables concerned with community size and degree of planned characteristics.

Figure 4.3 indicates a more equitable balance of social and environmental factors influencing overall social patterns satisfaction. Here the most important variables related to overall social satisfaction are concerned with education, marital status, and, to some extent, time— length of residency, age of neighborhood, and woman's travel time to work.

As shown in Figure 4.4, overall psychological well-being is almost entirely dominated by social influences, the most important of which is the life cycle cluster of variables. Only the modest 0.100 level relationship of age of neighborhood represents the total of environmental influences on psychological well-being. The individual variables that appear to have the greatest correlations are ethnic identity and age of woman.

In sum, it appears that the environmental factors have the greatest impact on the housing environment and community services, a moderate influence on social patterns, and a marginal effect on psychological well-being. By contrast, the social factors are overwhelmingly the most significant influences on psychological well-being, moderately important for the satisfaction with the housing environment and social patterns, and somewhat related to satisfaction with community services. The principle set of social forces appears to be those associated with the life cycle; and the least important appears to be subcultural influences.

These findings of the relationships between the theory-related clusters of independent variables and overall satisfaction indexes corroborate the findings of other recent studies:[14] While environmental factors can influence substantially satisfaction with housing and community services, such factors tend to have a limited impact on the more global feelings of psychological well-being. For this latter, and perhaps most important aspect of the quality of life, it seems that we must depend on the characteristics of the people themselves.

NOTES

1. Proposition 13 is the Jarvis-Gann Property Tax Initiative passed in California in 1978 in order to limit the expenditures of local government.

2. Nathan Glazer and Daniel Patrick Moynihan, *Beyond the Melting Pot* (Cambridge, Mass.: MIT Press, 1963).

3. See Melvin M. Webber, "Order in Diversity: Community Without Propinquity," in *Cities and Space*, ed. Lowdon Wingo (Baltimore, Md.: Johns Hopkins Press, 1963), pp. 23–56; and "The Urban Place and the Non-Place Urban Realm," in *Explorations into Urban Structure*, ed. Melvin M. Webber et al. (Philadelphia: University of Pennsylvania Press, 1964), pp. 79–153.

4. Angus Campbell, Philip E. Converse, and Willard L. Rodgers, *The Quality of American Life* (New York: Russell Sage Foundation, 1976).

5. Ibid., p. 414.

6. Helen Z. Lopata, *Occupation Housewife* (New York: Oxford University Press, 1971), p. 71.

7. Campbell, Converse, and Rodgers, *Quality of American Life*, p. 411.

8. Ibid., p. 421.

9. Lynne M. Jones, "The Labor Forge Participation of Married Women" (Masters thesis, University of California, Berkeley, 1974).

10. Claude S. Fischer and Robert M. Jackson, "Suburbs Networks and Attitudes," in *The Changing Face of the Suburbs*, ed. Barry Schwartz (Chicago: University of Chicago Press, 1976), pp. 279–307.

11. W. Bruce Shepard, "Metropolitan Political Decentralization: A Test of the Life-Style Value Model," *Urban Affairs Quarterly* 10 (1975): 297–313.

12. William Michelson, *Environmental Choice, Human Behavior and Resident Satisfaction* (New York: Oxford University Press, 1977).

13. See, for example, Fischer and Jackson, "Suburbs Networks and Attitudes"; and Robert B. Zehner *Indicators of the Quality of Life in New Communities* (Cambridge, Mass.: Ballinger, 1977).

14. Zehner, *Quality of Life*.

5

IMPLICATIONS FOR WOMEN AND THE FUTURE OF URBAN AMERICA

At the outset of our work we expressed a concern for women in suburbia. In particular, we asked ourselves how women with small children are faring in the environments purported to be especially designed for them—middle and upper middle-class suburbs of the United States. How could these environments be improved to make life more rewarding for women? What are the implications of these changes for our metropolitan areas? We addressed these questions from three different perspectives: an historical framework of suburbanization, changes in women's status, and our own cross-sectional study of suburban women. Our historical approach suggests that we may be at the end of an expansive era of suburban growth and on the threshold of a period of measured development heavily constrained by increasingly severe economic and resource-oriented burdens.

While our historical view portrays a future of women increasing their labor force participation for primarily economic reasons, a feminist analysis sees this phenomenon as the logical outgrowth of increased female independence. Indeed, we have seen how rapidly the consciousness of women has been raised as a mass movement in the United States during the last two decades. Changes in social structures also suggest that an increasing number of households will be headed by women. All indications are that while there may be some short-run contradictions due to cultural carry-overs of longstanding women's roles, women will continue to press for and attain a more equitable share of our nation's social and economic rewards outside the home.

Our own study of women in suburbia indicates that environmental factors have little impact on women's overall sense of happiness or psychological well-being. Social influences (particularly the life cycle factors of age of women, marital status, and age of children) and ethnic identity and education seem to be the independent variables most strongly related to overall sense of well-being. However, environmental influences appear to be important in other aspects of our study. We found that either older inlying neighborhoods of single-family homes or new, outlying, planned, higher density residential areas provide more satisfying housing for women than conventional suburban developments, new, low density areas of single-family homes built in small, less planned increments near the edge of metropolitan area. While it seems clear that residents of smaller suburban political units do enjoy greater satisfaction with community services compared to their central city counterparts, we also discovered that older inlying neighborhoods can provide superior social rewards, such as a rich friendship pattern and a deep sense of belonging.

What do these multi-faceted views suggest for the future of women and urban America?

SOCIAL IMPLICATIONS

Life cycle variables appear to be the social variables with the greatest impact on satisfaction with suburban life. Specifically, marital status appears most often as the variable explaining satisfaction of every kind. The problems of unmarried women will persist for as long as social, religious, and political institutions continue to support the nuclear family lifestyle as superior to all others. Whether or not one believes that it is possible or desirable for the single-parent home to be as satisfying as the two-parent home, one must acknowledge that there will continue to be many divorces for the foreseeable future and that many more women than men will have primary custody of children. Public policy should continue to provide economic support for women and children who need it and most specifically should fund public childcare facilities and adequate public transportation systems. Educational and occupational discrimination against women must be eliminated in order to give the children of households headed by women a fair chance economically. Anti-discrimination legislation, affirmative action policies, and changing attitudes have had some impact in recent years, but as long as women earn only 57 cents for each dollar earned by men, it is evident that there is still much to be done.[1]

While not all women wish to marry and not all divorced women wish to remarry, there are many people who prefer a married lifestyle and have lacked the skills (or luck) to make such a relationship work. If it is true that married women are substantially happier than unmarried women in a suburban setting, perhaps it would be desirable for public policy to provide greater assistance to married couples who are struggling to maintain their marriages. Rather than coercive economic and tax policies or pious pronouncements from national figures, we would recommend more publicly supported marriage counseling and wider education regarding the factors that lead to successful marriages. Many divorces appear to result from archaic conceptions of marriage relationships. We would in no way encourage any person to get married or to remain married, but we would like to see those who choose a conjugal lifestyle to have as much support as possible in building and maintaining a satisfactory relationship.

The other life cycle variables that have implications for our discussion are a woman's age and the number and ages of her children. A feminist analysis would suggest that women in their middle years ought to be happy, fulfilled, and eager to face a variety of challenging options. To the contrary, we found that age varied negatively with almost all indicators of psychological well-being. Because our sample was limited to women with at least one school-age child, we cannot compare their satisfaction levels to those with no children or those whose children have left the home. However, other studies, such as that conducted by Campbell, Converse and Rodgers, suggest that older women in all three categories are freed from some of the stresses that accompany the early years of the childrearing cycle.[2] Curiously, our study showed that women's sense of psychological well-being increased as their children got older but decreased as they them-selves got older. Of course, children cannot age without their mother aging as well. On the face of it, this paradoxical finding might seem to argue for bearing children while one is young. In fact, the trend is in the other direction, with testimonials from many women that delaying childrearing has allowed them to achieve educational goals, get started on a career, and to establish clearer values about the kind of lives they want to lead.

Women who want to raise a family and pursue a career are usually forced to delay one or the other. Some women who choose to establish their careers first later decide not to have children. Other women who have children early may never complete their education or enter a career. When the relin-quishing of one goal in favor of the other is a true matter of conscious choice no problem exists. But for some women this is a decision made by default as they assume the roles of wife and mother. Men, of course, may also delay the attainment of personal or professional goals because demands from the other domain, but the choices here are largely economic. Men usually are not asked to give up several years of their professional growth in order to be parents. At the policy level, then, we recommend that the tasks of caring for a home and nurturing children be presented through the media and education as tasks appropriate for any adult. Men and women together can decide which parent should fulfill the primary responsibilities for home and childcare at any point. A national acceptance of this assumption could induce employers to be more open to flexible working schedules, such as job sharing and full to part-time working arrangements that might change from year to year as family demands changed. Employers might be willing to excuse fathers as well as mothers for occasional parenting responsibilities, such as caring for a sick child or visiting a teacher.

A second major policy implication of our findings is that women should be encouraged to widen their options in their middle and later years. For men, the years between 30 and 50 are considered to be the most productive phase of their lives. It is unfortunate that women have been so influenced by the youth culture that some of them consider themselves to be past their peak when their last child starts school. Many universities offer special scholarships and re-entry programs for women who are returning to higher education after a long break in formal schooling. The national development of women's studies programs helps women to understand their own life experiences in a cultural and historical context and provides models of female achievement. Counseling programs for women and their families can ease the adjustment to new roles for women. Some industries are coming to recognize the special skills and insights of women who have managed homes and handled major responsibilities as community volunteers. In order to minimize the psychological distress implicit in our findings and to prevent an unconscionable waste of talent, we recommend the continuation and expansion of these programs which give financial and moral support to mature women.

Among the social class variables, education seemed to have more predictive power than income. The relatively minor impact of income on satisfaction should be viewed in the context of our sample population and of the rapid changes in the national economic picture that inevitably occur between the collection of data and the time it can be reported. It is almost certain that low-income groups' worries about providing for their most basic needs hamper their ability to find satisfaction in other aspects of life. For the relatively affluent participants in our study, though, it appears that additional increments of income buy larger and better housing but do not buy more satisfying friendships, psychological well-being, or humane and viable social services. However, gradually these people are starting to believe the environmentalists and economists who have been warning that our national and economic resources are finite and that we face an era when national and personal wealth may actually decrease.

At the policy level, we might add our voices to the chorus entreating national leaders to curb inflation and increase employment opportunities. More realistically, we also recommend that politicians, planners, and educators look to some models of other industrialized societies and groups within this country who have gracefully accepted the "less is more" philosophy. Ironically, a promising approach for dealing with the imperatives of a constricting economy may well lie in a social service greatly jeopardized by current trends—education.

Our research found that a woman's educational level correlated strongly with her satisfaction with community services, social patterns, and her psychological well-being. We do not believe that better educated women are happier because they are sitting in their living rooms reading Anais Nin. Education implies more than classical intellectual training or refined aesthetic standards. We suspect that educated women are happier in suburbia because they are better able to take advantage of the many opportunities available. A person who takes an essentially passive stance toward her environment will probably find suburbia bland and socially barren compared to either urban or small town life. An educated person is more likely to see herself in an active role with the power to shape her own experience. Education develops self-knowledge and an awareness of one's own preferences, skills, and needs. Education, particularly in the social sciences, develops an understanding of contemporary life and the social and cultural patterns that may differ from the time and place where one grew up. Education develops intellectual abilities needed for rewarding careers outside the house, and education provides the social and interpersonal skills to reach out to others and initiate friendships, organize groups, and also to set limits, resist domination, and protect one's own need for privacy. An educated person is more likely to know how to get the information she needs. She will call the sanitation department to complain about the storm sewers and the park and recreation department to find out about programs for her children. Consequently, community services seem more satisfactory to her. A well-educated person will seek out interesting classes, workshops, lectures, concerts, and art exhibits, many of which are free through community colleges or shopping centers. Just as women have to develop skills as consumers, suburban residents have to develop skills in using and appreciating the resources of their communities. Formal education, though not essential to the development of such skills, is certainly useful.

It is almost a cliché to recommend education as the solution for every social ill, from racism to sexism to environmental waste, and it is never a surprise when professional educators place a high value on the activity around which they have centered their lives. Nonetheless, the data from our own study and many others give us grounds for the particular urgency with which we press the following recommendation. Educational opportunities should be expanded for women at all levels in order to allow them to participate fully in the broad spectrum of qualitative benefits of society. Education for all persons, male and female, should emphasize personal autonomy and develop awareness of the cultural and environmental factors that can lead to fulfilling lives without constantly expanding material resources. Moreover, the funding of education must be pegged to some criteria other than enrollment due to bearish demographic trends. Elementary, secondary, and higher public education are all threatened by taxpayer's revolts as well, yet our study indicates that education, even as imperfectly conceived as it is at present, can enhance the quality of women's lives.[3]

Of the three sets of variables employed in our study that could be considered social factors, the subcultural variables had the least impact on the various indexes of satisfaction. However, the emergence of a relationship between a strong sense of ethnic identity and psychological well-being is a potentially important finding that bears further investigation. In a society where the price of mobility and flexibility may be the loss of stability, those who have strong ties with their ethnic heritage may have a sense of rootedness that serves an important psychic function. Our findings seem to offer tentative support for those educational and social programs aimed at fostering ethnic pride and identity. Rather than being divisive, as some might have feared, the encouragement of a sense of cultural identity appears to create a strong and healthy self-concept. It is important to note that our data refer to persons from many backgrounds who claimed a strong sense of ethnic or cultural identity, whether they are from traditionally oppressed groups, such as blacks and Mexican-Americans, or whether they belong to more culturally assimilated, "ex-ethnic" groups of European nationalities. Programs developing a sense of personal history and pride in heritage should be expanded for all persons as a possible antidote to the homogeneity and anonymity of suburban life.

ENVIRONMENTAL IMPLICATIONS

With regard to the influence of environmental factors, our study reveals that with the possible exception of age of neighborhood these factors have little effect on woman's overall sense of well-being. Perhaps this finding should not be surprising in that behavior has been shown to be more effectively explained by personal characteristics than by environmental variables.[4] Indeed, our findings corroborate those of Zehner in his study of quality of life in new communities: "Aspects of the residential environment (including whether or not an area is planned) have only a limited impact on overall life satisfaction."[5]

While these findings suggest limitations of environmental influences on the global sense of life satisfaction for a relatively well-off population, it is not clear that the same result would occur with different socioeconomic and cultural groups.[6] Moreover, our study finds that environmental factors are

often important influences on the satisfaction of other quality of life
aspects, such as housing, community services, and social patterns. Thus,
environmental planning and design may indeed make important contributions to a convenient and generally supportive context for our lives,
but it may be too much to expect that environmental factors themselves
would produce happier lives.

Our study also reveals the desirability of older, inlying, single-family
neighborhoods for women with children. Apparently, in such neighborhoods the benefits of design and visual familiarity, accessibility to the
metropolitan center, especially for employment opportunities, and a
supportive, diverse, and ongoing social structure can outweigh the costs of
lower satisfaction with home maintenance and certain public services, such
as schools. This finding is similar to what Michelson uncovered about the
desirability of single-family housing near downtown Toronto.[7] It suggests
that governments of central cities and perhaps inlying suburbs should
prevent the destruction of their older neighborhoods through urban
renewal (public or private) and explore the possibility of conserving and
rehabilitating such residential areas. This could be examined not only from
the perspective of improving the ease of home maintenance through
incentives for home repair (such as publicly supported loan programs), but
also with an eye to upgrading local public services, particularly schools. As
we discuss later, the forces to equalize the quality of metropolitan-wide
public services will probably make this inlying rehabilitation approach
more feasible over time.

This apparent desirability of older housing environments also suggests
the importance of building future new towns or large-scale housing
developments as extensions of existing communities, like the British
expanded towns, rather than as free-standing, totally new entities. Further,
an urban aesthetic in new development would create a sense of continuity
that is lacking in the raw venues of traditional speculative construction.
Such a philosophy of design has been heartily embraced in the Netherlands.
It is hoped that such an approach would tie the residents of new
development to the stability of the ongoing social structure in the existing
community.

Another major finding of our study is that in relatively new outlying
residential areas, planned higher density developments, such as condominiums and planned unit developments, appear to have more desirable
housing and community services than conventional single-family neighborhoods, not only for women who are single and working but for all women
with young children. These findings were based on the apparent superiority
of the higher density areas with regard to easier homeownership responsibilities, a greater sense of security, and the accessibility to other community
services, such as childcare and usable open space. Since these planned

areas offer housing and services which are more supportive and less demanding of women with children than are less planned areas, they tend to attract a relatively high percentage of women with considerable pressure on their time and energy—working women, especially those in demanding jobs, and women who are single parents.

As it seems likely that an increasing percentage of women will be working and will become more independent in the future, it seems probable that the demand for planned, higher density housing environments will increase substantially. Therefore, it would be useful for suburban communities to encourage increasing the supply of new higher density housing areas in the form of completely planned neighborhoods with appropriate support services and socializing facilities, as well as with transportation linkages to educational, cultural, employment, and shopping activities. Not only will this mean institutional changes, such as revising suburban ordinances and building codes which often discriminate against multi-family housing,[8] but it will also require broad citizen participation in order to educate the public and the building industry about the positive social, economic, and environmental aspects of such housing and the potential market for its development.

Man's travel time to work was shown to have a negative impact on woman's satisfaction with housing, community services, and social patterns. While this does have a female-male social role bias which may lessen in the future, long commutes are still likely to exact a toll on the quality of family life. In addition, it was shown that woman's travel time can have substantial direct negative social and psychological effects on her. This suggests that efforts should be made to encourage land use and transportation policies that foster a more spatially compact metropolitan area, such as locating jobs closer to housing, in-filling new development on under-utilized inlying open space, building new residential areas in higher densities than single-family housing, and expanding public transportation facilities in order to tie the regional land use structure together efficiently. This, in turn, calls for a level of regional planning and management which has heretofore been difficult to attain due to the decentralized, polycentric political structure of our metropolitan areas.[9] Considerable public participation and education will then be required to inform the diverse metropolitan-wide constituencies about the wisdom to trading off some local autonomy for the benefits of regional management.[10]

Our study indicated that the residents of smaller political units have greater satisfaction with their public services than their central city counterparts. It was also suggested that the differences in satisfactions with these two sets of public service systems were based, in part, on income differences between the average households in the smaller suburban communities and the central city and that these localized differences create public service inequities as well as great difficulty in regional planning and management of our metropolitan areas.

Yet, some long-term forces may be emerging which could narrow the differences between the suburban and central city public services. For example, the recent economy drives to limit the cost of local government,[11] legal decisions designed to equalize the quality of local services, such as public education,[12] and the general increase in pressure from environmental and regional planning institutions to regulate the activities of local government.[13] In addition, the rapidly increasing costs for commutation, land, and single-family housing in outlying areas are likely to make central city neighborhoods and their public services relatively more attractive in the future.

However, these changes will probably occur slowly, since it seems likely that, where possible, citizens will try to continue to have great control over their local governments and public services. Thus, if this situation remains unchanged in the near future, central city neighborhoods will continue to be less desirable in terms of public services than many outlying suburban communities. For this reason there has been a growth of pressure within central cities to decentralize some of the more socially sensitive public services, such as police patrol and schools, in order to facilitate community control of neighborhoods.[14] We therefore suggest that central cities do whatever they can not only to upgrade the quality of public services but, wherever feasible, to decentralize authority, or create the "equivalents of sovereignty" for their neighborhoods to control the management of local public services. Such policies are likely to attract women associated with middle and upper middle-class households to the more accessible central city neighborhoods.

Another set of environmental findings of our study suggests that, while public services are an important criterion used by households for initial residential location choices, these contextual services may become less important than the direct housing design experience within a few years. While more research will be needed to verify this finding, it suggests the growing importance of the micro-environment, especially housing satisfaction, in the lives of women. Yet, our study questions from a woman's perspective the desirability of the housing environments that characterize much of the metropolitan United States—new outlying, single-family tract developments. Indeed, such environments may well be outdated and dysfunctional with respect to the changes in the status of women that have occurred during the past decade and are likely to develop in the near future. Perhaps our preliminary re-examination of the quality of suburban life will enable us to begin to accommodate these changes with greater sensitivity than has been shown in the past.

CONCLUDING THOUGHTS

At one time this country might have been classified into regions that were clearly urban, rural, and suburban, according to certain definable physical and demographic characteristics. By the mid-1970s, a far greater proportion of our national population lived in the suburbs than ever before, but the suburbs had changed drastically from the bedroom communities of an earlier age. As the United States has become a nation of franchises, cities and small towns have each become suburbanized, and the suburbs, paradoxically, have become more like small towns and more urban in nature.

As population concentrated in the suburbs, shopping facilities, entertainment and employment soon followed. Buder reports that in some larger suburbs as many as 70 to 80 percent of the working people are employed within their own borders.[15] While many residents continue to commute to the nearby urban center for employment and cultural enrichment, more and more suburban residents appear to center their activities in their own communities. We cited Wood's observation of the limited use that suburban dwellers made of central city facilities.[16] One could argue that this behavior pattern is reminiscent of the provincialism of small town life. Fischer and Jackson are among the writers who have described suburbia as constellations of small towns.[17] Our results offer some support for the view that suburbia functions as a series of small towns. Those people who grew up in small towns seemed to find suburbia most satisfying, suggesting that they found the general social patterns familiar and comfortable. Our respondents who lived in the smaller suburban communities of Los Gatos and Cupertino were generally more satisfied with the social and community dimensions of their lives. Also highly satisfied were the residents of Willow Glen, formerly a separate municipality, which still retains much of the character of a small town within San Jose. Quality of life research shows that small town residents are among the groups expressing the greatest satisfaction with their community attributes.[18] Creating small towns within suburbia, whether the trend takes the form of separate municipalities or just groups of neighborhoods with some sort of central focus, may fill many people's need for a sense of community and identity.

At the same time that the physical layout and socialization patterns of suburbia are tending toward a small town orientation, the character of the population seems to be becoming more urbanized. While the traditional suburbs were dominated by nuclear families in the childrearing years of the life cycle, our research and review of literature show that contemporary suburbia attracts single adults, divorced parents, childless couples, senior citizens, and many other groups that characterize the heterogeneity of urban areas. These are the groups who do not seem to partake of the small town aspects of suburbia. Specifically, working women, single women, and women with strong ethnic ties report that they do most of their socializing outside their neighborhoods. For these nontraditional groups, suburbia works more like a greener and less dense urban area. They live in relative isolation from their immediate neighbors and seek friendship and group participation via non-spatial routes.

There is no need for conflict between those groups who wish to treat suburbia as a small town environment and those who wish to experience it as a more urban environment. Those areas between city and country can be envisioned as a checkerboard pattern of small town centers whose facilities are shared by residents of high and low density housing with both traditional and nontraditional lifestyles. As mentioned earlier, in terms of public policy it is important that the needs of the urban suburbanite not be subordinated to those of the small town suburbanite. Therefore, planned multi-family housing should be encouraged and not be relegated to undesirable areas, and public transportation should be expanded and not neglected in favor of the automobile.

Our society should not try to force all suburban women into the mold of the white, middle-class, full-time housewife and mother. That role as well as many others can easily be accommodated if creative planning and design provide for a variety of housing and lifestyles. One important step toward the achievement of this goal is the involvement of many more women in the professions of planning and architecture so that they may express their needs more directly.[19] Suburbia can represent the worst features of both rural and urban living or it can represent the best of both. Open and responsible social planning and a well-educated population can allow each suburban dweller to assemble a housing and social environment ideally tailored to her or his individual goals.

We realize that many of our proposals for the future development of urban areas are not new. For many years, others have argued in favor of regional planning for a more compact and socially and physically heterogeneous metropolitan area, for economic, social, political, and environmental reasons.[20] Indeed, as housing and commutation costs escalate, pressures for cost-reducing and energy-efficient inlying and planned higher density housing and for more public transportation are likely to mount anyway. What we have to add to this discussion about metropolitan areas is that these planning concepts make sense for still other very important reasons—for our urban society to facilitate equal opportunities for women and to accommodate the inevitable social changes related to this process. Perhaps now that we recognize the breadth of our community of interests, we will be able to effect these long sought after metropolitan changes.

NOTES

1. Lindsay Van Gelder, "Strains of 'Oh Promise Me' Emanating From the White House," *San Jose News* (February 8, 1979).

2. Angus Campbell, Philip E. Converse, and William L. Rodgers, *The Quality of American Life: Perceptions, Evaluations, and Satisfactions* (New York: Russell Sage Foundation, 1976), p. 405.

3. For another study with positive findings about the educational benefits for women, see Ibid., pp. 424–29.

4. Claude S. Fischer and Robert Max Jackson, "Suburbs, Networks and Attitudes," in *The Changing Face of the Suburbs,* ed. Barry Schwartz (Chicago: University of Chicago Press, 1976) pp. 279–309.

5. Robert B. Zehner, *Indicators of the Quality of Life in New Communities* (Cambridge, Mass.: Ballinger, 1977), p. 15.

6. Donald N. Rothblatt, "Improving the Design of Urban Housing," in *Urban Housing,* ed. Vasily Kouskoulas (Detroit, Mich.: National Science Foundation, 1973), pp. 149–54.

7. William Michelson, *Environmental Choice, Human Behavior, and Residential Satisfaction* (New York: Oxford University Press, 1977).

8. For a discussion on discriminatory zoning, see Paul Davidoff and Mary E. Brooks, "Zoning Out the Poor," in *Suburbia: The American Dream and Dilemma,* ed. Philip C. Dolce (New York: Anchor Press, 1976), pp. 135–66.

9. Donald N. Rothblatt, "Multiple Advocacy: An Approach to Metropolitan Planning," *Journal of the American Institute of Planners* 44 (April 1978): 193–99.

10. Ibid., pp. 196–98.

11. An example of economy drives for public sector activities is the Jarvis-Gann Property Tax Initiative (Proposition 13) passed in California in 1978 in order to limit the expenditures of local government.

12. Efforts to equalize the quality of local public services is demonstrated by the 1971 California Supreme Court decision, Serrano vs. Priest, which requires the equalization of available financial support per pupil in school districts throughout the state. Despite this trend, there is evidence suggesting that citizens may not be aware of qualitative differences in their local public services. See Brian Stipak, "Citizen Satisfaction with Urban Services: Potential Misuse as a Performance Indicator," *Public Administration Review* 39 (January-February 1979): 46–52.

13. Rothblatt, "Multiple Advocacy," p. 97.

14. Robert L. Bish and Hugh O. Nourse, *Urban Economics and Policy Analysis* (New York: McGraw-Hill, 1975), pp. 204–07.

15. Stanley Buder, "The Future of the American Suburbs," in Dolce, *Suburbia,* p. 205.

16. Robert C. Wood, *Suburbia: It's People and Their Politics* (Boston; Houghton-Mifflin, 1958) p. 107.

17. Fischer and Jackson, "Suburbs, Networks and Attitudes," pp. 299–304.

18. Campbell, Converse, and Rodgers, *Quality of American Life,* p. 236.

19. Rebecca Peterson, Gerda R. Wekerle, and David Morley, "Women and Environments: An Overview of An Emerging Field," *Environment and Behavior* 10 (December 1978): 511–34. Diana Sherman, "Feminists Advocate Rezoning, Transit: Suburbs Lambasted at UCLA Conference," *Los Angeles Times* (April 29, 1979): ix–2.

20. See, for example, the work of Luther Gulick, "Metropolitan Organization" *Annals of the American Academy of Political and Social Science* 314 (November 1957): 57–65.

APPENDIX A
QUESTIONNAIRE SCHEDULE

Address _____ Date _____

Census Tract _____ Household Number____

1. Background Information

    a. Marital Status _____   b. Duration of Marital Status (years)_____

Married	5
Widowed	4
Separated	3
Divorced	2
Single	1

    c.1 Number of children living in your home _____ c.2. Ages _____

    d. Do you rent or own this home? ____ Rent _1_ Own _2_

	Woman	Man	(if appropriate)

    e. Age (years)   _____ _____

    f. Length of Residence in Present
       Home (years)   _____ _____

    g. Years of Education Completed   ˙_____ _____

Grade School (0–8 yrs.)	1
High School (9–12 yrs.)	2
Some College (13–15 yrs.)	3
Bachelors Degree (16 yrs.)	4
Some Graduate School (17 yrs.)	5
Graduate Degree (18+ yrs.)	6

    h. Occupation   _____ _____

    i. Please tell me the letter of the group on this card that would indicate
       what the total income for your household was last year—1975—before
       taxes, that is. _____

a. $0 = 1,999	1	g. $22 = 23,999	12
b. $2 = 3,999	2	h. $12 = 13,999	7
c. $4 = 5,999	3	i. $14 = 15,999	8
d. $6 = 7,999	4	j. $16 = 17,999	9
e. $8 = 9,999	5	k. $18 = 19,999	10
f. $10 = 11,999	6	l. $20 = 21,999	11

m. $24 = 25,999	13	r. $34 = 35,999	18
n. $26 = 27,999	14	s. $36 = 37,999	19
o. $28 = 29,999	15	t. $38 = 39,999	20
p. $30 = 31,999	16	t. $38 = 39,999	20
q. $32 = 33,999	17	u. $40,000 and over	21+

j. About how far away is your place of work from here?

	Miles	Time
Woman	_____	_____
Man	_____	_____

k. Where did you live most of the time while you were growing up—in the country, in a small town, in a suburb of a large city, or in a large city?

_____

country __1__ small town __2__ suburb of a large city __3__
large city __4__

l.1. Was this in the San Jose area? ____ yes __2__ no __1__

   2. If no, where? _____

m. About how old is the house in which you now live? _____

n. Do you identify with any ethnic or cultural group? _____

   yes ___--___ no ___1___

If yes, which group? _____

How strongly do you identify with this group? _____

not strongly   very strongly

2. Housing Environment

   a. Personal and Family Privacy

      1. Do neighbors drop in when you'd rather they would not? _____

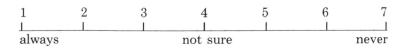

always   not sure   never

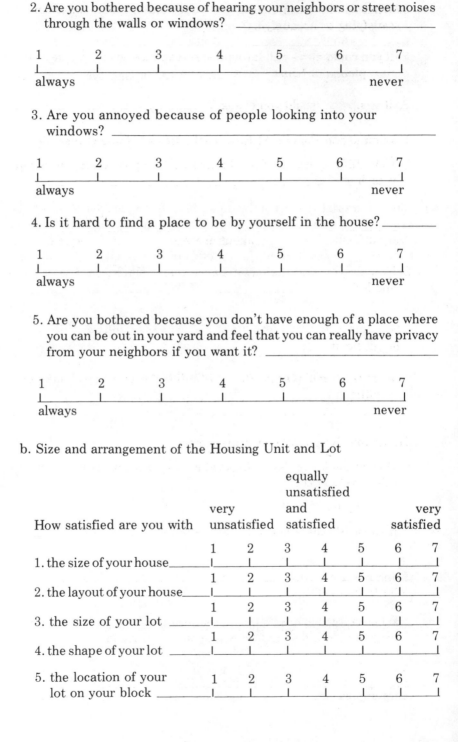

2. Are you bothered because of hearing your neighbors or street noises through the walls or windows? _____

1	2	3	4	5	6	7
always						never

3. Are you annoyed because of people looking into your windows? _____

1	2	3	4	5	6	7
always						never

4. Is it hard to find a place to be by yourself in the house?_____

1	2	3	4	5	6	7
always						never

5. Are you bothered because you don't have enough of a place where you can be out in your yard and feel that you can really have privacy from your neighbors if you want it? _____

1	2	3	4	5	6	7
always						never

b. Size and arrangement of the Housing Unit and Lot

How satisfied are you with	very unsatisfied		equally unsatisfied and satisfied			very satisfied	
	1	2	3	4	5	6	7
1. the size of your house_____							
2. the layout of your house____	1	2	3	4	5	6	7
3. the size of your lot _____	1	2	3	4	5	6	7
4. the shape of your lot _____	1	2	3	4	5	6	7
5. the location of your lot on your block _____	1	2	3	4	5	6	7

6. What is the main reason for your finding your house and lot satisfying or unsatisfying?

_____

7. If you could move walls around at no expense, would you be anxious to replan your house?   yes __1__ no __2__

8. If yes, what would you change? _____

c. Economic and Functional Responsibilities of Home Ownership

1. How difficult do you find the financial responsibilities of owning your home? _____

```
1        2        3        4        5        6        7
|_____|_____|_____|_____|_____|_____|
very difficult        about average        very easy
```

2. How do you find the maintenance responsibilities for your home and lot? _____

```
1        2        3        4        5        6        7
|_____|_____|_____|_____|_____|_____|
very difficult                          very easy
```

3. What is the main reason for your finding these responsibilities easy or difficult?

_____

d. House and Neighborhood Appearance

1. Do you think your house looks like most of the other houses within this development?

yes __1__ no __2__

How satisfied are you with this situation? _____

```
1        2        3        4        5        6        7
|_____|_____|_____|_____|_____|_____|
very dissatisfied                       very satisfied
```

2. When you go outside and look around at the streets and homes in the neighborhood, do you find what you see pleasant? _____

```
1        2        3        4        5        6        7
|_____|_____|_____|_____|_____|_____|
very unpleasant                         very pleasant
```

3. What is the main reason for your finding the appearance of your house and neighborhood pleasant or unpleasant?

_____

e. Location

1. Would you indicate the four most important reasons (in order of importance) you have for living where you do? (Please indicate "1" next to the most important reason, and so on.)

   (1) quality of public schools _____
   (2) location of work _____
   (3) cost of housing _____
   (4) type or design of house _____
   (5) social style of neighborhood _____
   (6) appearance of neighborhood _____
   (7) prestige of area _____
   (8) close to shopping _____
   (9) near friends and or relatives _____
  (10) near church or temple _____
  (11) near cultural activities _____
  (12) near the country _____
  (13)   near parks and recreation _____

2. Where did you live just before you moved to your present home— in the country, in a small town, in a suburb of a large city or in a large city? _____

country __1__ small town __2__ suburb or large city __3__
large city __4__

3. Was this in the San Jose area? ____ yes __2__ no __1__

b. If no, where? _____

4. All things considered, are you happier here, or in your previous home? _____

1	2	3	4	5	6	7
much unhappier			about the same			much happier

5. Would you indicate the four most important reasons (in order of importance) you have for feeling this way about your present home compared to your previous home? (Please indicate "1" next to the most important reason, and so on.) __

   (1) quality of public schools _____
   (2) location of work _____
   (3) cost of housing _____
   (4) type or design of house _____
   (5) social style of neighborhood _____
   (6) appearance of neighborhood _____
   (7) prestige of area _____
   (8) close to shopping _____
   (9) near friends and or relatives _____
 (10) near church or temple _____
 (11) near cultural activities _____
 (12) near the country _____
 (13) near parks and recreation _____

3. Community Services

  a. Parks and open space

    1. One of the things I like about this neighborhood is that parks are no further than a convenient walk away. _____

1	2	3	4	5	6	7
strongly disagree			no opinion			strongly agree

    2. I believe nearby parks are safe. _____

1	2	3	4	5	6	7
strongly disagree						strongly agree

    3. Our parks have what I consider to be sufficient facilities and activity programs for people of all ages. _____

1	2	3	4	5	6	7
strongly disagree						strongly agree

    4. How many times during an average month do you and your family use neighborhood parks? _____

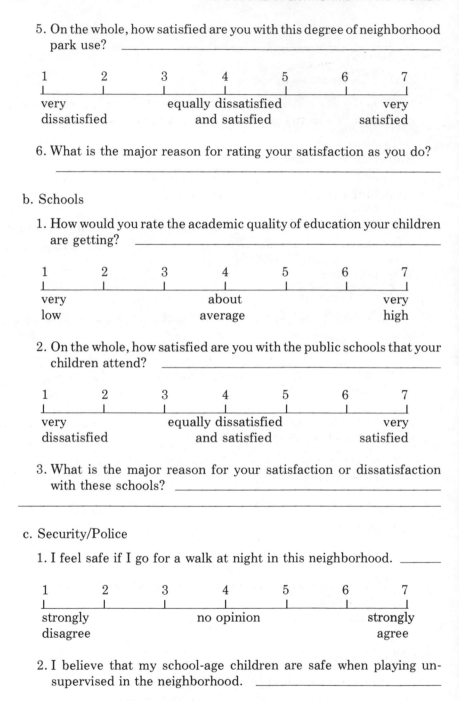

5. On the whole, how satisfied are you with this degree of neighborhood park use? _____

```
1        2        3        4        5        6        7
|_____|_____|_____|_____|_____|_____|
very              equally dissatisfied              very
dissatisfied          and satisfied              satisfied
```

6. What is the major reason for rating your satisfaction as you do?
_____

b. Schools

1. How would you rate the academic quality of education your children are getting? _____

```
1        2        3        4        5        6        7
|_____|_____|_____|_____|_____|_____|
very                     about                      very
low                     average                     high
```

2. On the whole, how satisfied are you with the public schools that your children attend? _____

```
1        2        3        4        5        6        7
|_____|_____|_____|_____|_____|_____|
very              equally dissatisfied              very
dissatisfied          and satisfied              satisfied
```

3. What is the major reason for your satisfaction or dissatisfaction with these schools? _____

c. Security/Police

1. I feel safe if I go for a walk at night in this neighborhood. _____

```
1        2        3        4        5        6        7
|_____|_____|_____|_____|_____|_____|
strongly             no opinion                 strongly
disagree                                           agree
```

2. I believe that my school-age children are safe when playing un-supervised in the neighborhood. _____

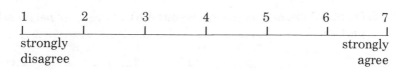

```
1        2        3        4        5        6        7
L_____L_____L_____L_____L_____L_____L
strongly                                         strongly
disagree                                           agree
```

3. On the whole, how satisfied are you with the police protection and sense of security you have in your neighborhood? _____

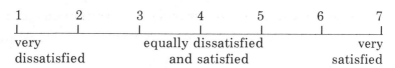

```
1        2        3        4        5        6        7
L_____L_____L_____L_____L_____L_____L
very              equally dissatisfied            very
dissatisfied        and satisfied              satisfied
```

4. What is the major reason for rating your satisfaction as you do?

_____

d. Child Care

1. Our community does enough to help the working mother. _____

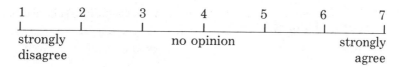

```
1        2        3        4        5        6        7
L_____L_____L_____L_____L_____L_____L
strongly              no opinion              strongly
disagree                                         agree
```

2. How many times during an average week do you use day care facilities (including baby sitters)? _____

3. On the whole, how satisfied are you with day care facilities available to you? _____

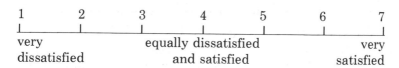

```
1        2        3        4        5        6        7
L_____L_____L_____L_____L_____L_____L
very              equally dissatisfied            very
dissatisfied        and satisfied              satisfied
```

4. What is the major reason for your satisfaction or dissatisfaction with these facilities? _____

_____

e. Transportation

1. How many cars does your family have? _____

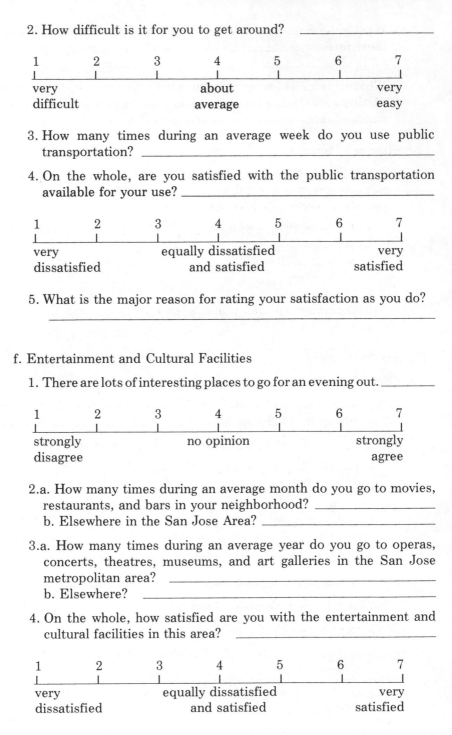

2. How difficult is it for you to get around? _____

```
1        2        3        4        5        6        7
|_____|_____|_____|_____|_____|_____|
very                    about                    very
difficult               average                  easy
```

3. How many times during an average week do you use public transportation? _____

4. On the whole, are you satisfied with the public transportation available for your use? _____

```
1        2        3        4        5        6        7
|_____|_____|_____|_____|_____|_____|
very              equally dissatisfied          very
dissatisfied        and satisfied               satisfied
```

5. What is the major reason for rating your satisfaction as you do?

_____

f. Entertainment and Cultural Facilities

1. There are lots of interesting places to go for an evening out. _____

```
1        2        3        4        5        6        7
|_____|_____|_____|_____|_____|_____|
strongly                no opinion              strongly
disagree                                        agree
```

2.a. How many times during an average month do you go to movies, restaurants, and bars in your neighborhood? _____
b. Elsewhere in the San Jose Area? _____

3.a. How many times during an average year do you go to operas, concerts, theatres, museums, and art galleries in the San Jose metropolitan area? _____
b. Elsewhere? _____

4. On the whole, how satisfied are you with the entertainment and cultural facilities in this area? _____

```
1        2        3        4        5        6        7
|_____|_____|_____|_____|_____|_____|
very              equally dissatisfied          very
dissatisfied        and satisfied               satisfied
```

5. What is the major reason for your satisfaction or dissatisfaction with these facilities? _____

   _____

6. What other kind of entertainment activity do you and/or your family participate in? _____

   _____

g. Finance of Services

1. Of all these services, which would you be willing to spend more money on (either tax dollars or your own)? Please check the appropriate services listed below.

   a. Parks and Open Space _____
   b. Schools _____
   c. Security/Police _____
   d. Child Care _____
   e. Transportation _____
   f. Entertainment and Cultural Facilities _____
   g. Other (specify) _____

4. Social Patterns

a. Friendships

1. How many people within this neighborhood (within 5 minutes from your home) do you speak to? _____

2. With how many of your intimate neighbors could you:

   a. talk to about topics of general interest? _____

   b. borrow things from? _____

   c. call on for aid during a crisis (such as illness), child care, errands, etc.? _____

   d. ask help with a project such as home repair? _____

   e. talk to about a personal problem? _____

3. How many close friends do you have:

   a. in your neighborhood? _____

   b. in other sections of the San Jose metropolitan area (Santa Clara County)? _____

   c. outside the San Jose metropolitan area, but within an hour's drive? _____

d. farther away? _____

4. How difficult do you find meeting people and establishing friendships? _____

```
1        2        3        4        5        6        7
|_____|_____|_____|_____|_____|_____|
very                    about                      very
difficult               average                    easy
```

5. What is the major reason for your finding meeting people and
   establishing friendships easy or difficult?

   _____

6. On the whole, how satisfied are you with:

```
1        2        3        4        5        6        7
|_____|_____|_____|_____|_____|_____|
very                                              very
dissatisfied                                      satisfied
```

   a. the kind of friendships you have in your neighborhood? _____

   b. the kind of friendships you have in the rest of the San Jose
      metropolitan area? _____

7. What is the major reason for your satisfaction or dissatisfaction
   with these patterns of friendships?

   _____

b. Group Participation

   1. How involved are you in each of these kinds of groups:

```
1        2        3        4        5        6        7
|_____|_____|_____|_____|_____|_____|
not involved                          organizer
at all                                or leader
```

   a. informal social groups in your neighborhood (bridge clubs,
      etc.) _____

   b. action projects in your neighborhood (co-ops, child care,
      improvement assoc.) _____

   c. groups related to your children's activities (P.T.A., cub
      scouts) _____

   d. religious groups _____

e. political organizations _____

f. informal groups outside your neighborhood _____

g. action groups outside your neighborhood (League of Women Voters, Sierra Club) _____

h. organized social groups outside your neighborhood (Sororities, lodges, clubs) _____

i. other organized groups _____

2. On the whole, how satisfied are you with:

```
1         2         3         4         5         6         7
|_____|_____|_____|_____|_____|_____|
very                  equally dissatisfied            very
dissatisfied             and satisfied             satisfied
```

a. the kind of opportunities for group participation in your neighborhood? _____

b. the kind of opportunities for group participation available in the San Jose Metropolitan Area? _____

3. What is the major reason for your satisfaction or dissatisfaction with these group involvements? _____

_____

c. Sense of Belonging

1. How closely do you identify with (feel in tune with) your neighborhood? _____

```
1         2         3         4         5         6         7
|_____|_____|_____|_____|_____|_____|
not closely                                          very
at all                                             closely
```

2. On the whole, how satisfied are you with this degree of identification? _____

```
1         2         3         4         5         6         7
|_____|_____|_____|_____|_____|_____|
very                  equally dissatisfied            very
dissatisfied             and satisfied             satisfied
```

3. What is the major reason for rating your satisfaction as you do?

_____

5. Psychological Well-Being

Please indicate your personal feelings (ranked 1 to 10) during the past month for the following categories:

a.　Fullness vs. Emptiness of Life (how emotionally satisfying, abundant or empty, your life felt) _____
10. Consummate fulfillment and abundance.
9. Replete with life's abundant goodness.
8. Filled with warm feelings of contentment and satisfaction.
7. My life is ample and satisfying.
6. Life seems fairly adequate and relatively satisfying.
5. Some slight sense of lack, vague and mildly troubling.
4. My life seems deficient, dissatisfying.
3. Life is pretty empty and barren
2. Desolate, drained dry, impoverished.
1. Gnawing sense of emptiness, hollowness, void.

b.　Receptivity towards and Stimulation by the World (how interested and responsive you felt to what was going on around you) _____
10. Passionately absorbed in the world's excitement. My sensations and feelings incredibly intensified.
9. Tremendously stimulated. Enormously receptive.
8. Senses lively. Great interest and delight in everything around me.
7. Open and responsive to my world and its happenings.
6. Moderately interested and fairly responsive.
5. Slightly disinterested and unresponsive.
4. Bored. Life is pretty monotonous and uninteresting.
3. Dull and apathetic. Almost no interest or desire for anything.
2. Mired down in apathy. My only desire is to shut out the world.
1. Life is too much trouble. Sick of everything, want only oblivion.

c.　Social Respect vs. Social Contempt (how you felt other people regarded you, or felt about you) _____
10. Excite the admiration and awe of everyone who matters.
9. Stand extremely high in the estimation of people whose opinions count with me.
8. People I admire recognize and respect my good points.
7. Confident that some people think well of me.
6. Feel I am appreciated and respected to some degree.
5. Some people don't seem to see much value in me.
4. I am looked upon as being of small or of no account.
3. People have no respect for me at all.
2. I am scorned, slighted, pushed aside.
1. Everyone despises me and holds me in contempt.

d. Personal Freedom vs. External Constraint (how much you felt you were free or not free to do as you wanted) _____

    10. Absolutely free to consider and try any new and adventuresome prospect.

    9. Independent and free to do as I like.

    8. Ample scope to go my own way.

    7. Free, within broad limits, to act as I want to.

    6. Can do a good deal on my own initiative and in my own fashion. No particularly restrictive limitations.

    5. Somewhat constrained and hampered. Not free to do things my own way.

    4. Checked and hindered by too many demands and constraints.

    3. Hemmed in, cooped up. Forced to do things I don't want to do.

    2. Trapped, oppressed.

    1. Overwhelmed, smothered. Can't draw a free breath.

e. Own Sociability vs. Withdrawal (how socially outgoing or withdrawn you felt _____

    10. Immensely sociable and outgoing.

    9. Highly outgoing, congenial and friendly.

    8. Very sociable and involved in things.

    7. Companionable. Ready to mix with others.

    6. Fairly sociable. More or less accessible.

    5. Not particularly outgoing. Feel a little bit unsociable.

    4. Retiring, would like to avoid people.

    3. Feel detached and withdrawn. A great distance between myself and others.

    2. Self-contained and solitary.

    1. Completely withdrawn. Want no human contact.

f. Companionship vs. Being Isolated (the extent to which you felt emotionally accepted by, or isolated from other people) _____

    10. Complete participation in warm, intimate friendship.

    9. Enjoy the warmth of close companionship.

    8. Thoroughly and genuinely liked.

    7. Feel accepted and liked.

    6. More or less accepted.,

    5. Feel a little bit left out.

    4. Feel somewhat neglected and lonely.

    3. Very lonely. No one seems to care much about me.

    2. Tremendously lonely. Friendless and forlorn.

    1. Completely isolated and forsaken. Abandoned. Ache with loneliness.

g.   Present Work (how satisfied or dissatisfied you were with your work).

_____

10. Tremendous, intense delight in my work. Proud of my purpose, skill, and accomplishment.
 9. Great pleasure and enjoyment in my work. Much fulfillment through work.
 8. Considerable satisfaction with my work. Eager to continue.
 7. Satisfied with my work. Encouraged to go on with it.
 6. More or less satisfied with my work. Keep plugging along.
 5. Somewhat dissatisfied with my work. Not much enjoyment doing it.
 4. Dissatisfied with my work. Can't see much good in it. Moderately frustrated.
 3. Greatly dissatisfied with my work. Not doing a good job. Markedly frustrated.
 2. Tremendously dissatisfied and frustrated in my work. Befuddled. Disorganized.
 1. Completely dissatisfied and frustrated in my work. Hopeless, useless chaos.

h.   Tranquility vs. Anxiety (how calm or troubled you felt)   _____
10. Perfect and complete tranquility. Unshakably secure.
 9. Exceptional calm, wonderfully secure and carefree.
 8. Great sense of well-being. Essentially secure, and very much at ease.
 7. Pretty generally secure and free from care.
 6. Nothing particularly troubling me. More or less at ease.
 5. Somewhat concerned with minor worries or problems. Slightly ill at ease, a bit troubled.
 4. Experiencing some worry, fear, trouble, or uncertainty. Nervous, jittery, on edge.
 3. Considerable insecurity. Very troubled by significant worries, fears, uncertainties.
 2. Tremendous anxiety and concern. Harassed by major worries and fears.
 1. Completely beside myself with dread, worry, fear. Overwhelmingly distraught and apprehensive. Obsessed or terrified by insoluble problems and fears.

i.   Personal Moral Judgment (how self-approving, or how guilty, you felt)   _____
10. Have a transcendent feeling of moral perfection and virtue.
 9. I have a sense of extraordinary worth and goodness.
 8. In high favor with myself. Well up to my own best standards.
 7. Consider myself pretty close to my own best self.

6. By and large, measuring up to most of my moral standards.

5. Somewhat short of what I ought to be.

4. I have a sense of having done wrong.

3. Feel that I have failed morally.

2. Heavy laden with my own moral worthlessness.

1. In anguish. Tormented by guilt and self-loathing.

j. Self-Confidence vs. Feeling of Inadequacy (how self-assured and adequate, or helpless and inadequate, you felt) _____

10. Nothing is impossible to me. Can do anything I want.

9. Feel remarkable self-assurance. Sure of my superior powers.

8. Highly confident of my capabilities.

7. Feel my abilities sufficient and my prospects good.

6. Feel fairly adequate.

5. Feel my performance and capabilities somewhat limited.

4. Feel rather inadequate.

3. Distressed by my weakness and lack of ability.

2. Wretched and miserable. Sick of my own incompetence.

1. Crushing sense of weakness and futility. I can do nothing.

k. Energy vs. Fatigue (how energetic, or tired and weary, you felt)____

10. Limitless zeal. Surging with energy. Vitality spilling over.

9. Exuberant vitality, tremendous energy, great zeal for activity.

8. Great energy and drive.

7. Very fresh, considerable energy.

6. Fairly fresh. Adequate energy.

5. Slightly tired. Indolent. Somewhat lacking in energy.

4. Rather tired. Lethargic. Not much energy.

3. Great fatigue. Sluggish. Can hardly keep going. Meager resources.

2. Tremendously weary. Nearly worn out and practically at a standstill. Almost no resources.

1. Utterly exhausted. Entirely worn out. Completely incapable of even the slightest effort.

l. Elation vs. Depression (how elated or depressed, happy or unhappy, you felt) _____

10. Complete elation. Rapturous joy and soaring ecstasy.

9. Very elated and in very high spirits. Tremendous delight and bouyancy.

8. Elated and in high spirits.

7. Feeling very good and cheerful.

6. Feeling pretty good, "O.K."

5. Feeling a little bit low. Just so-so.

4. Spirits low and somewhat "blue."

3. Depressed and feeling very low. Definitely "blue."
2. Tremendously depressed. Feeling terrible, miserable, "just awful."
1. Utter depression and gloom. Completely down. All is black and leaden.

APPENDIX B
DEPENDENT VARIABLES

Housing Environment

1. Personal and Family Privacy
   a. Unwanted Visits
   b. Audio Privacy
   c. Visual Privacy
   d. Indoor Privacy
   e. Outdoor Privacy

2. Size and Arrangement of Housing Unit and Lot

   a. Size of House
   b. Layout of House
   c. Size of Lot
   d. Shape of Lot
   e. Location on Block

3. Economic and Functional Responsibilities of Home Ownership

   a. Financial Responsibilities
   b. Maintenance Responsibilities

4. House and Neighborhood as a Physical Symbol of Tastes and Personality

   a. House Alikeness
   b. Neighborhood Appearance

Community Services

1. Parks and Open Space

   a. Accessibility
   b. Safety
   c. Accommodates All Age Groups
   d. Satisfaction with Usage

2. Schools

   a. Academic Quality
   b. Satisfaction with Schools

3. Security/Police

a. Safe Walking at Night
b. Children Safe in Neighborhood
c. Satisfaction with Security

4. Child Care

    a. Community Helps Working Mother
    b. Satisfaction with Day Care Facilities

5. Transportation

    a. Ease of Transport
    b. Satisfaction with Transit

6. Entertainment and Culture

    a. Availability of Entertainment and Cultural Facilities
    b. Satisfaction with Entertainment and Cultural Facilities

Social Patterns

1. Friendships

    a. Difficulty Making Friends
    b. Satisfaction with Friends in Neighborhood
    c. Satisfaction with Friends in Metropolitan Area

2. Group Activity

    a. Satisfaction with Group Opportunities in Neighborhood
    b. Satisfaction with Group Opportunities in Metropolitan Area

3. Sense of Belonging

    a. Identification with Neighborhood
    b. Satisfaction with Neighborhood Identification

Psychological Well-Being

1. Fullness vs. Emptiness of Life
2. Receptivity towards the world
3. Social Respect vs. Social Contempt
4. Personal Freedom vs. Constraint
5. Sociability vs. Withdrawal
6. Companionship vs. Isolation
7. Work Satisfaction
8. Tranquility vs. Anxiety
9. Self-Approving vs. Guilty
10. Self-Confidence vs. Inadequacy
11. Energy vs. Fatigue
12. Elation vs. Depression

APPENDIX C
INDEPENDENT VARIABLES

Social Class Influences

1. Income
2. Education
3. Occupational Status

Subcultural Influences

1. Ethnic Identity
2. Regional Origin
   a. Extent of Urban Origins
   b. Distance to San Jose Area
3. Length of Residency

Life Cycle Influences

1. Age
2. Marital Status
3. Number and Age of Children

Suburban Environmental Influences

1. Residential Density
2. Household Distance from the Central City Center
3. Age of Neighborhood
4. Distance to Work
5. Mean Neighborhood Income and Educational Levels
   a. Ratio of Family Income to Mean Neighborhood Family Income
   b. Ratio of Woman's Education to Mean Neighborhood Woman's
      Education
6. Population size of Political Unit
7. Design and Site Plan Characteristics.

APPENDIX D
EXPLORATORY VARIABLES

Housing Environment
1. Desire to Replan House
2. Reasons for Present Location
   a. First
   b. Second
   c. Third
   d. Fourth
3. Extent of Urban Character of Prior Location
4. Distance to San Jose Area of Prior Location
5. Happier at Present Location
6. Reasons for Satisfaction of Present Home
   a. First
   b. Second
   c. Third
   d. Fourth

Community Services

1. Park Usage per Month
2. Child Care Usage per Week
3. Number of Cars
4. Public Transport Usage per Week
5. Evenings out per Month in Neighborhood
6. Evenings out per Month in Metropolitan Area
7. Cultural Events per Year in Metropolitan Area
8. Cultural Events per Year Elsewhere
9. Willingness to Spend More Money On:
   a. Parks and Open Space
   b. Schools
   c. Security Police
   d. Child Care
   e. Transportation
   f. Entertainment and Cultural Facilities
   g. Other

Social Patterns

1. Speaking Acquaintances in Neighborhood
2. Neighbors to Talk about General Topics
3. Neighbors to Borrow from
4. Neighbors to Aid in Crises

5. Neighbors to Help in Project
6. Neighbors to Discuss Personal Problems
7. Close Friends in Neighborhood
8. Close Friends in Metropolitan Area
9. Close Friends One Hour Away
10. Close Friends Farther Away
11. Involved in Neighborhood Informal Groups
12. Involved in Neighborhood Action Groups
13. Involved in Children's Activity Groups
14. Involved in Religious Groups
15. Involved in Political Organizations
16. Involved in outside Informal Groups
17. Involved in outside Action Groups
18. Involved in outside Social Organization
19. Involved in Other Organized Groups

Background

1. Duration of Marital Status
2. Rent or Own
3. Age of Man
4. Length of Residency Man
5. Education Man
6. Working Woman (percent working)
7. Occupation Status of Man
8. Ethnic Identity (percent identified)
9. Man's Education to Mean Neighborhood Man's Education
10. Woman's Occupation to Mean Neighborhood Woman's Occupation
11. Man's Occupation to Mean Neighborhood Man's Occupation
12. Occupation–Education Ratio Woman
13. Occupation–Education Ratio man
14. Education Ratio Woman–Man
15. Occupation Ratio Woman–Man

APPENDIX E

DEPENDENT VARIABLE MEAN SCORES BY NEIGHBORHOOD

				Neighbors					
Dependent Variable	Inlying S.F.(S.J.)	Outlying S.F.(S.J.)	Outlying PUD(S.J.)	Outlying CON(S.J.)	S.F.(L.G.)	CON(L.G.)	S.F.(Cup)	CON(Cup.)	Total
Housing Environment	5.91	5.32	5.51	5.72	5.39	5.80	5.40	5.65	5.59
Privacy	6.21	5.66	5.78	5.81	5.75	5.91	5.79	5.64	5.82
Unwelcomed visits	6.23	5.89	6.03	6.07	6.02	6.06	5.73	5.80	5.98
Audio privacy	6.15	5.43	5.61	5.50	5.23	5.77	5.39	5.36	5.55
Visual privacy	6.77	6.35	6.31	6.37	6.61	6.58	6.36	5.99	6.42
Indoor privacy	5.97	5.88	5.44	5.68	5.50	5.71	5.71	5.62	5.65
Outdoor privacy	5.94	5.06	5.49	5.44	5.37	5.45	5.77	5.43	5.50
House and lot	6.02	5.41	5.49	5.51	5.42	5.75	5.61	5.29	5.56
Size of house	5.91	5.58	5.77	5.51	5.37	5.48	5.40	5.08	5.51
Layout of house	5.88	5.59	5.89	5.66	5.42	5.77	5.59	5.29	5.63
Size of lot	5.91	4.68	4.46	5.12	5.08	5.54	5.38	4.95	5.15
Shape of lot	5.98	5.33	5.33	5.43	5.28	5.93	5.82	5.39	5.57
Location on block	6.42	5.87	6.01	5.78	5.96	6.02	5.87	5.74	5.96
Home ownership responsibility	4.90	4.82	5.27	5.86	4.81	5.63	4.71	5.76	5.22
Financial responsibilities	5.16	4.91	5.19	5.52	4.92	5.20	4.81	5.31	5.13
Maintenance responsibilities	4.66	4.73	5.35	6.20	4.67	6.08	4.61	6.20	5.31
Symbol of taste	6.52	5.40	5.59	5.67	5.59	5.91	5.50	5.91	5.77
House alikeness	6.54	5.27	5.33	5.55	5.34	5.65	5.39	5.66	5.62

Neighborhood appearance	6.51	5.56	5.86	5.79	5.64	6.17	5.62	6.15	5.91
Community services	5.07	4.45	4.95	4.96	5.16	5.30	5.30	5.36	5.10
Parks and open spaces	5.60	3.71	4.59	4.70	4.91	5.30	5.42	5.27	4.97
Accessibility	6.31	3.69	4.40	4.85	5.15	5.20	5.84	5.02	5.08
Safety	5.35	3.99	5.10	5.18	4.60	5.22	5.15	5.28	5.00
Accomodate all ages	5.39	3.15	4.02	4.09	4.94	5.34	5.17	5.30	4.71
Satisfaction with usage	5.37	3.71	4.83	4.68	4.95	5.44	5.51	5.51	5.02
Schools	4.75	4.83	5.28	4.94	5.68	5.07	5.23	5.54	5.18
Academic quality	4.92	4.74	5.31	5.01	5.84	5.17	5.31	5.59	5.25
Satisfaction with schools	4.55	4.91	5.24	4.86	5.53	4.98	5.16	5.49	5.10
Security/Police	5.08	4.55	5.00	5.26	5.18	5.66	5.28	5.81	5.24
Safe walking at night	4.85	4.40	4.92	5.26	4.76	5.50	5.14	5.75	5.08
Children safe in neigh.	5.23	4.79	5.22	5.36	5.31	5.64	5.41	6.01	5.38
Satisfaction with security	5.22	4.36	4.69	5.06	5.45	5.86	5.28	5.71	5.22
Childcare	4.42	4.04	4.41	4.31	3.90	4.05	4.14	4.23	4.18
Community helps working mother	4.36	4.36	4.69	4.45	3.58	3.86	4.02	4.01	4.15
Satisfaction with day care facilities	4.42	3.89	4.07	4.30	4.35	4.21	4.29	4.48	4.26
Transportation	5.47	4.83	5.53	5.14	5.54	5.77	5.72	5.23	5.42
Ease of transit	6.48	6.25	6.44	6.38	6.51	6.69	6.56	6.32	6.46
Satisfaction with transit	4.41	3.45	4.64	3.84	4.60	4.86	4.88	4.13	4.37
Entertainment and culture	5.06	4.98	5.04	4.90	5.83	5.93	5.89	6.16	5.49

Neighborhood

Dependent Variable	Inlying S.F.(S.J.)	Outlying S.F.(S.J.)	Outlying PUD(S.J.)	Outlying CON(S.J.)	S.F.(L.G.)	CON(L.G.)	S.F.(Cup.)	CON(Cup.)	Total
Availability	5.16	4.92	5.31	5.05	5.96	5.99	5.84	6.11	5.55
Satisfaction	4.93	5.01	4.81	4.74	5.71	5.85	5.95	6.21	6.42
Social patterns	5.67	5.33	5.14	4.96	5.29	5.42	5.37	5.40	5.33
Friendships	5.92	5.72	4.32	5.43	5.66	5.73	5.74	5.71	5.66
Difficulty making friends	5.25	7.28	5.17	5.20	5.35	5.36	5.39	5.45	5.31
Satisfaction with neighborhood friends	6.11	5.94	5.19	5.19	5.72	5.75	5.84	5.53	5.64
Satisfaction with metro area friends	6.36	6.09	5.63	5.91	5.91	6.08	6.00	6.14	6.02
Group participation	5.41	5.11	5.13	4.77	5.06	5.65	5.18	5.68	5.25
Satisfaction with group opportunities in neighborhood	5.25	4.91	5.16	4.66	4.76	5.48	5.06	4.43	5.09
Satisfaction with group opportunities in metro area	5.59	5.33	5.06	4.93	5.36	5.81	5.30	5.93	5.42
Sense of belonging	5.60	5.07	4.89	4.69	5.15	4.87	5.19	4.82	5.04
Identification with neighborhood	5.07	4.62	4.54	4.19	4.79	4.33	5.09	4.55	4.65
Satisfaction with neighborhood identity	6.12	5.51	5.25	5.18	5.51	5.40	5.28	5.09	5.42

Psychological well-being	7.13	6.84	6.93	6.85	6.86	6.82	6.90	7.17	6.94
Fullness vs. emptiness	7.34	6.94	6.94	6.95	7.21	6.85	7.21	7.19	7.08
Receptivity towards the world	7.05	6.73	6.86	6.86	6.96	6.92	6.99	7.10	6.94
Social respect vs. social contempt	7.58	7.55	7.48	7.19	7.54	7.43	7.41	7.68	7.48
Personal freedom vs. constraint	6.69	6.49	7.14	6.80	6.60	6.70	6.58	7.02	6.75
Sociability vs. withdrawal	7.13	7.00	7.08	6.89	6.91	6.85	6.94	7.41	7.03
Companionship vs. isolation	7.90	7.51	7.59	7.36	7.31	7.42	7.35	7.77	7.53
Work satisfaction	7.75	7.36	7.39	7.13	7.15	7.24	7.14	7.36	7.31
Tranquility vs. anxiety	6.49	6.01	6.34	6.31	6.08	6.23	6.26	6.39	6.26
Self-approving vs. guilty	6.93	6.72	6.58	6.73	6.65	6.49	6.76	6.91	6.72
Self-confidence vs. inadequacy	7.18	7.05	7.26	6.90	7.04	6.86	7.03	7.38	7.09
Energy vs. fatigue	6.63	6.16	6.60	6.42	6.43	6.38	6.50	6.74	6.48
Elation vs. depression	6.89	6.56	6.65	6.53	6.47	6.52	6.73	6.86	6.65

Note: Inlying S.F.(S.J.) = Inlying single-family neighborhood in San Jose; Outlying S.F.(S.J.) = Outlying single-family neighborhood in San Jose; Outlying PUD(S.J.) = Outlying planned unit developments in San Jose; Outlying CON(S.J.) = Outlying condominiums in San Jose; S.F.(L.G.) = Single-family neighborhood in Los Gatos; CON(L.G.) = Condominiums in Los Gatos; S.F.(CUP.) = Single-family neighborhood in Cupertino; CON(CUP.) = Condominiums in Cupertino. Range of possible scores are 1.000 to 7.000 for all variables except for Psychological Well-Being variables, which cover a range of 1.000 to 10.000.

Source: compiled by the authors.

APPENDIX F
INDEPENDENT VARIABLE MEAN SCORES BY NEIGHBORHOOD

Independent Variables	Neighborhood								
	Inlying S.F.(S.J.)	Outlying S.F.(S.J.)	Outlying PUD(S.J.)	Outlying CON(S.J.)	S.F.(L.G.)	CON(L.G.)	S.F.(Cup.)	CON(Cup.)	Total
Social class influences									
Income (1975) (in thousands of dollars)	23.21	21.42	22.04	25.38	22.70	25.34	23.78	21.66	23.20
Education[a]	3.23	2.96	3.00	3.25	3.33	3.40	3.21	3.60	3.25
Occupational status[b]	2.43	2.25	2.07	2.80	2.46	2.97	2.43	3.05	2.56
Subcultural influences									
Ethnic identity (1.0 = lowest identity; 7.0 = highest)	1.81	1.50	1.43	2.19	1.74	1.71	1.89	2.11	1.80
Regional origin									
Extent of urban origins[c]	2.64	2.63	2.63	2.85	2.57	2.85	2.68	2.71	2.70
Distance to San Jose area[d]	3.54	4.29	4.95	3.92	4.26	3.52	3.73	4.54	4.09
Length of residency (years)	5.92	4.60	3.02	2.14	8.00	2.35	7.55	2.38	4.54
Life cycle influences									
Age (years)	35.59	33.32	31.90	33.88	37.06	35.84	35.38	34.31	34.70
Marital status (percent married)	96.2	89.0	95.7	77.2	90.5	72.8	88.1	75.2	85.4

	1	2	3	4	5	6	7	8	9
Children Number	2.12	2.42	2.33	1.80	2.43	1.93	2.30	1.59	2.12
Mean age	8.25	7.88	6.84	7.86	10.24	9.70	9.07	8.37	8.55
Suburban environmental influences									
Residential density (housing unit/net residential acre)	6.4	5.8	6.2	15.1	6.3	14.6	5.8	13.8	9.3
Household distance from the central city center (miles)	2.0	8.2	8.5	7.9	7.8	7.7	7.8	8.0	7.2
Age of neighborhood (years)	35.58	6.57	4.47	3.15	24.27	3.50	15.36	4.11	13.36
Travel time to work (minutes)									
Woman's	5.59	4.92	7.43	11.83	6.13	12.50	9.70	11.97	8.77
Man's	14.76	22.50	23.58	25.47	24.62	20.94	20.83	23.25	21.93
Mean neighborhood income and educational levels									
Ratio of family income to mean neighborhood family income	1.000	1.000	1.079	1.000	1.071	1.000	1.000	1.000	1.018
Ratio of woman's education to mean neighborhood woman's education	1.000	1.000	1.000	1.000	1.000	1.000	1.000	1.000	1.000
Population size of political unit (thousands)	551.2	551.2	551.2	551.2	23.9	23.9	22.0	22.0	287.1

	Neighborhood								
Independent Variable	Inlying S.F.(S.J.)	Outlying S.F.(S.J.)	Outlying PUD(S.J.)	Outlying CON(S.J.)	S.F.(L.G.)	CON(L.G.)	S.F.(Cup.)	CON(Cup.)	Total
Design and site plan characteristics (P = planned neighborhood; LP = less planned)	LP	LP	P	P	LP	P	LP	P	—

Note: Inlying S.F.(S.J.) = Inlying single-family neighborhood in San Jose; Outlying S.F.(S.J.) = Outlying single-family neighborhood in San Jose; Outlying PUD(S.J.) = Outlying planned unit developments in San Jose; Outlying CON(S.J.) = Outlying condominiums in San Jose; S.F.(L.G.) = Single-family neighborhood in Los Gatos; CON(L.G.) = Condominiums in Los Gatos; S.F.(Cup.) = Single-family neighborhood in Cupertino; CON(Cup.) = Condominiums in Cupertino.

[a] For years of education completed, the following scores are applicable: 1.0 = grade school (0–8 years); 2.0 = high school (9–12 years); 3.0 = some college (13–15 years); and 4.0 = college graduate (16 years); 5.0 = some graduate school (17 years); 6.0 = graduate degree (18 years).

[b] For occupational status, scores were estimated by research staff from descriptions of employment activities on questionnaires using the following scale: 1.0 = housewife; 2.0 = unskilled worker; 3.0 = semi-skilled worker; 4.0 = skilled worker; 5.0 = manager or owner; 6.0 = professional.

[c] Extent of urban origins is represented by the following scores: 1.0 = country; 2.0 = small town; 3.0 = suburb of large city; 4.0 = large city.

[d] Distance of regional origins to San Jose is based on actual mileage measurement and the following scale: 1.0 = within the San Jose metropolitan area (Santa Clara County); 2.0 = within a 50-mile radius; 3.0 = 51–250 miles; 4.0 = 251–500 miles; 5.0 = 501–1,000 miles; 6.0 = 1,001–1,500 miles; 7.0 = 1,501–2,000 miles; 8.0 = 2,001–3,000 miles; 9.0 = 3,001+ miles.

APPENDIX G
EXPLORATORY VARIABLE MEAN SCORES BY NEIGHBORHOOD

Exploratory Variable	Neighborhood								
	Inlying S.F.(S.J.)	Outlying S.F.(S.J.)	Outlying PUD(S.J.)	Outlying CON(S.J.)	S.F.(L.G.)	CON(L.G.)	S.F.(Cup.)	CON(Cup.)	Total
Housing environment									
Desire to replan house (percent no)	52.9	45.0	57.7	63.7	39.0	71.6	56.9	55.2	55.3
Reasons for present location[a]									
First	h.d.	h.c.	h.d.	h.c.	sch.	sch.	sch.	sch.	h.c.
Second	a.n.	h.c.	sch.	h.d.	sch.	sch.	h.c.	work	h.c.
Third	a.n.	h.d.	sch.	h.c.	shop	a.n.	work	a.n.	a.n.
Fourth	park	a.n.	a.n.	a.n.	shop	park	shop	a.n.	a.n.
Extent of urban character of prior location[b]	3.17	3.13	3.13	3.14	2.65	2.89	2.94	2.98	3.00
Distance to San Jose area of prior location[c]	1.86	2.14	2.34	1.77	1.94	1.87	1.97	1.97	1.98
Happier at present location	6.38	5.99	5.58	5.48	5.81	5.56	6.05	5.44	5.79
Reasons for satisfaction of present home[a]									
First	h.d.	h.d.	h.d.	h.c.	sch.	h.d.	h.d.	sch.	h.d.

| | Neighborhood | | | | | | | | |
Exploratory Variable	Inlying S.F.(S.J.)	Outlying S.F.(S.J.)	Outlying PUD(S.J.)	Outlying CON(S.J.)	S.F.(L.G.)	CON(L.G.)	S.F.(Cup.)	CON(Cup.)	Total
Second	a.n.	h.c.	a.n.	h.d.	sch.	h.d.	work	h.d.	h.d.
Third	a.n.	h.d.	h.d.	h.d.	a.n.	a.n.	a.n.	a.n.	a.n.
Fourth	park	a.n.	a.n.	a.n.	h.d.	h.d.	shop	a.n.	a.n.
Community services									
Park usage per month	4.83	2.35	4.49	3.42	3.79	4.97	7.39	4.99	4.56
Child care usage per week	1.46	1.16	1.40	1.53	1.27	1.72	1.10	2.14	1.47
Number of cars	1.96	1.97	1.89	1.83	2.07	1.80	1.94	1.79	1.91
Public transport usage per week	0.53	0.11	0.24	0.19	0.33	0.65	0.50	0.57	0.04
Evenings out per month in neighborhood	2.67	2.27	2.20	2.77	2.54	3.53	2.78	3.88	2.84
Evenings out per month in metro area	3.09	2.62	2.45	3.07	2.43	3.17	2.38	2.64	2.73
Cultural events per year metro area	3.56	3.18	3.79	4.08	6.86	6.39	6.12	7.28	5.19
Cultural events per year elsewhere	2.82	3.14	2.94	3.80	2.66	3.09	2.82	2.90	3.02
Willingness to spend more money on:									
Parks and open space	48.6	64.0	54.6	46.0	52.4	42.7	44.0	45.7	49.8
Schools	56.2	45.0	69.1	52.0	57.1	65.0	48.6	61.0	56.7
Security police	38.1	45.0	56.7	45.0	41.6	27.2	33.9	34.3	40.8
Childcare	20.0	25.0	29.9	33.0	26.7	35.0	12.8	36.2	27.2

Transportation	28.6	29.0	24.7	26.0	35.2	32.0	23.9	32.4	29.0
Entertainment and cultural facilities	36.2	29.0	42.3	32.0	29.5	37.9	15.6	25.7	30.8
Other	36.2	29.0	42.3	32.0	29.5	37.9	15.6	25.7	30.8
Social Patterns									
Speaking aquaintances in neighborhood	21.35	20.50	27.16	14.06	24.19	27.51	25.03	21.35	22.67
Neighbors to talk about general topics	9.86	11.29	8.40	6.64	10.95	7.89	9.62	7.68	9.06
Neighbors to borrow from	4.08	4.83	4.14	2.69	7.06	3.81	4.14	3.59	4.30
Neighbors to aid in crises	5.51	5.30	4.82	2.55	7.28	4.37	4.04	3.50	4.67
Neighbors to help in project	3.00	3.36	2.34	1.50	3.56	1.87	2.35	1.93	2.49
Neighbors to discuss personal problems	1.77	1.84	1.32	1.22	2.02	1.34	1.77	1.36	1.58
Close friends in neighborhood	2.79	3.06	2.22	1.87	2.15	1.77	2.61	2.16	2.33
Close friends in metropolitan area	11.91	8.30	6.77	9.49	9.75	7.48	8.70	7.20	8.72
Close friends one hour away	6.12	4.68	5.29	6.20	5.60	3.99	5.26	4.48	5.20
Close friends farther away	9.64	9.59	7.66	6.34	8.90	6.41	8.01	9.18	8.23
Involved in neighborhood informal groups[d]	1.72	2.05	2.27	2.10	1.79	1.83	2.55	2.40	2.09
Involved in neighborhood action groups[d]	2.26	1.90	2.10	2.08	2.11	2.07	2.00	2.91	2.18

| | Neighbors | | | | | | | | |
Exploratory Variable	Inlying S.F.(S.J.)	Outlying S.F.(S.J.)	Outlying PUD(S.J.)	Outlying CON(S.J.)	S.F.(L.G.)	CON(L.G.)	S.F.(Cup)	CON(Cup.)	Total
Involved in children's activity groups[d]	3.52	3.33	3.35	2.93	3.94	3.23	4.14	3.68	3.52
Involved in religious groups[d]	2.87	2.72	2.23	2.55	2.73	2.25	2.89	2.84	2.64
Involved in political organizations[d]	1.76	1.52	1.62	1.67	1.62	1.75	1.50	1.89	1.67
Involved in outside informal groups[d]	2.58	2.68	2.65	3.00	2.87	2.34	2.73	3.53	2.80
Involved in outside action groups[d]	1.97	1.60	1.58	2.05	2.01	1.80	1.69	2.17	1.86
Involved in outside social organizations[d]	2.00	1.85	1.87	1.98	1.94	2.01	1.81	2.15	1.95
Involved in other organized groups[d]	1.75	1.73	1.37	2.11	2.13	2.08	2.27	2.64	2.02
Background									
Duration of marital status (years)	12.69	10.60	10.00	9.05	14.31	11.01	12.38	8.13	11.04
Rent or own (percent own)	92.4	97.0	93.7	91.1	90.4	85.4	96.3	81.0	90.9
Age of man	38.13	35.69	34.94	35.76	40.5	37.87	37.95	37.70	37.30

Length of residency of man	5.99	5.45	2.99	2.13	8.06	2.37	7.18	2.38	4.73
Education of man[e]	3.99	3.41	3.76	3.72	4.16	4.16	4.18	4.22	3.95
Working women (percent working)	46.3	43.0	41.3	60.2	45.7	67.6	44.0	63.5	51.3
Occupation status of man[f]	4.64	4.62	4.58	4.44	4.71	4.60	5.19	4.84	4.71
Ethnic identity (percent identified)	19.5	12.0	14.3	28.3	26.0	20.7	23.0	30.5	21.7
Man's education to mean neighborhood man's education	1.29	1.38	1.28	1.43	1.27	1.51	1.20	1.37	1.34
Woman's occupation to mean neighborhood woman	1.03	1.00	1.00	1.00	1.07	1.03	1.00	1.03	1.02
Man's occupation to mean neighborhood man's occupation	1.18	1.25	1.26	1.32	1.22	1.45	1.15	1.32	1.27
Occupation-education ratio of woman	0.78	0.79	0.72	0.86	0.75	0.91	0.80	0.87	0.81
Occupation-education ratio of man	1.26	1.40	1.36	1.33	1.22	1.21	1.34	1.23	1.29

				Neighbors					
Exploratory Variable	Inlying S.F.(S.J.)	Outlying S.F.(S.J.)	Outlying PUD(S.J.)	Outlying CON(S.J.)	S.F.(L.G.)	CON(L.G.)	S.F.(Cup)	CON(Cup.)	Total
Education ratio woman–man	0.87	0.85	0.87	0.98	0.87	0.85	0.81	0.86	0.87
Occupation ratio woman–man	0.52	0.46	0.46	0.63	0.53	0.67	0.46	0.63	0.54

Note: Inlying S.F.(S.J.) = Inlying single-family neighborhood in San Jose; Outlying S.F.(S.J.) = Outlying single-family neighborhood in San Jose; Outlying PUD(S.J.) = Outlying planned unit developments in San Jose; Outlying CON(S.J.) = Outlying condominiums in San Jose; S.F.(L.G.) = Single-family neighborhood in Los Gatos; CON(L.G.) = Condominiums in Los Gatos; S.F.(Cup.) = Single-family neighborhood in Cupertino; CON(Cup.) = Condominiums in Cupertino.

[a]Sch. = quality of public schools; work = location of work; h.c. = cost of housing; h.d. = type or design of house; a.n. = appearance of neighborhood; shop = close to shopping; park = near parks and recreation.

[b]Extent of urban origins is represented with the following scores: 1.0 = country; 2.0 = small town; 3.0 = suburb of large city; 4.0 = large city.

[c]Distance of regional origins to San Jose is based on actual mileage measurement and the following scale: 1.0 = within the San Jose metropolitan area (Santa Clara County); 2.0 = within a 50-mile radius; 3.0 = 51–250 miles; 4.0 = 251–500 miles; 5.0 = 501–1,000 miles; 6.0 = 1,001–1,500 miles; 7.0 = 1,501–2,000 miles; 8.0 = 2,001 = 3,000 miles; 9.0 = 3,001+ miles.

[d]Range of possible scores are 1.00 for no involvement in group activities to 7.00 for organizing or leadership role.

[e]For years of education completed, the following scores are applicable: 2.0 = high school (9–12 years); 3.0 = some college (13–15 years); 4.0 = college graduate (16 years).

[f]For occupational status, scores were estimated by research staff from descriptions of employment activities on questionnaires using the following scale: 1.0 = housewife; 2.0 = unskilled worker; 3.0 = semi-skilled worker; 4.0 = skilled worker; 5.0 = manager or owner; 6.0 = professional.

Source: compiled by the authors.

APPENDIX H
NEIGHBORHOOD DESCRIPTIONS

1. Inlying Single-Family Neighborhood in San Jose

This area, built in the 1920s, 1930s, and 1940s, is located approximately two miles from the center of San Jose. It consists of tree-lined streets with varied one and two-story houses of traditional architecture with a net residential density of about six units per net residential acre. Known as Willow Glen, it is reminiscent of residential areas in many typical U.S. small towns. It still exists on a pedestrian scale with a local shopping street within a short walk of most dwellings. It appears to have a strong sense of physical and social identity.

2. Outlying Single-Family Neighborhood in San Jose

Consisting of mass-produced single-family tract houses, this neighborhood was built around 1970. With a density slightly less than six per net residential acre, this neighborhood is located on the southern edge of the city, is approximately eight miles from the center of San Jose, and is sparsely served by public transportation. In appearance it is typically suburban with standard, ranch-style, one and two-story homes arranged on a modified grid pattern. Immature landscaping gives the area a somewhat raw ambience.

3. Outlying Planned Unit Developments in San Jose

These areas consist of two developments of single-family homes built to a slightly higher density than the adjacent outlying single-family neighborhood. Built in the early 1970s, they are designed around community and socializing facilities, such as schools, parks, recreation halls, and swimming pools. Street patterns attempt to minimize pedestrian and auto contact. The houses are typically suburban in appearance.

4. Outlying Condominiums in San Jose

Comprised of several condomium developments built in the early 1970s, these areas are situated nearly eight miles from the center of San Jose. They are typically 80 to 150 attached housing units arranged around community and social facilities. Homeowners associations manage the maintenance of these communally owned facilities and the attractively landscaped grounds. The average densities here are approximately 15 units per net residential acre, or roughly three times the density of our single-family areas.

5. Single-Family Neighborhood in Los Gatos

This neighborhood lies in the older adjacent suburb of Los Gatos which, in the postwar era, became engulfed in the rapid growth of the San Jose metropolitan area. Like Willow Glen, Los Gatos in general is imbued with a strong sense of physical and social identity. The study neighborhood was built in the early 1950s and is approximately eight miles from downtown San Jose and about one mile from central Los Gatos. It consists primarily of one-story ranch-style homes with a density of about 6 units per net residential acre. Laid out on a modified grid, the streets present a mature but casual appearance.

6. Condominiums in Los Gatos

These consist of several developments, ranging from 60 to 150 units each. Nearly eight miles from downtown San Jose, they are slightly further from central Los Gatos than are the single-family homes. These units were designed around communal facilities as were the San Jose condominiums. In building type, density, and appearance they are similar to the San Jose condominium units.

7. Single-Family Neighborhood in Cupertino

Comprised of undifferentiated suburban development, primarily one-story, single-family homes, this area lies within the new suburb of Cupertino, incorporated in 1955. The housing was constructed in the early 1960s at about six units per net residential acre, is situated almost eight miles from downtown San Jose, and is but a short drive from the numerous shoping centers developed since that time. Unlike Los Gatos, Cupertino does not possess an older focal point of community identity. It is characterized by a heavy reliance on the automobile, which is typical of this nation's new suburbs.

8. Condominiums in Cupertino

Consisting of several condominium developments similar to those examined in San Jose and Los Gatos, these areas are located about eight miles from downtown San Jose. In appearance they are one and two-story, attached, single-family units grouped around community and social facilities. Built in the early 1970s, they have an average net residential density of nearly 14 units per acre, and the landscaping is extensive and attractive.

BIBLIOGRAPHY

BOOKS

Adams, Elsie, and Mary Louise Briscoe. *Up Against the Wall, Mother....* Beverly Hills, Calif.: Glencoe Press, 1971.

Aries, Phillippe. *Centuries of Childhood: A Social History of Family Life.* New York: Alfred A. Knopf, 1962.

Andreas, Carol. *Sex and Caste in America.* Englewood Cliffs, N.J.: Prentice-Hall, 1971.

Ballentyne, Sheila. *Norma Jean the Termite Queen.* New York: Bantam Books, 1976.

Bardwick, Judith M., ed. *Readings in the Psychology of Women.* New York: Harper and Row, 1972.

Baxendale, Rosalyn, Linda Gordon, and Susan Reverby, eds. *America's Working Women.* New York: Random House, 1976.

Bequaert, Lucie H. *Single Women Alone and Together.* Boston: Beacon Press, 1976.

Beauvoir, Simone de. *The Second Sex.* New York: Alfred A. Knopf, 1953.

Berger, Bennett M. *Working Class Suburb.* Berkeley: University of California Press, 1971.

Birmingham, Stephen. *The Golden Dream: Suburbia in the 1970's.* New York: Harper and Row, 1978.

Bish, Robert L. *The Public Economy of Metropolitan Areas.* Chicago: Markham, 1971.

_____, and Hugh O. Nourse. *Urban Economics and Policy Analysis.* New York: McGraw-Hill, 1975.

Bloomberg, William Jr., and Henry J. Schmandt, eds. *The Quality of Urban Life.* Beverly Hills, Calif.: Sage, 1969.

Bollens, John C., and Henry J. Schmandt. *The Metropolis: Its People, Politics, and Economic Life.* 3rd ed. New York: Harper and Row, 1975.

Bourne, Larry S., ed. *Internal Structure of the City.* New York: Oxford University Press, 1971.

Callow, Alexander B., ed. *American Urban History.* New York: Oxford University Press, 1973.

Campbell, Angus, Philip E. Converse, and William L. Rodgers. *The Quality of American Life: Perceptions, Evaluations, and Satisfactions.* New York: Russell Sage Foundation, 1976.

Chamberlin, Everett. *Chicago and Its Suburbs.* New York: Arno Press, 1974.

Chudacoff, Howard P. *The Evolution of American Urban Society.* Englewood Cliffs, N.J.: Prentice-Hall, 1975.

Clark, S.D. *The Suburban Society.* Toronto: University of Toronto Press, 1966.

Clark, Terry N., ed. *Community Structure and Decision Making.* San Francisco: Chandler, 1968.

Cole, Doris. *From Tipi to Skyscraper: A History of Women in Architecture.* Boston: i Press, 1973.

Dennis, Wayne, et al., eds. *Current Trends in Social Psychology.* Pittsburgh, Penn.: Pittsburgh University Press, 1951.

Dobriner, William M., ed. *The Suburban Community.* New York: G.P. Putnam's Sons, 1958.

Dolce, Philip C., ed. *Suburbia: The American Dream and Dilemma.* New York: Anchor Press, 1976.

Downs, Anthony. *Opening Up the Suburbs: An Urban Strategy for America.* New Haven, Conn.: Yale University Press, 1973.

Duhl, Leonard J., ed. *The Urban Condition.* New York: Basic Books, 1963.

Economic and Social Opportunities, Inc. *Female Heads of Household and Poverty in Santa Clara County.* San Jose, Calif.: Economic and Social Opportunities, 1974.

Edel, Matthew, and Jerome Rothenberg, eds. *Readings in Urban Economics.* New York: Macmillan, 1972.

Eichler, Edward P., and Marshall Kaplan. *The Community Builders.* Berkeley: University of California Press, 1967.

Epstein, Cynthia. *Woman's Place.* Berkeley: University of California Press, 1970.

Ewald, William R., ed. *Environment for Man.* Bloomington: Indiana University Press, 1967.

Fava, Sylvia J., ed. *Urbanism in World Perspective.* New York: Crowell, 1968.

Festinger, Leon, et al. *Social Pressures in Informal Groups.* Stanford: Stanford University Press, 1951.

Figes, Eva. *Patriarchal Attitudes.* New York: Stein and Day, 1970.

Firestone, Shulamith. *The Dielectic of Sex.* New York: William Morrow, 1970.

French, Marilyn. *The Woman's Room.* New York: Jove/HBJ Books, 1978.

Friedan, Betty. *The Feminine Mystique.* New York: Dell, 1963.

Gans, Herbert J. *The Levittowners.* New York: Vintage Books, 1967.

_____. *The Urban Villagers.* New York: Free Press of Glencoe, 1962.

Gilmour, Robert S., and Robert B. Lamb. *Political Alienation in Contemporary America.* New York: St. Martin's Press, 1975.

Glazer, Nathan, and Daniel P. Moynihan. *Beyond the Melting Pot.* Cambridge, Mass.: MIT Press,1963.

Goffman, Erving. *The Presentation of Self in Everyday Life.* New York: Doubleday, 1959.

Goheen, Peter J. *Victorian Toronto, 1850 to 1900.* Chicago: University of Chicago Press, 1970.

Gordon, R.E., et al. *The Split Level Trap.* New York: Dell, 1962.

Gornick, Vivian, and Barbara K. Moran, eds. *Women in Sexist Society.* New York: Basic Books. 1971.

Greer, Scott. *The Urbane View: Life and Politics in Metropolitan America.* New York: Oxford University Press, 1972.

Haar, Charles, ed. *The President's Task Force on Suburban Problems.* Cambridge, Mass.: Ballinger, 1974.

Hapgood, Karen, and Judith Getzels, eds. *Planning, Women, and Change.* Chicago: American Society of Planning Officials Planning Advisory Service, 1974.

Hareven, Tamara K., ed. *Family and Kin in Urban Communities, 1700–1930.* New York: New Viewpoints, 1977.

Hawley, Amos H., and Vincent P. Rock, eds. *Metropolitan American in Contemporary Perspective.* New York: Halsted Press, 1975.

Hirsch, Werner Z., ed. *Los Angeles: Viability and Prospects for Metropolitan Leadership.* New York: Praeger, 1971.

Holland, Laurence B., ed. *Who Designs America?* Garden City, N.Y.: Anchor Books, 1966.

Hoyt, Homer. *One Hundred Years of Land Values in Chicago.* New York: Arno Press, 1970.

Ibsen, Henrik. *A Doll's House.* The Oxford Ibsen, vol. 5, translated and edited by James Walter McFarlane. London: Oxford University Press, 1961.

Jackson, Kenneth L. and Stanley K. Schultz, eds. *Cities in American History.* New York: Alfred A. Knopf, 1972.

Keats, John. *The Crack in the Picture Window.* Boston: Houghton-Mifflin, 1956.

Kouskoulas, Vasily, ed. *Urban Housing.* Detroit, Mich.: National Science Foundation, 1973.

Kreps, Juanita. *Sex in the Market Place.* Baltimore, Md.: Johns Hopkins Press, 1971.

Lansing, John B., et al. *Planned Residential Environments.* Ann Arbor: University of Michigan Press, 1970.

Lapin, Howard S. *Structuring the Journey to Work.* Philadelphia: University of Pennsylvania Press, 1964.

Levin, Ira. *The Stepford Wives.* New York: Random House, 1972.

Lewis, Sinclair. *Main Street.* New York: Harcourt, Brace and Howe, 1920.

Lineberry, Robert L., and Ira Sharkansky. *Urban Politics and Public Policy.* New York: Harper and Row, 1971.

Lopata, Helena Z. *Occupation Housewife.* New York: Oxford University Press, 1971.

Lubove, Roy. *The Progressives and the Slums.* Pittsburgh, Penn.: University of Pittsburgh Press, 1962.

McFadden, Cyra. *The Serial.* New York: Alfred A. Knopf, 1977.

Marsden, Dennis. *Mothers Alone: Poverty and the Fatherless Family.* London: Allen Lane, The Penguin Press, 1969.

Masotti, Louis H., and Jeffrey K. Hadden, eds. *The Urbanization of the Suburbs.* Beverly Hills, Calif.: Sage, 1973.

Mead, Margaret. *Male and Female.* New York: William Morrow, 1949.

Meier, Richard L. *A Communications Theory of Urban Growth.* Cambridge, Mass.: MIT Press, 1962.

Meyer, John R., John F. Kain, and Martin Wohl. *The Urban Transportation Problem.* Cambridge: Harvard University Press, 1965.

Michelson, William. *Environmental Choice, Human Behavior, and Residential Satisfaction.* New York: Oxford University Press, 1977.

_____. *Man and His Urban Environment.* Reading, Mass.: Addison-Wesley, 1976.

Millet, Kate. *Sexual Politics.* Garden City, N.Y.: Doubleday, 1970.

Moos, Rudolf H., and Paul M. Insel, eds. *Issues in Human Ecology: Human Milieus.* Palo Alto, Calif.: National Press Books, 1973.

Morgan, Robin, ed. *Sisterhood is Powerful: An Anthology of Writings From the Women's Liberation Movement.* New York: Vintage Books, 1970.

Moustakas, Clark E. *Loneliness and Love.* Englewood Cliffs, N.J.: Prentice-Hall, 1972.

Nye, F. Ivan, and Lois Wladis Hoffman. *The Employed Mother in America.* Chicago: Rand McNally, 1963.

O'Neill, William, ed. *The Women's Movement: Feminism in the United States and England.* Chicago: Quadrangle Paperbacks, 1969.

Owens, Bill. *Suburbia.* San Francisco: Straight Arrow Press, 1973.

Packard, Vance. *The Status Seekers*. New York: Dell, 1962.

Page, Alfred N., and Warren R. Segfried, eds. *Urban Analysis*. Glenview, Ill.: Scott, Foresman, 1970.

Pahl, R.E., ed. *Readings in Urban Sociology*. London: Pergamon Press, 1968.

Porteous, J. Douglas. *Environment and Behavior: Planning and Everyday Urban Life*. Reading, Mass.: Addison-Wesley, 1977.

Proshansky, Harold, et al., eds. *Environmental Psychology: People and Their Settings*. New York: Holt, Rinehart and Winston, 1976.

Reisman, David, et al. *The Lonely Crowd*. New Haven, Conn.: Yale University Press, 1950.

Rennie, Thomas A.C., et al. *Mental Health in the Metropolis*. New York: McGraw-Hill, 1962.

Ricks, David F., and Alden E. Wessman. *Mood and Personality*. New York: Holt, Rinehart and Wilson, 1966.

Riis, Jacob. *How the Other Half Lives*. New York: Hill and Wang, 1957.

Rothblatt, Donald N., ed. *National Policy for Urban and Regional Development*. Lexington, Mass.: D.C. Heath, 1974.

Rousseau, Jean-Jacques. *Emile*. London: J.M. Dent and Sons, 1974.

Salper, Roberta, ed. *Female Liberation, History and Current Politics*. New York: Alfred A. Knopf, 1972.

Scanzoni, John. *Sexual Bargaining: Power Politics in the American Marriage*. Englewood Cliffs, N.J.: Prentice-Hall, 1972.

Schmitt, Peter J. *Back to Nature: The Arcadian Myth in Urban America*. New York: Oxford University Press, 1969.

Schneir, Miriam, ed. *Feminism: The Essential Historical Writings*. New York: Vintage Books, 1972.

Schnore, Leo F. *The New Urban History*. Princeton, N.J.: Princeton University Press, 1975.

Schwartz, Barry, ed. *The Changing Face of the Suburbs*. Chicago: University of Chicago Press, 1963.

Seeley, John, et al. *Crestwood Heights*. New York: Basic Books, 1956.

Sennett, Richard. *Families Against the City: Middle Class Homes of Industrial Chicago, 1872–1890*. New York: Vintage Books, 1974.

Shevsky, Eshref, and Wendell Bell. *Social Area Analysis*. Stanford, Calif.: Stanford University Press, 1955.

Schmandt, Henry J., and Warner Bloomberg, Jr., eds. *The Quality of Urban Life.* Beverly Hills, Ca.: Sage, 1969.

Slater, Phillip. *The Pursuit of Loneliness: American Culture at the Breaking Point.* Boston: Beacon Press, 1970.

Somner, Robert. *Personal Space: The Behavioral Basis of Design.* Englewood Cliffs, N.J.: Prentice-Hall, 1969.

Spectorsky, A.C. *The Exurbanites.* Philadelphia: Lippincott, 1955.

Stanford Environmental Law Society. *San Jose: Sprawling City.* Stanford, Calif.: Environmental Law Society, 1971.

Sternlieb, George, et al. *The Affluent Suburb: Princeton.* New Brunswick, N.J.: Transaction Books, 1971.

Stoll, Clarice Stasz. *Female and Male Socialization, Social Roles, and Social Structure.* Dubuque, Iowa: Wm C. Brown, 1974.

Terleckyi, Nestor E. *Improvements in the Quality of Life: Estimates of Possibilities in the United States.* Washington, D.C.: National Planning Association, 1975.

TeSelle, Sallie, ed. *The Rediscovery of Ethnicity: Its Implications for Culture and Politics in America.* New York: Harper and Row, 1973.

Torre, Susanna, ed. *Women in American Architecture: A Historic and Contemporary Perspective.* New York: Whitney Library of Design, 1977.

Tunnard, Christopher, and Henry Hope Reed. *American Skyline: The Growth and Form of Our Cities and Towns.* New York: Mentor Books, 1956.

Ural, Oktal, ed. *Proceedings of the Second International Symposium on Lower-Cost Housing Problems.* St. Louis: University of Missouri-Rolla, 1972.

Wapner, Seymour, Saul B. Cohen, and Bernard Kaplan, eds. *Experiencing the Environment.* New York: Plenum Press, 1976.

Ward, David. *Cities and Immigrants: A Geography of Change in Nineteenth Century America.* New York: Oxford University Press, 1971.

Warner, Sam Bass. *The Private City: Philadelphia in Three Periods of Growth.* Philadelphia: University of Pennsylvania Press, 1968.

_____. *Streetcar Suburbs: The Process of Growth in Boston, 1870–1900.* New York: Atheneum, 1969.

_____. *The Urban Wilderness.* New York: Harper and Row, 1972.

Webber, Melvin, et al., eds. *Explorations into Urban Structure.* Philadelphia: University of Pennsylvania Press, 1964.

Weiss, Robert S., et al., eds. *Loneliness.* Cambridge, Mass.: MIT Press, 1973.

Werthman, Carl, et al. *Planning and the Purchase Decision: Why People Buy in Planned Communities.* Berkeley: University of California Press, 1965.

Westermarck, Edward. *The History of Human Marriage.* New York: The Allerton Book Company, 1922.

Wheaton, William L.C., et al., eds. *Urban Housing.* New York: Free Press, 1966.

Wheelis, Allen. *The Quest for Identity.* New York: Norton, 1958.

Whyte, William H., Jr. *The Last Landscape.* New York: Doubleday, 1969.

_____. *The Organization Man.* Garden City, N.Y.: Anchor Books, 1957.

Williams, Oliver P. *Metropolitan Political Analysis.* New York: Free Press, 1971.

Wilner, Daniel M., et al. *The Housing Environment and Family Life.* Baltimore, Md.: Johns Hopkins Press, 1962.

Wilson, James Q., ed. *The Metropolitan Enigma.* Washington, D. C.: U.S. Chamber of Commerce, 1967.

Wingo, Lowdon, ed., *Cities and Space.* Baltimore, Md.: Johns Hopkins Press, 1963.

Wood, Robert C. *Suburbia: Its People and Their Politics.* Boston: Houghton-Mifflin, 1958.

_____. *1400 Governments.* Cambridge: Harvard University Press, 1961.

Woods, Robert A., and Albert J. Kennedy. *The Zone of Emergence.* ed. and abridged by Sam Bass Warner, 2nd ed. Cambridge, Mass.: MIT Press, 1969.

Zehner, Robert B. *Indicators of the Quality of Life in the New Communities.* Cambridge, Mass.: Ballinger, 1977.

ARTICLES AND PERIODICALS

Abu-Lughod, Janet L. "Designing a City For All." In *Planning, Women, and Change*, edited by Karen Hapgood and Judith Getzels, p. 37. Chicago: Planning Advisory Service, 1974.

Alonso, William. "Metropolis Without Growth." *The Public Interest* 53 (1978): 68–86.

_____. "A Theory of the Urban Land Market." In *Readings in Urban Economics*, edited by Matthew Edel and Jerome Rothenberg, pp. 104–11. New York: MacMillan, 1972.

Appleyard, Donald. "A Planners Guide to Environmental Psychology: Review Essay." *Journal of the American Institute of Planners* 43 (April 1977): 184–89.

Baldassare, Mark, and Claude S. Fischer. "Suburban Life: Powerlessness and a Need for Affiliation." *Urban Affairs Quarterly* 10 (March 1975): 314–26.

Bedell, Madelon. "Supermom." *Ms.* (May 1973): 84.

Bell, Wendell. "Familialism and Suburbanization." *Rural Sociology* 21 (September-December 1956): 276–83.

_____, and Marian Boat. "Urban Neighborhoods and Informal Social Relations." *American Journal of Sociology* 62 (January 1957): 391–98.

Belser, Karl. "The Making of Slurban America." *Cry California* 5 (Fall 1970): 1–21.

Blood, Robert O., and Robert L. Hamblin. "The Effect of the Wife's Employment on the Family Power Structure." In *Social Forces* 36 (May 1958): 347–52.

Brandwein, Ruth A., Carol A. Brown, and Elizabeth Maury Fox. "Woman and Children Last: The Social Situation of Divorced Mothers and Their Families." *Journal of Marriage and the Family* 36 (August 1974): 498–514.

Brown, Connie, and Jane Seitz. " 'You've Come a Long Way Baby': Historical Perspectives." In *Sisterhood is Powerful: An Anthology of Writings From the Women's Liberation Movement*, edited by Robin Morgan, p. 6. New York: Vintage Books, 1970.

Buder, Stanley. "The Future of the American Schools." In *Suburbia: The American Dream and Dilemma*, edited by Philip C. Dolce, pp. 193–216. New York: Anchor Press, 1976.

Bylinsky, Gene. "California's Great Breeding Ground for Industry." *Fortune* 89 (June 1974): 129–35, 216–24.

Caplow, T., and R. Foreman. "Neighborhood Interaction in a Homogeneous Community." *American Sociological Review* 15 (June 1950): 357–65.

Carro, Geraldine. "The Wage-Earning Mother." *Ladies Home Journal* (December 1978): 56.

Craik, Kenneth H. "The Comprehension of the Everyday Physical Environment." *Journal of the American Institute of Planners* 34 (January 1968): 29–37.

Davidoff, Paul, and Mary E. Brooks. "Zoning Out the Poor." In *Suburbia: The American Dream and Dilemma*, edited by Philip C. Dolce, pp. 135–66. New York: Anchor Press, 1976.

Downes, Bryan T. "Suburban Differentiation and Municipal Policy Choices." In *Community Structure and Decision-Making*, edited by Terry N. Clark, pp. 243–67. San Francisco: Chandler, 1968.

Ekland, Kent E., and Oliver P. Williams. "The Changing Distribution of Social Classes in a Metropolitan Area." *Urban Affairs Quarterly* 13 (March 1978): 313–41.

Engels, Frederich. "The Monogamous Family." In *Up Against the Wall, Mother...*, edited by Elsie Adams and Mary Louise Bricoe, pp. 266–77. Beverly Hills, Calif.: Glencoe Press, 1971.

Erickson, Julia A. "An Analysis of the Journey to Work for Women." *Social Problems* 24 (April 1977): 428–35.

Fava, Sylvia. "Beyond Suburbia." *Annals of American Academy of Political and Social Science* 422 (November 1975): 10–24.

Feldman, Arnold, and Charles Tilly. "The Interaction of Social and Physical Space." *American Sociological Review* 25 (1966): 877–84.

Ferree, Myra Marx. "The Confused American Housewife." *Psychology Today* (September 1976): 76ff.

Fischer, Claude S. "Toward a Subcultural Theory of Urbanism." *American Journal of Sociology* 80 (May 1975): 1319–41.

_____., and Robert Max Jackson. "Suburbs, Networks and Attitudes." In *The Changing Face of the Suburbs*, edited by Barry Schwartz, pp. 279–309. Chicago: University of Chicago Press, 1976.

Fuller, Margaret. "Women in the Nineteenth Century." In *Feminism: The Essential Historical Writings*, edited by Miriam Schneir, pp. 62–71. New York: Vintage Books, 1972.

Galbraith, John Kenneth. "How the Economy Hangs on Her Apron Strings." *Ms.* (May 1974): 64.

Gans, Herbert J. "Effects of the Move From City to Suburb." In *The Urban Condition*, edited by Leonard J. Duhl, pp. 184–98. New York: Basic Books, 1963.

Garr, Daniel J. "A Frontier Agrarian Settlement: San José de Guadalupe, 1777–1850." *San Jose Studies* 2 (November 1976): 93–105.

Gilman, Charlotte Perkins. "The Home: Its Work and Influence." In *Female Liberation, History and Current Politics*, edited by Roberta Salper, p. 115. New York: Alfred A. Knopf, 1972.

Gove, Walter R., and Jeanette F. Tudor. "Adult Sex Roles and Mental Illness." In *Changing Women in a Changing Society*, edited by Joan Huber, pp. 50–73. Chicago: University of Chicago Press, 1973.

Greenhouse, Linda. "These Wives Found Cure to Some of the Ills of Suburbia." *New York Times*, October 1, 1971.

Greer, Scott. "The Family in Suburbia." In *The Urbanization of the Suburbs*, edited by Louis H. Masotti and Jeffrey K. Hadden, pp. 149–70. Beverly Hills, Calif.: Sage, 1973.

Guest, Avery M. "The Changing Racial Composition of the Suburbs: 1950–1970." *Urban Affairs Quarterly* 14 (December 1978): 195–206.

Gutman, Robert. "Population Mobility in the American Middle Class." In *The Urban Condition*, edited by Leonard J. Duhl, pp. 172–83. New York: Basic Books, 1963.

_____. "Site Planning and Social Behavior." *Journal of Social Issues* 22 (Winter 1966): 103–15.

Hartley, Ruth E. "Some Implications of Current Changes in Sex Role Patterns." In *Readings in the Psychology of Women*, edited by Judith W. Bardwick, pp. 119–29. New York: Harper and Row, 1972.

Havens, Elizabeth M. "Women, Work, and Wedlock: A Note on Female Marital Patterns in the United States." In *Changing Women in a Changing Society*, edited by Joan Huber, pp. 213–19. Chicago: University of Chicago Press, 1973.

Hayghe, Howard. "Families and the Rise of Working Wives: An Overview." *Monthly Labor Review* 99 (May 1976): 12–19.

Hoffman, Lois Wladis. "The Decision to Work." In *The Employed Mother in America*, edited by Ivan F. Nye and Lois Wladis Hoffman, p. 18. Chicago: Rand McNally, 1963.

Holahan, Carole, and Lucie Gilbert. "In Two Career Marriages, Happy Wives Aim Low." *Psychology Today* (November 1978): 28–34.

Hopkins, Richard J. "Status, Mobility, and the Dimensions of Change in a Southern City: Atlanta: 1870–1910." In *Cities in American History*, edited by Kenneth L. Jackson and Stanley K. Schultz, p. 217. New York: Alfred A. Knopf, 1972.

Jackson, Kenneth L. "Urban Deconcentration in the Nineteenth Century: A Statistical Inquiry." In *The New Urban History*, edited by Leo F. Schnore, pp. 110–11. Princeton, N.J.: Princeton University Press, 1975.

Jones, Beverly. "The Dynamics of Marriage and Motherhood." In *Sisterhood is Powerful: An Anthology of Writings from the Women's Liberation Movement*, edited by Robin Morgan, pp. 46–61. New York: Vintage Books, 1970.

Kain, John F. "The Distribution and Movement of Jobs and Industry." In *The Metropolitan Enigma*, edited by James O. Wilson, pp. 1–31. Washington, D.C.: U.S. Chamber of Commerce, 1967.

_____. "The Journey to Work as a Determinant of Residential Location." In *Urban Analysis*, edited by Alfred N. Page and Warren R. Segfried, pp. 207–26. Glenview, Ill.: Scott, Foresman, 1970.

Kaniss, Phyllis, and Barbara Robins. "The Transportation Needs of Women." In *Planning, Women and Change*, edited by Judith Getzels and Karen Hapgood, pp. 63–70. Chicago: American Society of Planning Officials Planning Advisory Service, 1974.

Kantrowitz, Nathan. "Ethnic and Racial Segregation in the New York Metropolis, 1960." *American Journal of Sociology* 74 (1969): 685–95.

Kay, Jane Holtz. "The House That Woman Built." *Ms.* (July 1974): 93.

Kilborn, Peter T. "Corporate Grants Invade the Residential Market." *The New York Times*, February 4, 1979.

Ktsanes, T., and L. Reissman. "Suburbia: New Homes for Old Values." *Social Problems* 7 (Winter 1959–60): 187–94.

Lamare, James, and Francine Rabinovitz. "After Suburbia, What?" In *Los Angeles: Viability and Prospects for Metropolitan Leadership*, edited by Werner Z. Hirsch, pp. 169–206. New York: Praeger, 1971.

Lasch, Christopher. "Family as Haven in Heartless World." *Salmagundi* 34 (Fall 1976): 42–55.

McEaddy, Beverly Johnson. "Women Who Head Families: A Socioeconomic Analysis." *Monthly Labor Review* (June 1976): 3–9.

Mainardi, Pat. "The Politics of Housework." In *Sisterhood is Powerful: An Anthology of Writings from the Women's Liberation Movement*, edited by Robin Morgan, p. 450. New York: Vintage Books, 1970.

Maisel, Sherman, and Louis Winnick. "Family Housing Expenditures: Illusive Laws and Intrusive Variances." In *Urban Housing*, edited by William L.C. Wheaton, et al., pp. 139–53. New York: Free Press, 1966.

Manis, Jerome, and Leo Stine. "Suburban Residence and Political Behavior." *Public Opinion Quarterly* 22 (Winter 1958): 483–98.

Marshall, Harvey. "Suburban Life Styles: A Contribution to the Debate." In *The Urbanization of the Suburbs*, edited by Louis H. Masotti and Jeffrey K. Hadden, pp. 123–48. Beverly Hills, Calif.: Sage, 1973.

Masotti, Louis H. "Suburbia Reconsidered: Myth and Counter Myth." In *The Urbanization of the Suburbs*, edited by Louis H. Masotti and Jeffrey K. Hadden, pp. 15–22. Beverly Hills, Calif.: Sage, 1973.

_____., and D. Bowen. "Communities and Budgets: The Sociology of Municipal Expenditures." *Urban Affairs Quarterly* 1 (December 1965): 38–58.

Merton, Robert K. "Social Psychology of Housing." In *Current Trends in Social Psychology*, edited by Wayne Dennis, et al., pp. 163–217. Pittsburgh, Penn.: Pittsburgh University Press, 1951.

Meyer, John R. "Urban Transportation." In *The Metropolitan Enigma*, edited by James O. Wilson, pp. 34–75. Washington, D.C.: U.S. Chamber of Commerce, 1967.

Miller, Darla. "Most Men Still 'Kings' in San Jose Homes." *San Jose Mercury*, December 6, 1978.

Morgan, Robin. "The Changeless Need—A Conversation with Dorothy Dinnerstein." *Ms.* (August 1978): 44–46.

Ms. staff. "Who is the Real Family?" *Ms.* (August 1978): 43.

Novak, Michael. "How American Are You If Your Grandparents Came from Serbia in 1888?" In *The Rediscovery of Ethnicity: Its Implications for Culture and Politics in America*, edited by Sallie TeSelle, pp. 1–20. New York: Harper and Row, 1973.

Olson, David. "The (New) Cost of Being a Woman." *Mother Jones* (January 1977): 14.

O'Reilly, Jane. "The Housewife's Moment of Truth." *Ms.* (Spring 1972): 54–69.

Osmund, Humphrey. "Some Psychiatric Aspects of Design." In *Who Designs America?*, edited by Lawrence B. Holland, pp. 281–318. Garden City, N.Y.: Anchor Books, 1966.

Parr, A. E. "Psychological Aspects of Urbanology." *Journal of Social Issues* 22 (October 1966): 39–45.

Peterson, Rebecca, Gerda R. Wekerle, and David Morley. "Women and Environment: An Overview of an Emerging Field." *Environment and Behavior* 10 (December 1978): 511–34.

Pfeil, E. "The Patterns of Neighboring in Dortmund-Norstadt." In *Readings in Urban Sociology*, edited by R.E. Dahl, pp. 136–58. London: Pergamon Press, 1968.

Pray, Marilyn. "Planning and Women in the Suburban Setting." In *Planning, Women and Change*, edited by Judith Getzels and Karen Hapgood, p. 52. Chicago: American Society of Planning Officials Planning Advisory Service, 1974.

Raven, John. "Sociological Evidence on Housing (2: The Home Environment)." *The Architectural Review* 142 (1967): 236ff.

Reisman, David. "The Suburban Sadness." In *The Suburban Community*, edited by William M. Dobriner, pp. 375–408. New York: G.P. Putnam's Sons, 1958.

Ritter, Kathleen V. and Lowell E. Hargens. "Occupational Positions and Class Identifications of Married Working Women: A Test of the Asymmetry Hypothesis." *American Journal of Sociology* (January 1975): 934–47.

Rossi, Alice. "The Roots of Ambivalence in American Women." In *Readings in the Psychology of Women*, edited by Judith M. Bardwick, pp. 119–31. New York: Harper and Row, 1972.

Rothblatt, Donald N. "Housing and Human Needs." *Town Planning Review* 42 (April 1971): 130–44.

_____. "Improving the Design of Urban Housing." In *Urban Housing*, edited by Vasily Kouskoulas, pp. 149–54. Detroit, Michigan: National Science Foundation, 1973.

_____. "Multiple Advocacy: An Approach to Metropolitan Planning." *Journal of the American Institute of Planners* 44 (April 1978): 193–99.

Rushing, William. "Two Patterns in the Relationship Between Social Class and Mental Hospitalization." *American Sociological Review* 34 (August 1969): 533–41.

Sadalla, Edward K., and David Stea. "Approaches to a Psychology of Urban Life." *Environment and Behavior* 10 (June 1978): 139–46.

Sanoff, Henry. "Neighborhood Satisfaction: A Study of User Assessments of Low Income Residential Environment." In *Proceedings of the Second International Symposium on Lower-Cost Housing Problems*, edited by Oktal Ural, pp. 119–24. St. Louis: University of Missouri-Rolla, 1972.

Schmandt, Henry J., and G. Stephens. "Measuring Municipal Output." *National Tax Journal* 61 (December 1960): 369–75.

Schnore, Leo F. "The Growth of Metropolitan Suburbs." *American Sociological Review* 22 (April 1957): 165–73.

_____ , and Vivian Zelig Klaff. "Suburbanization in the Sixties: A Preliminary Analysis." *Land Economics* 40 (February-November 1972): 23–33.

Schulman, Norman. "Mutual Aid and Neighboring Patterns: The Lower Town Study." *Anthropologica* 9 (1967): 51–60.

Scott, Ann Crittendon. "The Value of Housework for Love or Money." *Ms.* (July 1972): 59.

Shephard, W. Bruce. "Metropolitan Political Decentralization: A Test of the Life-Style Value Model." *Urban Affairs Quarterly* 10 (1975): 297–313.

Sherman, Diana, "Feminists Advocate Rezoning, Transit: Suburbs Lambasted at UCLA Conference." *Los Angeles Times*, April 29, 1979, p. ix-2.

Siembieda, William J. "Suburbanization of Ethics of Color." *Annals of the American Academy of Political and Social Science* 422 (November 1975): 118–28.

Smith, Timothy L., "Religion and Ethnicity in America." *American Historical Review* 63 (December 1978): 1155–85.

Sommer, Robert. "Man's Proximate Environment." *Journal of Social Issues* 22 (October 1966): 59–70.

Stipak, Brian. "Citizen Satisfaction With Urban Services: Potential Misuse as a Performance Indicator." *Public Administration Review* 39 (January-February 1979): 46–52.

Syfers, Judy. "I Want a Wife." *Ms.* (Spring 1972): 56.

Tarr, Joel Arthur. "From City to Suburb: The 'Moral' Influence of Transportation Technology." In *American Urban History*, edited by Alexander B. Callow, p. 202. New York: Oxford University Press, 1973.

Tax, Meredith. "Woman and Her Mind: The Story of Daily Life." In *Female Liberation, History and Current Politics*, edited by Roberta Salper, pp. 228–33. New York: Alfred A. Knopf, 1972.

Temple, Charlotte. "Planning and the Married Woman With Children—A New Town Perspective." In *Planning, Women and Change*, edited by Judith Getzels and Karen Hapgood, p. 47. Chicago: American Society of Planning Officials Planning Advisory Service, 1974.

Thernstom, Stephan. "Urbanization, Migration and Social Mobility in Late Nineteenth Century America." In *American Urban History*, edited by Alexander B. Callow, p. 399. New York: Oxford University Press, 1973.

Tiebout, C.M. "A Pure Theory of Local Expenditures." In *Readings in Urban Economics*, edited by Matthew Edel and Jerome Rothenberg, pp. 513–23. New York: MacMillan, 1972.

Tilly, Charles. "Occupational Rank and Grade of Residence in a Metropolis." *American Journal of Sociology* 67 (1961): 323–30.

Tomeh, Aida K. "Empirical Considerations on the Problems of Social Integration." *Sociological Inquiry* 39 (Winter 1969): 65–76.

_____. "Informal Group Participation and Residential Patterns." *American Journal of Sociology* 70 (July 1965): 28–35.

Torre, Susanna, Cynthia Rock, and Gwendolyn Wright. "Rethinking Closets, Kitchens, and Other Forgotten Spaces." *Ms.* (December 1977): 55.

United Press. "Average Home Buyer—Young, Married, No Kids." San Francisco *Chronicle*, November 28, 1977.

Van Gelder, Lindsay. "Strains of 'Oh Promise Me' Emanating from the White House." San Jose *News*, February 8, 1979.

Webber, Melvin M. "Order in Diversity: Community Without Propinquity." In *Cities and Space*, edited by Lowdon Wingo, pp. 23–56. Baltimore, Md.: Johns Hopkins Press, 1963.

_____. "The Urban Place and the Nonplace Urban Realm." In *Explorations Into Urban Structure,* edited by Melvin Webber, pp. 79–153. Philadelphia: University of Pennsylvania Press, 1964.

Weiss, Robert, and Nancy Samuelson. "Social Roles of American Women: Their Contribution to a Sense of Usefulness and Importance." *Marriage and Family Living* 20 (November 1958): 358–66.

Weissman, Myrna M., and Eugene S. Paykel. "Moving and Depression in Women." In *Loneliness*, edited by Robert S. Weiss, et al., pp. 154–64. Cambridge, Mass.: MIT Press, 1973.

Wolforth, John. "Journey to Work." In *Internal Structure of the City*, edited by Larry S. Bourne, pp. 240–47. New York: Oxford University Press, 1971.

Wollstonecraft, Mary A. "A Vindication of the Rights of Women." In *Feminism: The Essential Historical Writings*, edited by Miriam Schneir, pp. 5–18. New York: Vintage Books, 1972.

Woolf, Virginia. "A Room of One's Own." In *Up Against the Wall, Mother...*, edited by Elsie Adams and Mary Louise Briscoe, pp. 388–99. Beverly Hills, Calif.: Glencoe Press, 1971.

Wright, James D. "Are Working Women Really More Satisfied?" *Journal of Marriage and the Family* 40 (May 1978): 301–14.

Zelan, Joseph. "Does Suburbia Make a Difference?" In *Urbanism in World Perspective*, edited by Sylvia F. Fava, pp. 401–08. New York: Crowell, 1968.

Zimmer, Basil. "The Urban Centrifugal Drift." In *Metropolitan America in Contemporary Perspective*, edited by Amos H. Hawley and Vincent P. Rock, pp. 23–92. New York: Halsted Press, 1975.

PUBLIC DOCUMENTS

Environmental Protection Agency. *The Quality of Life Concept.* Washington, D.C.: Government Printing Office, 1973.

Santa Clara County Housing Task Force. *Housing: A Call for Action.* San Jose, Calif.: Santa Clara County Planning Department, 1977.

Santa Clara County Planning Department. *Housing Characteristics, Cities, Santa Clara County, 1970.* San Jose, Calif.: Santa Clara County Planning Department, 1971.

_____. *1975 Countywide Census, Santa Clara County.* San Jose, Calif.: Santa Clara County Planning Department, 1976.

U.S., Department of Commerce, Bureau of the Census. *Consumer Income: Household Money Income in 1975 by Housing, Tenure and Residence for the United States, Regions, Divisions and States.* Washington, D.C.: Government Printing Office, 1977.

_____. *Household and Family Characteristics: March, 1976.* Washington, D.C.: Government Printing Office, 1977.

_____. *Household Income in 1972 and Selected Social and Economic Characteristics of Households.* Washington, D.C.: Government Printing Office, 1972.

_____. *Money Income in 1975 of Families and Persons in the United States.* Washington, D.C.: Government Printing Office, 1977.

U.S., House, *The Child Care Act of 1979,* H.R. 1121.

U.S., Senate, *The Child Care Act of 1979,* S. 4.

UNPUBLISHED MATERIAL

Anderson, James R., et al. "Residents' Satisfaction: Criteria for the Evaluation of Housing for Low and Moderate Income Families." Paper read at the American Institute of Planners Conference, Denver, Colorado, October 1974.

Bem, Darryl, and Sandra Bem. "The Power of a Nonconscious Ideology: Training a Woman to Know Her Place." Public speech, San Jose State University Women's Week, San Jose, California, 1972.

Bombeck, Irma. "The Grass Is Always Greener Over the Septic Tank," Television movie, 1978.

Carney, James M. "How to Evaluate the Impacts of the Combined General Plans of the Cities of Santa Clara County, California." Masters Planning Report, San Jose State University, 1978.

Freitas, Melanie. "Women in Suburbia." Masters Planning Report, San Jose State University, 1974.

Grumich, Susan. "Women in Limbo: Social Class and Life Cycle Perspectives of Feminine Roles." M. A. thesis, San Jose State University, 1972.

Jones, Lynne M. "The Labor Force Participation of Married Women." Masters thesis, University of California, Berkeley, 1974.

de Jonge, Derk. "Some Notes on Sociological Research in the Field of Housing." Mimeographed. Delft: Delft University of Technology, 1967.

Michelson, William. "Environmental Change." Research Paper no. 60. Centre for Urban and Community Studies, 1973.

Rothblatt, Donald N., Daniel J. Garr, and Jo Sprague. "The Quality of Suburban Life." Paper read at the American Institute of Planners Conference, Kansas City, Missouri, October 1977.

INDEX

ABOUT THE AUTHORS

DONALD N. ROTHBLATT chairs the Urban and Regional Planning Department at San Jose State University and is past president of the Association of Collegiate Schools of Planning. His other works include *Human Needs and Public Housing, Regional Planning: The Appalachian Experience, Allocation of Resources for Regional Planning*, and *National Policy for Urban and Regional Development*. He has studied planning in the United States and Europe and holds the Ph.D. in City and Regional Planning from Harvard University, where he was on the planning faculty.

DANIEL J. GARR is Associate Professor of Urban and Regional Planning at San Jose State University. He has published widely in the area of urban history and social policy. A winner of the Herbert E. Bolton Award of the Western History Association, he was a Senior Fulbright Research Scholar at the Institute for Town Planning Research, Delft University of Technology in the Netherlands. Dr. Garr holds graduate planning degrees from the University of California, Berkeley and Cornell University.

JO SPRAGUE is Associate Professor of Speech Communication at San Jose State University, where she is also on the faculty of the Women's Studies program. Her works include the co-authorship of *Speech Communication in the Secondary School*, articles in natural communication journals, and papers on women's issues at national and international conferences. She holds the Ph.D. in Communications from Purdue University.